$12.95

The Schmitts'

For Conference Information and
Group Prices, write:

CONFERENCE ON DISCIPLESHIP
ARTS PUBLICATIONS LTD
3800 E. Hampden Avenue
Englewood, Colorado 80110

CURRICULUM ON DISCIPLESHIP

Dynamics of Discipling

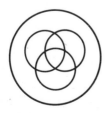

Copyright © 1978
CURRICULUM COMMITTEE OF DYNAMICS OF DISCIPLING
ARTS PUBLICATIONS LTD
Denver, Colorado
Second Edition

Dynamics of Discipling

Published by ARTS PUBLICATIONS LTD
Denver, Colorado

DEDICATED to the establishment and preservation of the belief that the Spirit-Filled Life may be UNDERSTOOD, EXPERIENCED, and SHARED by the earnest believer in *this* present day.

Didst Thou not die, that I might live,
  No longer to myself but Thee?
Might body, soul, and spirit give
  To Him who gave Himself for me?
Come then, my Master and my God,
Take the dear purchase of Thy blood.
                              —John Wesley

Preface

The Discipling concept is not new. A Disciple is a pupil, a follower, or adherent of any teacher or school of religion, learning or art (Webster). Great teachers have always had Disciples. Great causes have always necessitated both Disciples and Disciplers.

Jesus Christ is the *Personification* of the *Greatest Cause* ever revealed to man. He has had dedicated Disciples in the past. He has ardent Disciples today. The propagation of His Truth necessitates Disciples and Disciplers for the future.

Jesus Christ's earthly ministry commenced with the words, "Come, follow me . . . and I will make you fishers of men" (Matthew 4:19, NIV). His earthly ministry closed with the words, "go and make disciples" (Matthew 28:19, NIV). It is the duty, responsibility, and privilege of every born-again believer not only to be a *Disciple,* but also to be a *Discipler.*

The imperative of this command demands *personalized vision, crystallized objectives,* and *realistic methods.*

This study is a result of that vision being personalized in the heart and mind of a pastor and a "handful" of Spirit-filled staff and laymen. Working as a committee, these dedicated Disciplers crystallized their objectives and determined that, with God's help, they would produce a simple, but effective, procedure that would enable them to confront their city with the claims of the Gospel. They labored with prayerful seriousness as they shared the concept in small-group settings, and began to formulate a course of study.

The Discipling Curriculum Committee, who, individually, wish to remain anonymous, have worked for several years writing, rewriting, field-testing, and rewriting the material which is presented in this study.

That which is forever settled in Heaven (Psalm 119:89) must be made available to those of us here on earth. "Go and make disciples" is a direct mandate from Heaven. The prayer of the Committee is that the material included in the *Dynamics of Discipling* will better enable you to fulfill this mandate and to be assured that you can fully rely on the strength and character of the *ONE* Who said,

"And lo, I am with you always, even to the end of the age."
Matthew 28:20, NASB

Table of Contents

	INTRODUCTION	11
Premise		
	CHAPTER 1 Mandate of the Master	13
Basis		
	CHAPTER 2 The Word of God in the Life of a Disciple	25
Problem		
	CHAPTER 3 Man	51
Solution		
	CHAPTER 4 The Born-Again Life	85
	CHAPTER 5 The Spirit-Filled Life	113
Growth		
	CHAPTER 6 Faith	147
	CHAPTER 7 Prayer	181
	CHAPTER 8 Knowing God's Will	207
	CHAPTER 9 Commitment	221
	CHAPTER 10 Obedience	241
	CHAPTER 11 The Priorities of the Christian Life	265
	CHAPTER 12 Worship	277
	CHAPTER 13 Temptation	297
Share		
	CHAPTER 14 Personal Evangelism	315
	ACKNOWLEDGMENTS	359

Introduction

Saul of Tarsus was a man of great learning and eloquence. But when, on the Damascan Road, he was confronted with Jesus Christ Who turned his life inside out and ultimately gave him the commission to "go and make disciples," this scholar was overwhelmed with a sense of personal inadequacy.

In spite of his broad education . . . In spite of his training in persuasion . . . In spite of his enthusiasm for spreading the "Good News," this man knew that he, first, had to mentally and experientially take full measure of the God/man relationship before attempting to share. He perceived that he must BE a Disciple before he could "go and make disciples."

So, before he ever presented himself to Peter, he went into the desert for three years of study, meditation, and prayer. He felt an urgent need to explore all dimensions of the Great Commission and make them an integral part of himself. He could not lead on a path he did not know.

If such preparation was essential for the intellectual Saul of Tarsus, it must be an imperative for us today. Believing that to be true, we, the Discipling Curriculum Committee of Denver First Church, have "gone alone" to our deserts (individually and collectively) where we have studied, prayed, and attempted to understand all that was involved in Jesus' command. We have, now, tried to articulate our findings in such a way that we . . . and all who read . . . will have a formula by which we can, indeed, "go and make disciples."

In this book, we attempt to definitively explore Jesus' intentions in the Great Commission. We have striven to obtain an understanding of His Mandate as we have built a pyramid in which each block assists our comprehending, experiencing, and following that command in our personal lives.

Deleting pious platitudes and cutting through unrealistic cliches, we have tried to deal with the God/man relationship in the "nitty-gritty" of life's complexities. We have looked at life AS IT IS and shown God at work in the whole thing with us.

Once we intellectually understand and personally experience what is involved in BEING a Disciple, then we are best prepared to "go and make disciples." The last part of the book deals with specific ways and means we believe will enable us to go into "the highways and hedges" and "make disciples."

The purpose for this book is to prepare all of us who know Jesus Christ as personal Savior to be able to verbally and non-verbally COMMUNICATE the Good News to everyone we meet. The prayer of the Curriculum Committee is that, with the background of this intensive study . . . we may have training to match the purity of our motivation . . . we may have knowledge to match the dimension of our enthusiasm . . . we may have the expertise in Discipling so we can effectively obey the Great Commission: "Go and make disciples."

For several years we have labored toward this goal. We now send forth our efforts in this volume with the prayer that those who seriously study its pages will be enabled to become powerful respondents to Christ's call to "go and make disciples."

Mandate of the Master
(outline)

I. General Purpose of This Study

II. Definitions Essential to This Study
    A. A Christian Disciple
    B. Discipler
    C. Christian Discipling

III. Challenge of This Study

IV. Tools of This Study
    A. Syllabus
    B. Bible
    C. Marker

V. Method of This Study
    A. Understand
    B. Experience
    C. Communicate

VI. General Format of This Study

VII. Specific Objectives of This Study

Go and teach, i.e., disciple, all nations, and you cannot make disciples unless you are a disciple yourself.
—Oswald Chambers

Mandate of the Master

JESUS COMMISSIONED HIS FOLLOWERS TO
"MAKE DISCIPLES."

He told his disciples, "I have been given all authority in heaven and earth. Therefore go and make disciples in all the nations, baptizing them into the name of the Father and of the Son and of the Holy Spirit, and then teach these new disciples to obey all the commands I have given you; and be sure of this—that I am with you always, even to the end of the world."

Matthew 28:18-20, TLB

For this reason, it becomes the duty, responsibility, and privilege of every born-again believer not only to be a Disciple, but also to be a Discipler.

If you are willing to accept this Great Commission, we invite you to share in the structure of this study.

I. General Purpose of This Study

The purpose of this study is to identify yourself at your particular location in life currently (where you are now) . . . to identify the destination you would like to achieve (where you desire to be) . . . and to help answer the urgent question:

"How Do I Get There From Here?"

This demands honest personal evaluation.

You may begin such evaluation by looking at four groups of individuals. Although it is difficult to categorize completely, from a general point of view, every person falls into one of the following categories:

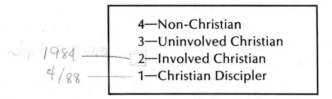

When you look at these categories, there are general questions that rise to your conscious mind:

1. Where am I now?
2. Where do I want to be?
3. How do I get there from here?

This study is designed to help you answer these questions. The purpose of this study will have been achieved when:

1. Your Christian life has been deepened, broadened, and enriched.
2. Under the leadership of the Holy Spirit, you have sensed the call of God to become a Discipler and have responded in obedience to that call.

II. Definitions Essential to This Study

A. A Christian Disciple (Follower of Christ)

A true Disciple is a person who has a deep abiding love for the Person of Christ, an unshakable faith and confidence in the Word of Christ, and is committed to Christ in obedience and service.

A brief profile of a Disciple would be:

1. He is totally committed to Jesus Christ. This means that every activity and every thing in his life are surrendered to Christ's Lordship (Luke 14:26-27, 33). — *according to this passage, can I have a husby + child and fulfill His plan for me to disciple?*

2. He is diligently saturating his life with the Word of God through consistent Bible intake (John 8:31).

3. He is developing his devotional life by consistently having a daily quiet time and is growing in his prayer life (Psalm 5:3; Mark 1:35). — *morning prayer - watch throughout day for His responses*

4. Love (demonstrated by a servant-heart) and loyalty characterize his regular involvement in the fellowship of the local church (I John 1:3; Hebrews 10:24-25). — *Be encouraging!*

5. He demonstrates his desire to make Christ known to others by regularly sharing his personal testimony and the Gospel with increasing skill (John 15:8). *Glorify God by bringin "much fruit"*

B. Discipler

A true Discipler is a *Disciple* who is consciously allowing *(+ unconsciously - everything about self)* Christ to reproduce His life, through him, into the lives of others.

A brief profile of a Discipler would be:

1. He is measurably growing in each area listed under "Disciple" (II Peter 3:18). *Grow in grace and knowledge - to Him be the glory.*

2. He has demonstrated his ability to be effective in personal evangelism by *leading men* to Christ (Acts 8:29-30, 37-38).

3. He has Discipled another person (as defined under "Disciple") (I Thessalonians 2:11-13).

4. He is currently Discipling others (Colossians 1:28-29). *striving through HIS power.*

C. Christian Discipling

Discipling is reproducing in the lives of others what Christ has shown us through His Word and through the Holy Spirit. It is the process of investing oneself in the lives of others.

III. Challenge of This Study

In order to see the potential and significance of this program, the following geometric progression should prove enlightening.

If you were to train 100 people in this course of Discipling for a period of one year, and these 100 people were to become Disciplers, the effects would look like this:

Time in Training	Disciplers	Disciples	To Become Disciplers	Accumulative Total Lives Touched
1 year	100	800	100	900
2 years	200	1,600	200	2,500
3 years	400	3,200	400	5,700
4 years	800	6,400	800	12,100
5 years	1,600	12,800	1,600	24,900
6 years	3,200	25,600	3,200	50,500
7 years	6,400	51,200	6,400	101,700
8 years	12,800	102,400	12,800	204,100

Time in Training	Disciplers	Disciples	To Become Disciplers	Accumulative Total Lives Touched
1 year	100	800	200	900
2 years	300	2,400	600	3,300
3 years	900	7,200	1,800	10,500
4 years	2,700	21,600	5,400	32,100
5 years	8,100	64,800	16,200	96,900
6 years	24,300	194,400	48,600	291,300
7 years	72,900	583,200	145,800	874,500
8 years	218,700	1,749,600	437,400	2,624,100

EXPLANATION: The first table is based on the fact that one Disciple out of each small group of eight Disciples would become a Discipler. The second table is based on the fact that two Disciples out of each small group of eight Disciples would become Disciplers.

The point is not so much that these percentages will be the actual average, but rather that when everyone does a little the effect is startling.

If you were to use the same type of table for only one person (you or me), and you worked at it with eight people in your first group, let us suppose two of them became Disciplers. Then each of the two Disciplers would develop a group of eight for one-year intervals. The result in eight years would be that your groups would have trained 26,241 people.

There is an old saying: "By the yard it's hard, but by the inch it's a cinch." There was never a time when this saying could be truer or more thrilling than today!

It would not be wise or profitable to God's Kingdom to get all "caught up" in these large figures. Instead, there is need to realize that the approach to this entire concept is described in two simple steps:

1. Commit yourself to study earnestly the material in this course.

2. Relax about the future and leave the rest to the Lord.

ARE YOU SECURE WITH THAT APPROACH? Very Much

> In all thy ways acknowledge him and he will direct thy paths.
> Proverbs 3:6, KJV

IV. Tools of This Study

A. **Syllabus**—This is your guide for all that is done in Discipling. Study your syllabus and bring it to class.

B. **Bible**—You will be using the Word in every session; therefore, bring your favorite translation or translations. The following are excellent:

> *The King James Version*
> *The Living Bible*
> *The New American Standard Bible*
> *The New International Version*

C. **Marker**—You will want to develop a marking color and code which will prove indispensable in the future as you use the Word in your Discipling ministry.

V. Method of This Study

It will be the pattern to do three things with any Scripture or concept explored in these sessions:

A. **Understand**—What does this passage teach? Do I clearly understand what this passage is really teaching? Do I understand this concept?

B. **Experience**—Do I experience this truth in my life now? How does my life "stack up" when put alongside this truth?

C. **Communicate**—Do I know how to convey this truth? Can I articulate this to others? How do I organize this to share with my family and friends?

VI. General Format of This Study

In these sessions, time will be spent in both training, using the Discipling material, and a devotional time of sharing Scriptures, problems, concerns, and burdens. As a rule of thumb, your time will be spent in:

> Two-thirds of the time—Discipling Curriculum Training
> One-third of the time—Devotions and Sharing

VII. Specific Objectives of This Study

The specific objectives of these classes are to help you fulfill the Great Commission in your own life by *following Christ* and *investing your life* in the lives of other people.

When you have completed these Discipling sessions, it is our prayer that you will:

A. Be a New Testament Disciple of Jesus Christ—one who has placed himself at the Master's disposal.

B. Be able to feed yourself from the Word of God.

C. Believe that the Great Commission is for all believers.

D. Know how to Disciple others and to become continually involved in Discipling others.

E. Understand that New Testament Christians must have:

    1. New spiritual insights and instruction.

    2. Worship (private and public).

    3. Fellowship (large and small group).

    4. Expression (ministry or service).

F. Recognize that QUALITY is the key to the multiplying process in training the Disciple. Multiplication is assured only when there is the proper training of people who can carry the training process into succeeding generations.

G. Understand that Discipling others cannot be done *solely* through a *classroom setting*. It must also include on-the-job training, which is the imparting of one life into another.

H. Recognize that a Disciple must:

1. Know his doctrine (I Peter 3:15).

2. Keep in daily touch with Headquarters (Acts 2:42-47).

3. Have a strategic, effective plan for making new converts (Acts 8:4; 20:20).

4. Know how to use a variety of tools and methods in helping people grow spiritually.

I. Be able to evaluate your *own* spiritual growth and maturity.

J. Develop an awareness level and an active concern for the spiritual growth and maturity of others. *Be sensitive to others needs and their stresses.*

The Word of God in the Life of a Disciple

(outline)

I. Hearing the Word of God

    A. Six Practical Methods for Effectively Hearing God's Word

    B. Assignment

II. Reading the Word of God

    A. Reading and Marking Your Bible

    B. Develop a Consistent Reading Plan

III. Studying the Word of God

    A. Begin to Memorize a Verse

    B. Proceed to Memorize the Verse

IV. Meditating on the Word of God

    A. Results of Meditation

    B. Practical Application

The whole Bible was given to us by inspiration from God and is useful to teach us what is true and to make us realize what is wrong in our lives; it straightens us out and helps us do what is right.

II Timothy 3:16, TLB

The Word of God in the Life of a Disciple

When by faith you invited Jesus Christ into your life to be your personal Savior, you became a Child of God by virtue of being born of the Spirit. As a member of the Family of God, you have entered into a brand new relationship with Jesus Christ.

Within this new association you have the personal responsibility to vigorously and aggressively develop a growing relationship with Christ. As you pursue this development, you will mature into your full potential in Christ.

You may immediately wonder, "How is this vital, growing relationship to be pursued? What tools are available to me, and how do I employ them?"

Two sources of strength are available to you to assure your success in reaching your full potential in Christ. They are the Word of God and the Holy Spirit.

As stated on page 17, one of the points of the profile of a Disciple is "he is diligently saturating his life with the Word of God through consistent Bible intake." This is a Biblical absolute, as indicated in John 8:31-32.

> *If* ye continue in my word, *then* are ye my disciples indeed; and ye shall know the truth, and the truth shall make you free.
>
> John 8:31-32, KJV

Ezra's method of saturating his life with the Word of God included studying, practicing, and teaching God's Word. This method correlates with the pedagogy of this Discipling course—i.e., understand, experience, and communicate.

> For Ezra had set his heart *to study* the law of the Lord, and *to practice* it, and *to teach* His statutes and ordinances in Israel.
>
> Ezra 7:10, NASB

Jeremiah, too, had committed himself to filling up his life with God's Word, with this resulting heart-cry:

> Thy words were found and I *ate* them, and Thy words became for *me a joy* and the *delight of my heart;* For I have been called by Thy name, O Lord God of hosts.
>
> Jeremiah 15:16, NASB

One of God's choice men, George Mueller, once indicated that the position the Bible holds in your life and thoughts directly reflects the intensity of your spiritual life (or your relationship to Christ). He stated this axiom in light of his own personal experience. For the first four years following his conversion, he neglected the Word of God, resulting in his remaining a babe, both in knowledge and grace. Following these four years, he began diligently searching the Scriptures which led to growth and blessing.

In considering these statements, you may now ask:

- What is the *Word of God?*
- •• What does it mean to *saturate my life with the Word of God?*
- ••• *How do I* saturate my life with the Word of God?

• WHAT IS THE WORD OF GOD?

The identity of the Word of God may be determined by close study of the Biblical correlation between Jesus Christ and the Scriptures listed in the box.

JESUS CHRIST	THE SCRIPTURES
The Word became flesh . . . John 1:14, NIV . . . and his name is the Word of God. Revelation 19:13, NIV	All Scripture is God-breathed . . . II Timothy 3:16, NIV
. . . and your years will never end. Hebrews 1:10, 12, NIV	". . . but my words will never pass away." Matthew 24:35, NIV
. . . and this life is in his Son . . . I John 5:11-12, NIV	". . . the words I have spoken to you . . . are life." John 6:63, NIV
. . . of the Son he loves . . . all things were created by him and for him. Colossians 1:13, 16, NIV	. . . the universe was formed at God's command . . . Hebrews 11:3, NIV
In him we have redemption through his blood . . . Ephesians 1:7, NIV	. . . you have been born again . . . through the . . . word of God . . . I Peter 1:23-25, NIV
. . . he is faithful . . . will . . . purify us . . . I John 1:9, NIV	"You are already clean because of the word I have spoken to you." John 15:3, NIV
". . . the Father . . . has entrusted all judgment to the Son." John 5:22, NIV	". . . that very word which I spoke will condemn him at the last day." John 12:48, NIV

> ## CONCLUSIONS
>
> 1. Any attack against Scripture is an attack against Jesus Christ (John 5:39).
> 2. Spiritual growth requires that Jesus Christ and the written/spoken Word of God never be separated (I Peter 2:2-3).
> 3. The Word must not be used for information only (I Thessalonians 1:5).
> 4. Any concept of *Jesus* apart from the Word is a false "Christ" (Matthew 24:23-24).

Therefore, you can see that the *"Word"* which God used to speak the worlds into existence, the *"Word"* which has been written and has come down to us through history, and the *"Word"* which became Flesh and dwelt among us, are not different in substance and character, but, in fact, all these are one and the same.

•• WHAT DOES IT MEAN TO *SATURATE* MY LIFE WITH THE WORD OF GOD?

In studying the following diagrams, note how the saturation of the *Word* is possible in your life in a very practical way.

God's *written or spoken Word* may be taken in through your soul functions—i.e., mind, will, and emotions—by hearing, reading, studying, or memorizing.

The ultimate purpose is to feed your spirit which was created in God's own Image and longs to have that Image of God fulfilled. However, at this point there are two interesting factors to consider:

1. Even if the Word of God, written or spoken, is *rejected*, it still has an effect on the soul and spirit (Hebrews 4:12, NIV).

2. When the Word of God, written or spoken, is *accepted*, it not only affects the spirit, but also helps to bring the soul functions into meaning and balance.

God's Word not only enters from the external into the internal, but *also* Christ *Himself,* the *Incarnate Living Word,* living *in* the heart of every born-again Christian, finds expression and fulfillment as He lives His life through the spirit, the soul, and the body of every believer.

THE WORD IN US LIVES OUT HIS LIFE *THROUGH* US.

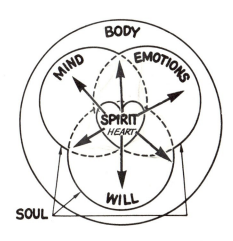

This is what Paul means when he states, "Christ in your hearts is your only hope of glory" (Colossians 1:27, TLB).

NOTES

For those who are relatively new to the Bible, a brief look at the contents of the Scriptures will be given. There have been many schemes devised to assist people in their understanding of the content and general breakdown of the Bible. One such device is included here.

THREE-POINT OUTLINE OF THE BIBLE
I. GOD'S INTENTION (Genesis 1 and 2) II. SIN'S INCEPTION (Genesis 3:1-13) III. GOD'S INTERVENTION (Genesis 3:13—Revelation)

A second scheme which will assist you in understanding the contents of the Scriptures is outlined on the following page.

OVERVIEW OF THE 66 BOOKS OF THE BIBLE

OLD TESTAMENT (39 Books) The Account of a Nation — Israel			About 400 years between Testaments	NEW TESTAMENT (27 Books) The Account of a Man — Christ Jesus			
Rise and Fall of the Hebrew Nation	Literature of the Nation's Golden Age	Literature of the Nation's Dark Age		GOSPELS The Story of the Man	HISTORY Activities of His First Century Church	EPISTLES The Man's Teaching and Principles	FORECAST The Man's Ultimate Universal Rule
17 Books	5 Books	17 Books		4 Books	1 Book	21 Books	1 Book
PENTATEUCH (LAW) 1 Genesis 2 Exodus 3 Leviticus 4 Numbers 5 Deuteronomy HISTORY 1 Joshua 2 Judges 3 Ruth 4 I Samuel 5 II Samuel 6 I Kings 7 II Kings 8 I Chronicles 9 II Chronicles 10 Ezra 11 Nehemiah 12 Esther	POETRY 1 Job 2 Psalms 3 Proverbs 4 Ecclesiastes 5 Song of Solomon	MAJOR PROPHETS 1 Isaiah 2 Jeremiah 3 Lamentations 4 Ezekiel 5 Daniel THE TWELVE PROPHETS 1 Hosea 2 Joel 3 Amos 4 Obadiah 5 Jonah 6 Micah 7 Nahum 8 Habakkuk 9 Zephaniah 10 Haggai 11 Zechariah 12 Malachi	The Old Testament looks forward to Christ's sacrifice on the Cross. CHRIST JESUS (cross) The New Testament is based on the work Christ finished on the Cross.	1 Matthew 2 Mark 3 Luke 4 John	Acts	Paul's Letters 1 Romans 2 I Corinthians 3 II Corinthians 4 Galatians 5 Ephesians 6 Philippians 7 Colossians 8 I Thessalonians 9 II Thessalonians 10 I Timothy 11 II Timothy 12 Titus 13 Philemon General Letters 1 Hebrews 2 James 3 I Peter 4 II Peter 5 I John 6 II John 7 III John 8 Jude	Revelation

"All Scripture is God-breathed and is useful for teaching, rebuking, correcting, and training in righteousness, so that the man of God may be thoroughly equipped for every good work." (II Timothy 3:16-17 NIV)

••• *HOW DO I* SATURATE MY LIFE WITH THE WORD OF GOD?

Four methods of saturating your life with the Word of God in a practical way will be considered as our study continues:

      x I. Hearing the Word of God

      II. Reading the Word of God

      x III. Studying the Word of God

      IV. Meditating on the Word of God

Pause right now and decide—on purpose—that, as you discover these four methods, you will choose to begin practicing these (or some derivatives thereof).

> I will put these four methods of Scripture intake into my life.
>
> check one:
>
> YES ✓   NO ___

I. Hearing the Word of God

God wants His people to hear His word. Seven times in Chapters 2 and 3 of Revelation, the admonition is given, "... <u>hear what the Spirit says to the churches</u> ..." (Revelation 2:7, 11, 17, 29 and 3:6, 13, 22, NASB).

Your own appetite for the Word is stimulated as you listen to the insight and applications resulting from the study of the Word by Godly pastors and teachers.

[Handwritten margin note: "God so loved ~~Jim~~ that He gave His only begotten Son."]

A. Six Practical Methods for Effectively Hearing God's Word

1. Be prepared to listen.
   a. Obtain sufficient rest, exercise, and nutrition.
   b. Spend some time in prayer.
   c. Ask yourself, "What do I already know about this subject?" and "What questions do I have?"
   d. Try to anticipate what you think the speaker will say.
   e. Arrive unrushed with your tools: Bible, pen, paper, and perhaps a cassette recorder.

x 2. Sit down front, in the middle of the listener's area.

3. As you listen, try determining the <u>main points</u> and <u>illustrations</u>.

4. You can hear at a faster rate of speed than a speaker can speak. Take advantage of this difference in speed by utilizing the following:
   a. Think back over what has already been said.
   b. Think aside, by asking, "How can I apply this?"

5. Take notes by priority—50% of forgetting takes place within the first 24 hours.
   a. List the Scripture references.
   b. List the main points.
   c. List the best illustrations.
   d. List whatever else you can get.

6. Decide on one major highlight, conclusion, or application from every message you hear.

Outline sermon and apply during weekly devotions

B. Assignment

> Use the form, "Effectively Hearing God's Word," as found on page 45, to take notes on the next sermon, message, or cassette that you hear.

II. Reading the Word of God

In Revelation 1:3 God tells us that He will bless that person who is obedient to what he *reads* in the Word. There is a difference between *reading* and *studying* the Word. We read the Bible in order to get an overview of God's Word. Reading should result in fun and refreshment. Bible reading can be exciting and profitable if we understand its purpose and apply a few simple, practical concepts. Consider the diagram below which graphically illustrates a vital relationship between Bible reading and prayer.

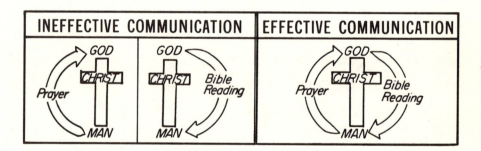

Dialogue requires two basic participants: someone to speak and someone to listen. For effective dialogue, the roles of speaker and listener must be passed back and forth between the participants. This concept is pertinent to Bible reading, as indicated in the previous diagram. If you resort only to letting God speak to you through Bible reading, there is no dialogue. It is also true that if you do all the talking to God through prayer, there is no dialogue. Effective dialogue occurs when you allow God to talk to you through Bible reading, and you then respond back to Him through prayer. Two helpful hints for making your Bible reading more effective for spiritual growth are described below.

A. Marking Your Bible

As you read your Bible, mark anything that impresses you. It may be a question, a conviction, or a new insight. Be assured that these impressions are given by the Holy Spirit. God is speaking to you! After you have read and marked, go back over what you have marked, responding back to God. Let this response be based on what impressed you. By so doing, Bible reading takes on a new dimension. Instead of a required exercise, Bible reading will become fun, refreshing, exciting, and profitable!

B. Develop a Consistent Reading Plan

You may want to use the form, "My Bible Reading Record," as found on page 46, to keep track of where you have read in your Bible. After you read a chapter of a particular book of the Bible, mark across that corresponding number on the chart. By maintaining your reading chart, you will know what you have already read and what you have left to read. Begin by reading one chapter out of the New Testament each day as a minimum.

> **ASSIGNMENT**
>
> 1. Begin reading and marking in your Bible.
> 2. Keep a record of your reading on "My Bible Reading Record," as found on page 46.
> 3. Share what you have read and marked in your small-group sharing time.

III. Studying the Word of God

Two New Testament letters were written to the Church at Thessalonica. Upon reading each of these letters, you may be impressed with the caliber of Christians that God had raised up. However, the Berean Christians excelled the Thessalonians in one major area—Bible study:

> Now the Bereans were of more noble character than the Thessalonians, for they received the message with great eagerness and examined the Scriptures every day to see if what Paul said was true.
>
> Acts 17:11, NIV

The study of God's Word brings you into personal discoveries of the truth of God. By writing down your discoveries (the distinctive characteristic of Bible study), you organize your thinking for better recall and practical application.

One simple, but effective, approach to Bible study is the "Three-Point Verse Analysis."

> ### THREE-POINT VERSE ANALYSIS
>
> 1. What does the verse say?
>   After choosing a particular portion of the Bible to study, write *in your own words* what the verse says.
>
> 2. What is the context?
>   Read the verses before and after the passage you are studying. Write *in your own words* the context of these verses.
>
> 3. What can be done to apply this passage?
>   Write a measurable, practical, personal application.

> ### ASSIGNMENT
> Do at least one "Three-Point Verse Analysis" Bible study per week for the next four weeks. Use the form provided on page 47.

Probably the most effective principle a Disciple can use to saturate his life with the Word of God is to consistently "write it on the table of his heart," i.e., memorize it! Many who have invested in consistent Scripture memory have heartily testified that, for the investment in time and effort, Scripture memory has returned some of the greatest dividends in their Christian lives. The Psalmist recognized the value of memorizing Scripture:

> Wherewithal shall a young man cleanse his way? by taking heed *thereto* according to thy word. With my whole heart have I sought thee: O let me not wander from they commandments. *Thy word have I hid in mine heart, that I might not sin against thee.*
>
> Psalm 119:9-11, KJV

Jesus Himself had memorized Scripture, as is clearly indicated by the way He used the Word during His wilderness temptation (Matthew 4:4, 7, 10).

Scripture memory is a skill and, as such, can be improved. However, the key to successfully memorizing Scripture on a consistent basis is determined by the desire of one's heart.

"Do I Really Want to Do This?" *Yes*

"Does God Want Me to Consistently Memorize His Word?" *Yes*

Once you are able to answer these questions with positive responses, you are ready to embark upon that most exciting path which enables you to

> . . . Always be prepared to give an answer to everyone who asks you to give the reason for the hope that you have.
> I Peter 3:15, NIV

By applying a few simple concepts, you will soon be experiencing the thrill of "hiding God's Word" in your heart!

A. Begin to Memorize a Verse By:

1. Reading it through aloud several times.

2. Making a conscious effort to obtain a grasp at what the verse means—try to visualize what the writer is trying to say.

3. Personalizing through applying the verse to your own life in a practical way.

B. Proceed to Memorize the Verse By:

1. Asking God to help you.

2. Working on the reference and first phrase.

3. Then adding the second phrase.

4. Continuing to add phrases until you finally have the verse *word perfect*.

5. Concluding with the reference again.

6. Reviewing the reference and verse several times immediately after you have completed steps 1 through 5.

7. Continuing to review the reference and verse at least once a day over the next several days.

8. Having someone check your recollection of the verse.

9. Reviewing—the only way to keep a verse sharp in your mind and ready to use.

You may have already established a different method of Scripture memorization which you feel more comfortable in using. If it works—use it!

> ## ASSIGNMENT
>
> Employing the principles previously given, memorize the following five verses:
>
> | | |
> |---|---|
> | Luke 9:23 | Follow Christ |
> | John 8:31 | The Word |
> | Mark 1:35 | Prayer |
> | Hebrews 10:25 | Fellowship |
> | Mark 16:15 | Witness |
>
> Write out these verses on the verse cards provided on page 361. You may choose your favorite translation of the Bible. Carry these verses with you each day in your pocket or purse, and choose extra moments each day to memorize and/or review your verses. To begin, memorize one new verse each week as a minimum.

IV. Meditating on the Word of God

God expects His people to spend time—a lot of it—meditating upon His Word. The Bible is abundantly clear about this:

> This book of the law shall not depart out of thy mouth; but thou shalt meditate therein day and night, that thou mayest observe to do according to all that is written therein: for then thou shalt make thy way prosperous, and then thou shalt have good success.
>
> Joshua 1:8, KJV

> Oh, the joys of those who do not follow evil men's advice, who do not hang around with sinners, scoffing at the things of God: But they delight in doing everything God wants them to, and day and night are always meditating on his laws and thinking about ways to follow him more closely.
>
> Psalms 1:1-2, TLB

A. Results of Meditation

The result of meditating upon God's Word is to lead you into practically applying the Word. Meditation is "spiritual digestion." It is the "tool" you have to get God's Word out of the realm of mere theory into "shoe leather." It takes you from merely being a "hearer" to becoming a "doer."

> Do not merely listen to the word, and so deceive yourselves. Do what it says.
>
> James 1:22, NIV

> But the man who looks intently into the perfect law that gives freedom, and continues to do this, not forgetting what he has heard, but doing it—he will be blessed in what he does.
>
> James 1:25, NIV

Without meditation and practical application, hearing, reading, or studying, or even memorizing the Word of God becomes a fruitless mental exercise. Never cheat yourself or God by failing to apply the Word of God to your life in a practical, measurable manner.

B. Practical Application

The following three suggestions will help you make a personal application from the Word of God.

HOW TO MAKE A PERSONAL APPLICATION FROM GOD'S WORD

1. Pray that God will give you a specific application and show you how to practically do it.

2. Once God speaks to you, *write out* how you fall short in that particular area. Use personal singular pronouns (I, me, etc.). Generally, your applications will be related to either your relationship with God or your relationship with people.

3. Write out specifically what God would have you do in order to correct what you wrote in number 2 above. It may take the form of memorizing a particular verse, doing a special Bible study, praying daily about the need, asking someone's forgiveness, etc. Insure that your course of action is specific, practical, and measurable. Set time limits as required. You may want to ask someone to hold you accountable.

ASSIGNMENT

For the next four weeks, make one major application from God's Word per week.

Use the form provided on page 49 and employ the suggestions previously discussed. You may draw your application from a sermon, your Bible reading, personal Bible study, or a memory verse. Be sure that your resulting application is practical and measurable. If not too personal, make yourself accountable by asking someone to check you out in your application.

EFFECTIVELY HEARING GOD'S WORD

Blessed is he who reads and those who *hear* the words of the prophecy, and heed the things which are written in it; for the time is near.
Revelation 1:3, NASB

MESSAGE TOPIC _____

SPEAKER _____ DATE _____

—SCRIPTURE REFERENCES—

—MAIN POINTS—

—ILLUSTRATIONS—

—MISCELLANEOUS—

—APPLICATION—

MY BIBLE READING RECORD

Book	Chapters
GENESIS	1 2 3 4 5 6 7 8 9 10 11 12 13 14 15 16 17 18 19 20 21 22 23 24 25 26 27 28 29 30 31 32 33 34 35 36 37 38 39 40 41 42 43 44 45 46 47 48 49 50
EXODUS	1 2 3 4 5 6 7 8 9 10 11 12 13 14 15 16 17 18 19 20 21 22 23 24 25 26 27 28 29 30 31 32 33 34 35 36 37 38 39 40
LEVITICUS	1 2 3 4 5 6 7 8 9 10 11 12 13 14 15 16 17 18 19 20 21 22 23 24 25 26 27
NUMBERS	1 2 3 4 5 6 7 8 9 10 11 12 13 14 15 16 17 18 19 20 21 22 23 24 25 26 27 28 29 30 31 32 33 34 35 36
DEUTERONOMY	1 2 3 4 5 6 7 8 9 10 11 12 13 14 15 16 17 18 19 20 21 22 23 24 25 26 27 28 29 30 31 32 33 34
JOSHUA	1 2 3 4 5 6 7 8 9 10 11 12 13 14 15 16 17 18 19 20 21 22 23 24
JUDGES	1 2 3 4 5 6 7 8 9 10 11 12 13 14 15 16 17 18 19 20 21
RUTH	1 2 3 4
I SAMUEL	1 2 3 4 5 6 7 8 9 10 11 12 13 14 15 16 17 18 19 20 21 22 23 24 25 26 27 28 29 30 31
II SAMUEL	1 2 3 4 5 6 7 8 9 10 11 12 13 14 15 16 17 18 19 20 21 22 23 24
I KINGS	1 2 3 4 5 6 7 8 9 10 11 12 13 14 15 16 17 18 19 20 21 22
II KINGS	1 2 3 4 5 6 7 8 9 10 11 12 13 14 15 16 17 18 19 20 21 22 23 24 25
I CHRONICLES	1 2 3 4 5 6 7 8 9 10 11 12 13 14 15 16 17 18 19 20 21 22 23 24 25 26 27 28 29
II CHRONICLES	1 2 3 4 5 6 7 8 9 10 11 12 13 14 15 16 17 18 19 20 21 22 23 24 25 26 27 28 29 30 31 32 33 34 35 36
EZRA	1 2 3 4 5 6 7 8 9 10
NEHEMIAH	1 2 3 4 5 6 7 8 9 10 11 12 13
ESTHER	1 2 3 4 5 6 7 8 9 10
JOB	1 2 3 4 5 6 7 8 9 10 11 12 13 14 15 16 17 18 19 20 21 22 23 24 25 26 27 28 29 30 31 32 33 34 35 36 37 38 39 40 41 42
PSALMS	1 2 3 4 5 6 7 8 9 10 11 12 13 14 15 16 17 18 19 20 21 22 23 24 25 26 27 28 29 30 31 32 33 34 35 36 37 38 39 40 41 42 43 44 45 46 47 48 49 50 51 52 53 54 55 56 57 58 59 60 61 62 63 64 65 66 67 68 69 70 71 72 73 74 75 76 77 78 79 80 81 82 83 84 85 86 87 88 89 90 91 92 93 94 95 96 97 98 99 100 101 102 103 104 105 106 107 108 109 110 111 112 113 114 115 116 117 118 119 120 121 122 123 124 125 126 127 128 129 130 131 132 133 134 135 136 137 138 139 140 141 142 143 144 145 146 147 148 149 150
PROVERBS	1 2 3 4 5 6 7 8 9 10 11 12 13 14 15 16 17 18 19 20 21 22 23 24 25 26 27 28 29 30 31
ECCLESIASTES	1 2 3 4 5 6 7 8 9 10 11 12
SONG of SOLOMON	1 2 3 4 5 6 7 8
ISAIAH	1 2 3 4 5 6 7 8 9 10 11 12 13 14 15 16 17 18 19 20 21 22 23 24 25 26 27 28 29 30 31 32 33 34 35 36 37 38 39 40 41 42 43 44 45 46 47 48 49 50 51 52 53 54 55 56 57 58 59 60 61 62 63 64 65 66
JEREMIAH	1 2 3 4 5 6 7 8 9 10 11 12 13 14 15 16 17 18 19 20 21 22 23 24 25 26 27 28 29 30 31 32 33 34 35 36 37 38 39 40 41 42 43 44 45 46 47 48 49 50 51 52
LAMENTATIONS	1 2 3 4 5
EZEKIEL	1 2 3 4 5 6 7 8 9 10 11 12 13 14 15 16 17 18 19 20 21 22 23 24 25 26 27 28 29 30 31 32 33 34 35 36 37 38 39 40 41 42 43 44 45 46 47 48
DANIEL	1 2 3 4 5 6 7 8 9 10 11 12
HOSEA	1 2 3 4 5 6 7 8 9 10 11 12 13 14
JOEL	1 2 3
AMOS	1 2 3 4 5 6 7 8 9
OBADIAH	1
JONAH	1 2 3 4
MICAH	1 2 3 4 5 6 7
NAHUM	1 2 3
HABAKKUK	1 2 3
ZEPHANIAH	1 2 3
HAGGAI	1 2
ZECHARIAH	1 2 3 4 5 6 7 8 9 10 11 12 13 14
MALACHI	1 2 3 4
MATTHEW	1 2 3 4 5 6 7 8 9 10 11 12 13 14 15 16 17 18 19 20 21 22 23 24 25 26 27 28
MARK	1 2 3 4 5 6 7 8 9 10 11 12 13 14 15 16
LUKE	1 2 3 4 5 6 7 8 9 10 11 12 13 14 15 16 17 18 19 20 21 22 23 24
JOHN	1 2 3 4 5 6 7 8 9 10 11 12 13 14 15 16 17 18 19 20 21
ACTS	1 2 3 4 5 6 7 8 9 10 11 12 13 14 15 16 17 18 19 20 21 22 23 24 25 26 27 28
ROMANS	1 2 3 4 5 6 7 8 9 10 11 12 13 14 15 16
I CORINTHIANS	1 2 3 4 5 6 7 8 9 10 11 12 13 14 15 16
II CORINTHIANS	1 2 3 4 5 6 7 8 9 10 11 12 13
GALATIANS	1 2 3 4 5 6
EPHESIANS	1 2 3 4 5 6
PHILIPPIANS	1 2 3 4
COLOSSIANS	1 2 3 4
I THESSALONIANS	1 2 3 4 5
II THESSALONIANS	1 2 3
I TIMOTHY	1 2 3 4 5 6
II TIMOTHY	1 2 3 4
TITUS	1 2 3
PHILEMON	1
HEBREWS	1 2 3 4 5 6 7 8 9 10 11 12 13
JAMES	1 2 3 4 5
I PETER	1 2 3 4 5
II PETER	1 2 3
I JOHN	1 2 3 4 5
II JOHN	1
III JOHN	1
JUDE	1
REVELATION	1 2 3 4 5 6 7 8 9 10 11 12 13 14 15 16 17 18 19 20 21 22

"All Scripture . . . is useful . . ." (II Timothy 3:16 NIV)

THREE-POINT VERSE ANALYSIS

PASSAGE _____ DATE _____

CONTENT (What does it say?):

CONTEXT (What do verses before and after say?):

APPLICATION:

PASSAGE _____ DATE _____

CONTENT (What does it say?):

CONTEXT (What do verses before and after say?):

APPLICATION:

PASSAGE _____ DATE _____

CONTENT (What does it say?):

CONTEXT (What do verses before and after say?):

APPLICATION:

PASSAGE _____ DATE _____

CONTENT (What does it say?):

CONTEXT (What do verses before and after say?):

APPLICATION:

PERSONAL APPLICATIONS

PASSAGE _____ DATE _____ PRAYED _____

FAULT (Where I fall short):

PLAN (What I'm going to do):

PASSAGE _____ DATE _____ PRAYED _____

FAULT (Where I fall short):

PLAN (What I'm going to do):

PASSAGE _____ DATE _____ PRAYED _____

FAULT (Where I fall short):

PLAN (What I'm going to do):

PASSAGE _____ DATE _____ PRAYED _____

FAULT (Where I fall short):

PLAN (What I'm going to do):

Man
(outline)

I. Principles to be Apprehended

   A. The Historical Background

      1. The Theory of Dichotomy
      2. The Theory of Trichotomy

   B. The Relevant Merger

II. Practics to be Applied

   A. The Body Function and Characteristics

      1. The body is amoral.
      2. The body is imperfectible.
      3. The body is mortal.

   B. The Soul Function and Characteristics

      1. The soul functions are amoral.
      2. The soul functions are imperfectible.
      3. The soul functions are mortal.

   C. The Spirit or Heart Function and Characteristics

      1. The spirit or heart function is moral.
      2. The spirit or heart function is perfectible.
      3. The spirit or heart function is immortal.

   D. Some Practical Examples

      1. Consider the physical body and its need for food.
      2. Consider the psychical need to be accepted.
      3. Consider the physical and psychical need for sexual relations.

   E. The Practical Aspect of the Functional Trichotomy as it Relates to Sin

*Didst Thou not die, that I might live,
No longer to myself but Thee?
Might <u>body</u>, <u>soul</u>, and <u>spirit</u> give
To Him who gave Himself for me?
Come then, my Master and my God,
Take the dear purchase of Thy blood.*
—John Wesley

Man

In the previous chapter, "The Word of God in the Life of a Disciple," you will recall a simple diagram which was used to illustrate how God's Word can saturate a human life (pages 30 and 31). In this chapter that diagram will be enlarged upon and explained as you discover how the constituent elements of man's nature can function in relationship to a spiritual God and His creation. You are going to enjoy this chapter as you discover some of the basic principles regarding God's most complex creation . . . Man. Throughout this chapter you will be called upon to use your "thinker" as these principles are presented. Comprehension of the material included in this chapter is mandatory if there is to be adequate understanding of such future subjects as "The Born-Again Life" and "The Spirit-Filled Life."

In this chapter you will have the opportunity to learn and deal with the following terms.

moral	that which deals with or is concerned with establishing principles of "<u>right</u>" and "<u>wrong</u>" in <u>behavior</u>
amoral	that which deals with concerns other than those of "right" and "wrong"

perfectible	capable of being made perfect, whole, or entire in this present life
imperfectible	incapable of being made perfect, whole, or entire in this present life
mortal	subject to death, destined to die
immortal	imperishable, destined to live, will not die
Dichotomy	the theory that holds that man is composed of two kinds of essence
Trichotomy	the theory that holds that man consists of three constituent elements

[Handwritten annotations: "non-christian or self-centered christian" next to imperfectible; "we are all" next to mortal; "by God's grace" next to immortal; "?" next to Dichotomy]

So . . . sharpen your wits, sharpen your pencils, and ask God for a "learner's attitude" as you discover the basic functional elements of man through:

    I. Principles to be Apprehended
    II. Practics to be Applied

I. Principles to be Apprehended

A. The Historical Background

For centuries early church leaders pondered and discussed the subject of man's nature. Just exactly what were the elements that constituted man's personality? They knew man had a body which was capable of carrying out physical functions, i.e., breathing, running, seeing, working, and even reproducing. Yet, there seemed to be more than just the outside observable flesh. Man could <u>think</u>; he could <u>reason</u>; he could <u>remember</u>. He could also feel pain, anger, excitement, and frustration. He had certain likes and dislikes, favorite foods, favorite colors, and favorite people. Man had a way of choosing certain occupations and life-styles, while rejecting others.

Man had all of this, and yet, there seemed to be more . . . something deeper. There seemed to be a reaching out for an identity with something or someone bigger than himself . . . a god. There were feelings of "rightness" and "wrongness" and "oughtness" that became the driving motivation for nearly all he did. Yet, there were some things he did that seemed to have nothing to do with "rightness" and "wrongness" . . . things he just did.

Questions would then arise: Do you feel pain with your body or your mind? Is frustration physical? Where does anger come from? Where does love come from? Does getting hungry have anything to do with morality? Is the drive for reproduction sinful? Why do some people have to wear glasses? Is it wrong to feel bad because you look funny? How will all this be affected in the life hereafter?

As you can see, that which constitutes man's nature, and how that nature affects man's behavior, posed some perplexing problems. Some of the early church leaders ran away from the problem and chose to study Creation or Armageddon. However, those who wrestled with this problem very adamantly and very decisively aligned themselves with one of two *very* separate and distinct camps of thought. Discussion cemented into polarization, for most held strongly to either one or the other of these two theories.

| Theory of Dichotomy | OR | Theory of Trichotomy |

In the following pages you will have the opportunity to examine the strengths and weaknesses of both these theories.

1. The Theory of Dichotomy

   This view holds that man is composed of two kinds of essence: a material portion (physical) and a non-material portion (spiritual). The Dichotomist insists that man consists of *two, and only two,* distinct elements, matter and non-matter, or material and spiritual.[1] If diagrammed, this position would be illustrated as follows.

   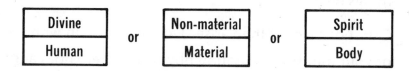

   Some confusion has arisen here out of the fact that in both the Old Testament and the New Testament, the terms *soul* and *spirit* have been translated almost interchangeably.

   The theory of Dichotomy is a very comfortable approach because it is so simplistic on the surface. And there is some consolation in being in this camp, since it is known for certain that man is at *least* dichotomic—material and non-material.

   However, there are some major limitations to the theory of Dichotomy.

   a. It makes neither allowance nor explanation for the moral and amoral aspects of the non-material, that is, mind, emotions, and will.

   b. It breaks down when applied to practical living.

   c. It unrealistically holds that if something is not material, then it is *spiritual*.

   d. It tends to break down, rather than support, the unity of the total person.

---

[1] H. Orton Wiley and Paul Culbertson, *Introduction to Christian Theology* (Kansas City, Mo.: Beacon Hill Press, 1957), p. 153.

Consequently, throughout the years, confusion has been the result whenever the theory of Dichotomy has been applied to practical everyday living.

2. The Theory of Trichotomy

This theory holds that man consists of three constituent elements: body (Greek, *soma*), soul (Greek, *psuche*), and spirit (Greek, *pneuma*).[2] Wiley and Culbertson refer to the three elements as "spirit, the animal soul, and the body."[3] In *Exploring Our Christian Faith,* W. T. Purkiser states:

> This theory holds that man consists of three component parts—body, soul, and spirit—and that the soul and spirit are almost as distinct from each other as soul and body. The spirit is declared to be the organ of divine life and of communion with God, the seat of the divine indwelling. The soul is seen as the seat of the natural life, where the natural faculties of the conscious being dwell. It is the intermediary between the body and the spirit.[4]

Many passages of Scripture seem to indicate that the nature of man is threefold. As an example:

> Now may the God of peace Himself sanctify you entirely; and may your *spirit* and *soul* and *body* be preserved complete, without blame at the coming of Lord Jesus Christ.
> I Thessalonians 5:23, NASB

If the theory of Trichotomy were to be diagrammed, it would appear something like this.

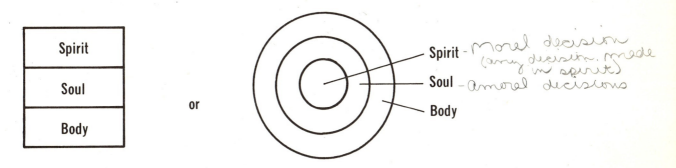

---

[2] A. M. Hills, *Fundamental Christian Theology, Volume 1* (Pasadena, Calif.: C. J. Kinne, 1931), p. 327.
[3] *Op. cit.,* Wiley and Culbertson, p. 153.
[4] W. T. Purkiser, *Exploring Our Christian Faith* (Kansas City, Mo.: Beacon Hill Press, 1960), p. 210.

As complete as the theory of Trichotomy would appear on the surface, it also suffers from severe limitations.

a. It makes no provision for integration of the total person, but rather, tends to segment or polarize the different characteristics of the individual.

b. It breaks down under application to practical life.

c. As was the case with Dichotomy, it does not distinguish between the moral and the amoral aspects of the mind, emotions, and will. (what body (physical) is made up of)

> NOTE: *Moral* simply means that which deals with or is concerned with establishing principles of "right" and "wrong" in behavior. Whereas, *amoral* (a = not + moral) would be that which is dealing with concerns other than those of "rightness" and "wrongness." In and of themselves, the things that are amoral can never become moral.

Well, you may now take a deep breath, sit up tall with your sharp pencil in hand, and say, "That's very interesting . . . but so what?"

The nineteenth-century theologian, Dr. John Miley, is quoted in the writing of A. M. Hills:

> Dr. Miley after discussing dichotomic and trichotomic divisions of human nature, closes by saying, "We have reached no dogmatic conclusion on the question. Indeed, it does not seriously concern any important doctrine of Christian theology. It is a question of speculative interest in biblical psychology, but has no doctrinal implications decisive of either its truth or falsity."[5]

---

[5] *Op. cit.*, Hills, p. 328.

Isn't it amazing how some of the "ho-hum"'s and "so-what"'s of science and medicine of fifty years ago have become the great "oh-my"'s of today's re-discoveries? The geometric progression of increased knowledge has taken some principles that once seemed very obscure and quite unimportant and suddenly made them acutely relevant and necessary. So it is with understanding the nature of man as it relates to behavior. Although there was once a time when the characteristics of man's nature did not concern most theologians, twentieth-century discoveries of behavioral psychology demand our understanding of these ageless and eternal biblical principles.

If you are to be effective Disciples and Disciplers today, you should revisit the old truths and see if they can be articulated and applied to the knowledge and needs of our present world. Today, it *does* make a difference whether or not you understand the nature of man in order to more fully understand what happens to that nature in "The Born-Again Life" and "The Spirit-Filled Life." The distinction must be understood between the things that are _changed_ and those that are _affected_ by the Holy Spirit as He deals with man's nature and his behavior.

B. The Relevant Merger

It must be clearly understood at the outset that *man is a unit and functions as such*. He is not a fragmented bunch of parts held together by some humanistic epoxy. The integration of man's total personality cannot be over-emphasized. Quite obviously, there is no way you can totally understand man's nature by a simple diagram. There is no way to adequately describe through graphs or charts man's complexity. However, from a *functional* point of view, man *can* be more practically understood by describing him according to his *functions* and then defining the *characteristics* of those functions. Therefore, from a *functional* point of view, man can be described as:

- **BODY**
  (PHYSICAL)

- **SOUL** *(dichotomy, material + non-material)*
  (PSYCHICAL)

- **SPIRIT** *(attitude of God)*
  (SPIRITUAL)

Now take a look at the *characteristics* that will be used in describing these functions. *(workable + operable)*

1	2	3
moral or amoral	perfectible or imperfectible	mortal or immortal

dichotic part of it

Definitions:

moral	that which deals with or is concerned with establishing principles of "right" and "wrong" in behavior
amoral	that which deals with concerns other than those of "right" and "wrong"
perfectible	capable of being made perfect, whole, or entire in this present life
imperfectible	incapable of being made perfect, whole, or entire in this present life
mortal	subject to death, destined to die
immortal	imperishable, destined to live, will not die

Man, then, <u>*functions* as a *trichotomy*</u>—body, soul, and spirit. Each of these functions has three characteristics used to describe it: i.e., (1) moral or amoral, (2) perfectible or imperfectible, and (3) mortal or immortal. However, *two* of these functions have the *same* characteristics. Now, then, if *two* of the *three functions* have the same common characteristics, then, in reality, man's nature is a *dichotomy*. <u>So it is—a *trichotomy* in *function* and a *dichotomy* in *characteristic!*</u> What you have just seen is a functional, relevant merger of two historically opposed camps of thought. *(Don't you just love a wedding)*

Look at the simple recap of man's nature:

- *Unity* from the standpoint of *Essence*
- *Dichotomy* from the standpoint of *Characteristic*
- *Trichotomy* from the standpoint of *Function*

And now for a name . . . you could call it: "The Threefold Functional Aspects and Characteristics of the Dichotomic Nature of Man" . . . or, you could simply call it: "Functional Trichotomy." Let's just call it "Functional Trichotomy." *(How's your "thinker" doing?)*

II. Practices to be Applied

In the following paragraphs you will examine the various aspects of the *Functional Trichotomy*. However, it is necessary that you keep in mind the *unity and integration* of the total person as his nature is expressed.

A. The Body Function and Characteristics

THE BODY/PHYSICAL	
FUNCTION	CHARACTERISTICS
	1. Amoral 2. Imperfectible 3. Mortal

> But this precious treasure ... is held in a perishable container, that is, in our weak bodies ...
> II Corinthians 4:7, TLB

1. The body is *amoral*.

   That is, in and of itself, the body is *neither righteous nor evil*. It is physical material only. You can touch it. You can see it. The Bible calls it "dust" that will one day return to the earth.

   > Then the dust will return to the earth as it was ...
   > Ecclesiastes 12:7, NASB

   Since the body is the amoral vessel housing the other functions, it is not in and of itself sinful. "Now, mistakes, and whatever infirmities flow from the corruptible state of the body, are no way contrary to love, nor therefore, in the Scripture sense, sin."[6]

---

[6]John Wesley, *Plain Account of Christian Perfection* (Boston, Mass.: McDonald, Gill & Co., 1766), p. 43.

2. The body is *imperfectible*.

   Some bodies appear to be "more perfect" than others. However, until these bodies die or otherwise are exchanged for perfect, *soma pneumatikon,* or spiritual bodies (I Corinthians 15:44), you can expect such imperfections as sickness, weakness, and fatigue. Won't it be wonderful when this imperfect, mortal body takes on the perfection of immortality?

   > For this perishable must put on the imperishable, and this mortal must put on immortality.
   > I Corinthians 15:53, NASB

3. The body is *mortal*.

   It will die.

   > And inasmuch as it is appointed for men to die once, and after this comes judgment.
   > Hebrews 9:27, NASB

B. The Soul Function and Characteristics

THE SOUL/PSYCHICAL	
FUNCTION	CHARACTERISTICS
(Venn diagram: MIND – to think, EMOTIONS – to feel, WILL – to act)	1. Amoral 2. Imperfectible 3. Mortal

[margin note: same as the body]

[margin note: psuche = soul; these act both dependent and interdependent of each other.]

The soul is comprised of

- The mind — the capacity to think and reason;
- The emotions — the capacity to experience feeling;
- The will — the capacity to desire and choose.

PLEASE NOTE: The characteristics of the soul function are the same as those of the body.

[margin note: What you think determines what you feel. How you feel determines the actions you take.]

The soul is the *psychical nature of man:* the Greek word *psuche* equals *soul.* You learned in the earlier portion of this chapter that one of the historical weaknesses of trying to explain the nature of man was the fact that, in the explanation of his different aspects, man was so separated and segmented that the result was unrealistic.

Look again at the preceding diagram. Notice how the different soul functions overlap each other. It can be described by a simple layman's term taken from the building-contracting field: "interfacing." <u>Interfacing</u> is simply where a common boundary is formed of two or more bodies of spaces. It is used here to show the absolute action and interaction, dependence and interdependence, of one soul function upon the other two. Your *mental* functions are definitely influenced by your emotional and volitional (willful) functions. Your *desires* are interlocked with your emotions and intellect. Your *emotions* are certainly affected by your desires and your intellect. To think that these functions can be totally separated in the everyday life is unrealistic.

1. The soul functions are *amoral*.

   a. The *mind* is the capacity to think and reason. There is a part of your mental function that has nothing to do with morality. On the scale of morality there is nothing righteous or evil about your capacity to learn that two times two equals four. There is nothing righteous or evil about your capacity to recognize that the sun is shining. This portion of your mental capacity is amoral.

   b. *Emotion* is the capacity to experience feeling. There is a part of your emotional function that has nothing to do with morality. It is neither righteous nor evil to be totally *surprised* when your friends give you an unexpected birthday party (unless you lied about your age). Being *grieved* when your favorite pet runs away has absolutely nothing to do with morality.

   c. The *will,* or volition, is the capacity to desire or choose. There is a part of your *volitional function* that has nothing to do with morality. You may *desire* to set your alarm clock in order to arise at six o'clock in the morning. Or, you may *choose* to put catsup on your french-fried potatoes at lunch. Certainly these volitional functions are neither righteous nor evil; rather, they are amoral.

2. The soul functions are *imperfectible*.

In this life, the human *mind* will always be imperfect. You will be subject to imperfect judgment and understanding. Upon occasion, the ragged edge of a frayed *emotion* will snag when you least expect it. And because of your imperfect human judgment, you may even make some amoral choices that are regrettable.

> We secondly believe that there is no such perfection in this life, as implies an entire deliverance, either from ignorance, or mistake, in things not essential to salvation, or from manifold temptations, or from numberless infirmities, wherewith the corruptible body more or less presses down the soul. We cannot find any ground in Scripture to suppose, that any inhabitant of a house of clay is wholly exempt either from bodily infirmities, or from ignorance of many things; or to imagine any is incapable of mistake, or falling into divers temptations.[7]

[Handwritten margin note: It does away with the idea that holiness churches become perfect.]

John Wesley goes on to state:

> A man may be filled with pure love, and still be liable to mistake. Indeed, I do not expect to be freed from actual mistakes, till this mortal puts on immortality. I believe this to be a natural consequence of the soul's indwelling in flesh and blood. For we cannot now think at all, but by the meditation of those bodily organs which have suffered equally with the rest of our frame. And hence we cannot avoid sometimes thinking wrong, till this corruptible shall have put on incorruption.

> But we may carry this thought further yet. A mistake in judgment may possibly occasion a mistake in practice . . . Yet, where every word and action springs from love, such a mistake is not openly a sin.[8]

[7] *Ibid.*, p. 27.
[8] *Ibid.*, p. 41.

3. The soul functions are *mortal.*

The functions of the mind, emotions, and will, *as they are known today,* will one day cease to operate as they do at the present. One day that gray cerebrum, cerebellum, and medulla will no longer receive stimuli, interpret, and emit commands. One day the motor neurons, correlating neurons, and the dendrites of the nervous system will all die and return to dust.

> My soul cleaves to the dust . . .
> Psalm 119:25, NASB

The mind, emotions, and will shall then take on different *characteristics,* inasmuch as these functions will result from an immortal, glorified source.

> . . . who will transform the body of our humble state into conformity with the body of His glory, by the exertion of the power that He has even to subject all things to Himself.
> Philippians 3:21, NASB

C. The Spirit or Heart Function and Characteristics

THE SPIRIT OR HEART/SPIRITUAL	
FUNCTION	CHARACTERISTICS
(Spirit or heart → Mind, Emotions, Will diagram)	1. Moral 2. Perfectible 3. Immortal

The spirit is the function of man's nature that deals with moral issues. Through the Scriptures the terms *spirit* and *heart* are usually used interchangeably.

That the *human soul* and *spirit* are *not identical* is proved by the fact that they are *divisible*.

> For the word of God is living and active and sharper than any two-edged sword, and piercing as far as the division of soul and spirit, of both joints and marrow...
>
> Hebrews 4:12, NASB

The soul and spirit are sharply distinguished in the burial and resurrection of the body.

> It is sown a natural body (*soma psuchikon* = psychical or soul body).
>
> It is raised a spiritual body (*soma pneumatikon* = spiritual body).
>
> I Corinthians 15:44, NASB

Every man is created with a heart or spirit. James tells us that the body without the *spirit* is dead (James 2:26). The writer of Ecclesiastes tells us that when we die, our *spirit* will return to God who gave it (Ecclesiastes 12:7). Daniel tells us:

> I Daniel was grieved in my *spirit* in the midst of my body...
>
> Daniel 7:15, KJV

We also read that when Christ came to the place of death, He "cried out again with a loud voice, and yielded up His *spirit*" (Matthew 27:50, NASB). Old wicked Pharaoh even had problems with his *spirit*.

> Now it came about in the morning that his *spirit* was troubled...
>
> Genesis 41:8, NASB

1. The spirit or heart function is *moral*.

   The *spirit* or *heart* is the function of man's nature where *moral business is transacted*. It is the center or the seat of the basic moral affections of man. Genesis 8:21 (NASB) states that "the intent of man's *heart* (spirit) is evil from his youth." In I Chronicles 28:9 (NASB) we are told that "the Lord searches all *hearts,* and understands every intent." ". . . For with the *heart* man believes . . ." (Romans 10:10, NASB). This is more than just the amoral mental assent of the psyche; this is dealing with a moral issue.

   The following are some important Scriptures regarding the heart or spirit function.

Jeremiah 24:7, NASB	". . . for they will return to Me with their whole *heart*."
Deuteronomy 4:29, NASB	"But from there you will seek the Lord your God, and you will find Him if you search for Him with all your *heart* and all your *soul*."
Zechariah 7:12, NASB	". . . they made their *hearts* like flint so that they could not hear the law and the words . . ."
Jeremiah 32:40, NASB	". . . I will put the fear of Me in their *hearts* so that they will not turn away from Me."
Psalm 119, NASB v. 2	. . . Who seek Him with all their *heart*.
v. 7	. . . uprightness of *heart* . . .
v. 10	With all my *heart* I have sought Thee . . .
v. 11	Thy word I have treasured in my *heart* . . .
	(total of 13 times in Psalm 119)
I Samuel 16:7, NASB	". . . man looks at the outward appearance, but the Lord looks at the *heart*."
I Kings 8:39, NASB	". . . Thou alone dost know the *hearts* . . ."
Luke 16:15, NASB	". . . God knows your *hearts* . . ."
I Kings 11:4, NASB	. . . when Solomon was old, his wives turned his *heart* . . . his *heart* was not wholly devoted to the Lord his God . . .
	(Also, I Kings 9:4 and 15:3)

Psalm 51:10, NASB	Create in me a clean *heart* . . . renew a steadfast spirit . . .
Ezekiel 11:19, NASB	". . . I shall give them one heart, and shall put a new *spirit* within them."
Philippians 4:7, NASB	. . . guard your *hearts* . . .
Romans 2:5, NASB	. . . stubbornness and unrepentant *heart* . . .
Romans 8:27, NASB	. . . He who searches the *hearts* knows . . .
Luke 24:25, NASB	". . . O foolish men and slow of *heart* to believe . . ."
Jeremiah 17:9, NASB	"The *heart* is more deceitful than all else . . ."
Matthew 15:8, NASB	". . . their *heart* is far away from Me."
Matthew 19:8, NASB	". . . Because of your hardness of *heart* . . ."

[handwritten annotation: "same thing mentioned twice" pointing to Ezekiel 11:19]

Perhaps the most classic Scripture which deals with the morality of the heart or spirit function is found in Proverbs.

> Keep thy heart with all diligence; for out of it are the issues of life.
>
> Proverbs 4:23, KJV

Please note again the diagram on page 30. You will observe that *all of the functions of the soul, i.e., mind, emotions, and will, are present and active in the heart*. This is the center of the interfacing.

> The capacity of the heart or spirit includes the functions of the mind, emotions, and will in regard to moral matters . . . matters dealing with "rightness" and "wrongness" and "oughtness."

It is true that there are some functions of the mind that have nothing to do with righteousness or evil. However, there are some other functions of the mind that have everything to do with morality. There are certain emotions which are not tied to morality . . . there are certain emotions which are essentially moral. As we observed earlier, there are some desires or choices which simply have to do with amoral decisions. However, there are certain choices where the volition is activated in regard to issues which are totally moral.

The heart is the citadel, or moral control room, where either Christ or sin is in command. *The domination of either Christ or sin over the spiritual nature of man will determine the observable and unobservable moral behavior of that man.* With this in mind, go back and review the Scriptures on the previous pages. As you can see, *the characteristic* which you have been studying, *of the heart or spirit function is definitely moral.*

2. The spirit or heart function is *perfectible*.

An entire chapter, entitled "The Spirit-Filled Life," will be devoted to this subject later. However, let it be stated at this point that when Christ commanded, "Therefore you are to be perfect, as your heavenly Father is perfect" (Matthew 5:48, NASB), He was not talking about a "someday," "if," or "maybe" situation. The good news is that in the moral areas of the spirit or heart—in matters dealing with *moral intent*—there is a possibility of purity based on the purity of Jesus Christ living His life through you via the Holy Spirit.

> God is love . . . if we love one another, God abides in us, and His love is *perfected* in us. By this we know that we abide in Him and He in us, because He has given us of His Spirit . . . God is love, and the one who abides in love abides in God, and God abides in him. By this, love is *perfected* with us, that we may have confidence in the day of judgment; because *as He is, so also are we in this world.*
> I John 4:8-17, NASB

3. The spirit or heart function is *immortal*.

This is the part of man's nature that will last eternally. *How it will be "re-housed" is not known.* But it is known that your spirit or heart will live on forever, and forever, and forever, and forever.

D. Some Practical Examples

How does all of this apply to you in your everyday living? How will this new insight help you to live a more victorious Christian life this next week?

Before looking at some very practical applications of these truths, a *quick review* is needed.

Below is a diagram of the Functional Trichotomy. This represents the totally unified and integrated person. Without looking back to the previous pages, label the three different functions as indicated by the arrows:

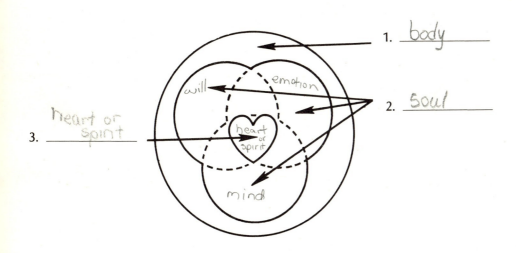

1. body
2. soul
3. heart or spirit

Now, fill in the three characteristics for each function:

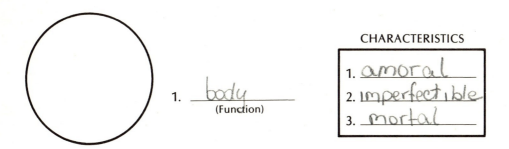

1. body
   (Function)

CHARACTERISTICS
1. amoral
2. imperfectible
3. mortal

NOTES 74

*Truth brings morality to a situation

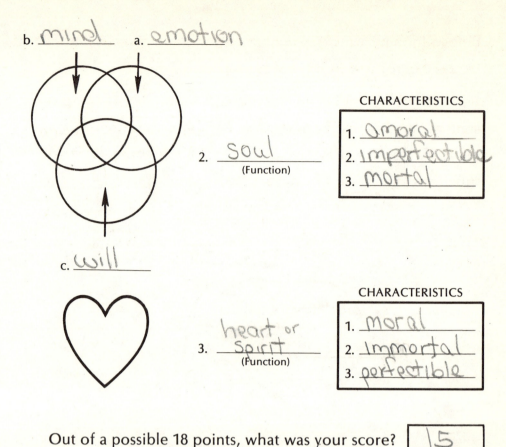

b. mind   a. emotion

2. soul (Function)

CHARACTERISTICS
1. amoral
2. imperfectible
3. mortal

c. will

3. heart or spirit (Function)

CHARACTERISTICS
1. moral
2. immortal
3. perfectible

Out of a possible 18 points, what was your score? 15 SCORE

NOTE: During the review you may have made an interesting discovery. All of the functions of the soul (mind, emotions, will) are also present and active in the heart. The capacity of the heart or spirit includes the functions of the mind, emotions, and will in regard to *moral matters* . . . matters dealing with "right" and "wrong." If you were to diagram this fact in regard to your *mind*, it would look like this:

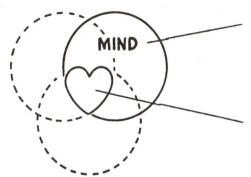

There are some activities of the mind that are amoral and have *nothing* to do with "right" and "wrong,"

—HOWEVER—

There are *some* activities of the mind that are moral and have *everything* to do with "right" and "wrong."

[margin notes: katsup on fries; abortion]

Can you think of some examples of each?

If you were to diagram this fact in regard to your *emotions*, it would look like this:

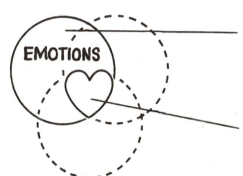

There are some functions of the emotions that are amoral and *are not tied to "right" and "wrong,"*

—HOWEVER—

There are certain emotions which *are moral and deal with "right" and "wrong."*

[margin notes: cry if pet dies; remorse at wrong decision]

Can you think of some examples of each?

If you were to diagram this fact in regard to your *will*, it would look like this:

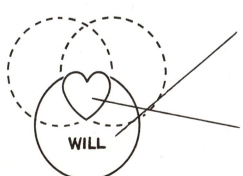

There are *some desires or choices* which simply have to do with *amoral issues and are not "right" or "wrong,"*

—HOWEVER—

There are *certain volitional choices* which are *totally moral and deal with "right" and "wrong."*

[margin notes: desire a clean house or eating; going where knowingly temptations are present]

Can you think of some examples of each?

As you can clearly see, the moral aspect of the heart is different from the amoral aspect of the soul *even though all three functions*—i.e., mind, emotions, and will—*are present and active in both.*

God created man in His own Image and in His own Likeness (Genesis 1:26; 5:1; 9:6). It is God Who is Spirit, manifesting Himself through His Word, either written, declared, or Living, that is the governing principle of morality in your heart. That God Himself is able to write His laws upon your heart is a fact which is impossible to fully understand or describe... but that is exactly what happens.

Look now at some practical examples of how these principles work in your everyday life.

1. Consider the *physical body* and its need for food. There is nothing inherently evil about the necessity to satisfy the pangs of hunger. This is a God-given safeguard against starvation.

    Suppose you go into your favorite supermarket to pick up a sandwich from the delicatessen. You are absolutely famished from the vigorous activities of the morning—and now it is lunch time—time to eat. With that delicious sandwich, piled high with meat, cheese, tomatoes, lettuce, etc. in hand, you head toward the check-out stand. Your mouth begins to water; you can hardly wait to bite into that sandwich. However, as you approach the check-out stand, you discover that your money is still on your dresser at home. "No problem," you say. You are still hungry... and fortunately your jacket has big pockets. So, with your mouth still watering, the sandwich goes into the big pocket... and you actually smile at the girl at the check-out stand as you and your unpaid-for-sandwich go out the door.

QUESTIONS:

a. Was this a moral issue? *Yes*

b. Is hunger moral or amoral? *amoral*

c. Was it justifiable to take the sandwich since the total price was not over $5.00? *No*

d. At what point did the situation change from amoral to moral: *when the will was tempted and chose to steal.*

   (1) when you decided to eat a cheap sandwich instead of a balanced meal?

   (2) when you chose the sandwich with meat, cheese, tomatoes, and lettuce?

   (3) when you decided in your heart to take the sandwich without proper compensation?

   (4) when you smiled at the girl as you went out the door?

   (5) other?

Look again at Hebrews 4:12, (NASB):

> For the word of God is living and active and sharper than any two-edged sword, and piercing as far as the *division* of *soul* and *spirit* . . .

The deciding factor which *always* divides the amoral soul function from the moral spirit or heart function is the *Word of God.*

God said, *"You shall not steal"* (Exodus 20:15, NASB).

There is absolutely nothing evil about the need for food. There is absolutely nothing evil about the food itself. *However,* when you <u>decided in your heart</u> to take something that was not yours . . . and without rendering the required compensation . . . <u>made it yours</u> . . . it then became a moral situation—<u>a decision of the heart</u>. Moral issues are always centered around the point of choice (volitional or willful act) and determined by the Word of God, either written or alive.

2. Consider now the *psychical* need to be accepted. There is nothing inherently evil about the need to be accepted.

Suppose you and several of your friends are gathered in the church parking lot or at a local restaurant discussing generalities. The name of a common acquaintance comes up in the discussion. You feel insecure and threatened by the very mention of this person. So you take the opportunity to employ some very subtle "leveling" devices.

Here are two of the most common ways that this could be accomplished:

    a. by innuendo, i.e., raising an eyebrow, shrugging the shoulders, etc., or

    b. by telling something about this person that may be true but should not be told.

Everybody laughs, and you feel *accepted* for being so clever.

> For the word of God is living and active and sharper than any two-edged sword, and piercing as far as the division of *soul* and *spirit* . . .
> Hebrews 4:12, NASB

Has this amoral *psychical need* to be accepted become a moral issue? The answer is "no." As stated previously, there is nothing inherently evil about the need to be accepted. However, it is a *moral issue* when, in the heart, you *choose* to deceive, exaggerate, or harm another in order to be accepted.

> "You shall not bear false witness . . ."
> Exodus 20:16, NASB

This is true in your sales record, your golf score, or any other way you *choose* to exaggerate or deceive.

Is it, then, a moral issue to drive a car you can't afford or live in a house you can't afford for the sole purpose of being accepted?

> "You must not tell lies."
> Deuteronomy 5:20, TLB

3. Consider now the *physical* and *psychical* need for sexual relations. Certainly there is nothing inherently evil about God's Plan to equip you with a sex drive.

Suppose you were Joseph, number eleven son of Jacob. Joseph was hundreds of miles away from home. No one really knew Joseph's situation and certainly, having been sold as a slave by his own family, it would appear as though no one really cared. No one, that is . . . except Potiphar's wife. With every imaginable method of seduction, she tried to persuade Joseph to choose evil. But Joseph realized that there was more to be considered than a physical or psychical need to be satisfied.

> For the word of God is living and active and sharper than any two-edged sword, and piercing as far as the division of soul and spirit . . .
>
> Hebrews 4:12, NASB

Even though the Ten Commandments had not been given, yet, it was the <u>Living, Active Word of God</u> that enabled Joseph to choose righteousness in this moral situation.

When does the *amoral sex drive* become involved in a *moral issue?* It becomes involved in a moral issue whenever it is contrary to the sanctity of marriage. However, the sex drive, in and of itself, can never be moral. The point of determination is God's Word and our volitional response to that truth.

> "You shall not commit adultery."
>
> Exodus 20:14, NASB

It is interesting to note that Jesus, in His "Sermon on the Mount," carried the thought even further by emphasizing the fact that the morality of the situation precedes the actual physical act.

> "You have heard that it was said, 'YOU SHALL NOT COMMIT ADULTERY'; but I say to you, that every one who looks on a woman to lust for her has committed adultery with her already in his *heart."*
>
> Matthew 5:27-28, NASB

Jesus is not declaring that the amoral sex drive or curiosity is evil. He is saying that when you decide in your heart that, if given the opportunity, you would respond to the physical and psychical drive outside the parameters of marriage, you have already committed adultery in your heart.

James, the brother of Jesus, likewise dealt with this issue:

> But each one is tempted when he is carried away and enticed by *his own lust*. Then when lust has *conceived*, it *gives birth to sin;* and when sin is accomplished, *it brings forth death.*
>
> James 1:14-15, NASB

Therefore, it is important to note that it is the volitional determination of the heart that gives any situation morality.

E. The Practical Aspect of the Functional Trichotomy as It Relates to Sin

If you are to become all that God intended through Christ for you to become, and if you are to live the victorious Christian life that is provisionally yours to live, then it is mandatory that you understand the differences between the amoral functions of the body and soul, and the moral function of the heart.

Historically, many have been led into believing that *"sin"* is any deviation from absolute perfection, whether known or unknown, voluntary or involuntary.

Dr. H. Orton Wiley states:

> Calling that sin which is not sin, opens the door also to actual sinning.[9]

If there is not a clear distinction between the amoral body and soul functions and the moral function of the heart, then you are forced to agree that every amoral thing human beings do is "sin," because, ideally, it could be better. It then falls short of an absolute standard of perfection.

---

[9] H. Orton Wiley, *Christian Theology, Volume II* (Kansas City, Mo.: Beacon Hill Press, 1953), p. 508.

But to make everything sin is, in effect, to make nothing sin. It is impossible to grade sins. *If forgotten promises, faulty judgment, and human limitations and infirmities are sins, then there is no qualitative distinction possible between such so-called sins on the one hand and lying, theft, or immorality on the other. The door then is left open wide to sin of all sorts.*[10]

Look again at the diagram:

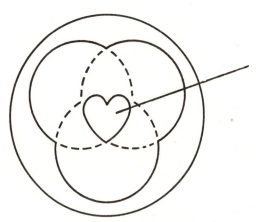

The heart is the function that deals with moral issues. It is the perfectible area that deals with motive and intent. It is the moral function of the mind, emotions, and will that has the capacity to choose righteousness or evil.

Sin is used to describe human conduct in the New Testament and implies conscious choice. The idea that *sin* is a conscious and moral act of the will is consistent with the entire teaching of the New Testament.

> No one who lives in him keeps on sinning . . . Dear children, do not let anyone lead you astray. He who does what is right is righteous, just as he is righteous. He who does what is sinful is of the devil, because the devil has been sinning from the beginning. The reason the Son of God appeared was to destroy the devil's work. No one who is born of God will continue to sin . . .
> I John 3:6-9, NIV

This Scripture is rendered meaningless if "sin" is to include all the amoral body and soul imperfections and deviations from absolute perfection, whether known or unknown, voluntary or involuntary.

---

[10] *Op. cit.*, Purkiser, p. 307.

John Wesley's concise and consistent summation of the New Testament teaching of sin is difficult to improve upon:

> Sin . . . a voluntary transgression of a known law.[11]

> The Christian consciousness and conscience recognize that there *is* a significant qualitative difference between mistakes, errors, and lapses on one side and voluntary transgressions of divine law on the other. When judged by the law of *objective right,* there is no difference between a forgotten promise and a broken promise. When judged by the law of *objective right,* there is no difference between a misstatement of fact made in ignorance and a lie. In each case, something promised has not been performed and an untruth has been stated.
>
> But there is a tremendous difference in these two types of situation subjectively and ethically. In the case of both forgotten promise and ignorant misstatement, *there is regret—but not guilt. There is sorrow but not sin.* Lapses of memory and ignorance are always deplorable and should be avoided as far as possible. But the Christian consciousness does not find in these infirmities anything which would interrupt its fellowship with God or bring to it condemnation and a sense of guilt. . . . *sin is fundamentally a matter of choice, of intention, and of purpose.*[12]

(Wesley's point of view)

```
SIN      ⎧ 1. A willful transgression against a known law of
AS AN   ⎨      God                      (James 4:17, NASB)
ACT      ⎪             ★ brings about ★
         ⎩ 2. Separation from God       (Isaiah 59:2, NASB)
```

The following two chapters will deal with the twofold aspect of sin—*the acts of sin* and *the nature of sin*—and the remedy for each.

Therefore, throughout this Discipling Curriculum, *sin* will be considered as an act and a nature of the heart involving the moral capacities of the mind, emotions, and will.

---

[11] *Op. Cit.*, Wesley, p. 43.
[12] *Op. Cit.*, Purkiser, pp. 307-308.

The Born-Again Life

(outline)

I. The Crisis of the Born-Again Life

　A. Crisis Commences with a Response

　　1. Divine Initiative
　　2. Awareness of Need
　　　a. Written Word
　　　b. Declared Word
　　　c. Living Word
　　3. Awareness of Moral Choice
　　4. Man's Response

　B. Crisis Culminates with a Result

　　1. Forgiveness
　　2. Justification
　　3. Regeneration
　　4. Adoption

II. The Continuation of the Born-Again Life

　A. Internal Adjustments Necessary to this Continuation

　　1. Steadfastness
　　2. Open-mindedness
　　3. Reverence and Godly Fear
　　4. Thankfulness
　　5. Testimony
　　6. Faithfulness in Prayer Life
　　7. Forgiveness
　　8. Self-Discipline and Willingness
　　9. Optimism

B. External Adjustments Necessary to this Continuation
    1. Regular Church Attendance
    2. Cultivate New Friendships
    3. Recreation
    4. Physical Habits
    5. Stewardship
        a. Time
        b. Money
        c. Talent
    6. Other
    7. Other

III. The Moral Conflict in the Born-Again Life

A. Original Sin is the Basis for Moral Conflict from Within
    1. General Terms to Describe the Condition of Original Sin
    2. Original Sin Is Displayed Through Contrary Choices

B. Diagrams of the Three Conditions of Man's Heart

C. Conclusion and Illustration

Redemption in His Blood
* He calls you to receive;*
"Come unto Me, the pard'ning God
* Believe," He cries, "believe!"*
—John Wesley

The Born-Again Life

The born-again life is described in different ways by different people. Bypassing such descriptions, we will specifically deal with basic facts about the born-again life.

There is no way you can totally understand man as shown in a simple diagram. There is no way to adequately describe through graphics or charts man's complexity. However, from a functional point of view, it can best be understood if man is viewed as a Functional Trichotomy. As you saw in chapter 3, there are three basic human functions that must be differentiated if you are to understand the born-again life as God has planned.

In order to understand these facts, please begin by looking at man as depicted in the previous chapter. In the space below draw and label the diagram of the Functional Trichotomy.

List the characteristics of each function in the boxes provided.

CHARACTERISTICS

BODY
1. A MORAL
2. IMPREFECTABLE
3. MORTAL

SOUL
1. A. MORAL
2. IMPREFECTABLE
3. MORTAL

SPIRIT
1. MORAL
2. PREFECTABLE
3. IMMORTAL

In regard to sin, fill in the box below.

A willful transgression against a known law of God

SIN AS AN ACT

1. 4-17 Therefore to him that knoweth to do good and doeth it not to him it is sin
   Scripture *James 4:17*
   willful transgression against God
   brings about

2. Iss 59-2 But your iniquities have separated you from your God.
   Scripture *Isaiah 59:2*
   Separation from God
   your sins have hidden his face from you,
   so that he will not hear

Separation from God

Now that we have reviewed the Functional Trichotomy and the definition of sin as an act, consider another aspect of sin. The following diagram illustrates this twofold aspect.

accumulative   *carnal*

S — Sorry
C — Confess
A — Ask (for forgiveness)
B — Believe

```
                    ┌─────┐
                    │ SIN │
                    └─────┘
                   ↙       ↘
```

Sinful Acts	Sinful Nature
willful transgressions for which we are responsible	original sin in the heart for which we were not responsible

Born-Again Life or Conversion — A New Relationship	Spirit-Filled Life or Entire Sanctification — A New Relationship
In response to repentance, confession, and faith, committed sins are forgiven by God.	In response to complete consecration and faith, there is a cleansing of the inner self and an empowering for service.

The chapter on "The Spirit-Filled Life" (chapter 5), deals with the *sin nature and its effect on man*. However, this chapter (chapter 4) will be devoted to explaining how the born-again life deals with the *problem of the acts of sin*.

There are three basic divisions in this chapter that describe the born-again life.

    I. The Crisis of the Born-Again Life
   II. The Continuation of the Born-Again Life
  III. The Moral Conflict in the Born-Again Life

I. The Crisis of the Born-Again Life

The word *crisis* in this study is defined as: a *turning point* in human life; a point in time when a person *changes directions;* a moment when *he chooses* one life-style over another.

In light of this definition, it may be clearly seen that the "crisis" of the born-again life begins the moment the Holy Spirit convicts you. You can no longer carry the guilt and pressure of the load of sin, and you *decide* to accept Christ as the Savior of your life. In that decisive moment of *separation* from sin, you are born anew spiritually.

"Crisis" is *decision* and *separation* from sin.

There are two considerations vital to understanding this *crisis:*

A. Crisis Commences with a Response

Look now at the following areas of response.

> 1. DIVINE INITIATIVE *God reaching to me 1975*
> 2. AWARENESS OF NEED
> 3. AWARENESS OF MORAL CHOICE
> 4. MAN'S RESPONSE

1. *Divine Initiative—God reaching out to man.*

    God reaches out to man by means of the ever-active presence of the Holy Spirit in the world. He does not desire that man should remain separated from Him, but rather, that man should be reconciled once again to Him in love.

> Whoever does not love does not know God, because God is love. This is how God showed his love among us: He sent his one and only Son into the world that we might live through him. This is love: not that we loved God, but that he loved us and sent his Son as an atoning sacrifice for our sins.
> I John 4:8-10, NIV

> "For God so loved the world that he gave his one and only Son, that whoever believes in him shall not perish but have everlasting life."
> John 3:16, NIV

God initiated the Plan of Salvation through the shed blood and sacrifice of Jesus Christ.

> But God commendeth his love toward us, in that, while we were yet sinners, Christ died for us.
> Romans 5:8, KJV

> ... that God was reconciling the world to himself in Christ, not counting men's sins against them. And he has committed to us the message of reconciliation.
> II Corinthians 5:19, NIV

God also takes the initiative in making that Plan become a reality in the heart of the sinner. He does not wait for man to make the first move, but rather, reaches down to man in an *act of love* with the *purpose* of *reconciliation* and *redemption*.

DEFINE:
Reconciliation — *so that we may begin – again – to walk with God in His light.* [to be brought back in right relationship]

Redemption — *In His act of love, He already is wanting to take us into His arms* [to buy back for a price]

2. *Awareness of Need—Man recognizing his sinful condition.*

It is the work of the Holy Spirit to bring man to the awareness of his needy condition. It is the Holy Spirit that helps man know the difference between *mistake* and *sin* by the use of either sorrow or guilt. The sinner must first be convinced that he is a sinner. There is no hope for the sinner as long as he presumes that he is all right.

> "And He, when He comes (the Holy Spirit), (He) will convict the world concerning sin, and righteousness and judgment."
>
> John 16:8, NASB

In convincing man of his sin, the Holy Spirit always works in conjunction with the Word of God, either written, declared, or Living.

a. *Written*—the Holy Spirit dealing with man through the printed page, i.e., either Scripture or written material based upon God's Word.

> List an example of the way the Holy Spirit has helped you become aware of your need through the *written* Word.
>
> *That I must pick up my cross + bear it daily — God can work in my life fully only if He is in control of everything*

b. *Declared*—the work of the Holy Spirit through the proclaimed Word. This proclamation may be made by a preacher, prophet, teacher—or simply shared by a friend. *(films, cassettes or example of someone else.)* The proclaimed Word is not limited to the spoken Word but also includes the declaration by example.

> List an example of the way the Holy Spirit has helped you become aware of your need through the *declared* Word.
>
> *The above preached on + discussed with others.*

c. *Living* (Christ in you)—a very powerful means which the Holy Spirit uses to make man aware of his need. Man was created in the Image of God, and the Holy Spirit works through that Image however tarnished it may be.

> List an example of the way the Holy Spirit has helped you become aware of your need through the *Living* Word.
> *experiences with different people at college—recognizing my need for knowledge*

Conviction is the word which most often is used in describing the work of the Holy Spirit in making man aware of his need. Sometimes the vehicle through which the Holy Spirit works is referred to as *conscience*. Conscience is <u>not always uniform but is universal</u>. The Holy Spirit, through conviction, may utilize the *written, declared,* or *Living* Word to help man become aware of his need.

[margin: That still small voice inside when you know God is speaking to you alone.]

3. *Awareness of Moral Choice—Man realizing his moral responsibility.*

   The Holy Spirit not only convicts man of his sin but also convinces man of *righteousness* and *judgment*.

   > "And He, when He comes (the Holy Spirit), (He) will will convict the world concerning sin, and righteousness and judgment."
   >
   > John 16:8, NASB

   To convict man simply of his sin, and then leave him with nothing better, would be to leave man in confusion and despair. Not only is man shown a "better way," a way of righteousness, but also the Holy Spirit is faithful to convince man that *if he does not break from sin,* he must face *judgment.* Man now has a problem: <u>he is faced with a choice, i.e., *sin—or—righteousness*. Man is presently and ultimately *responsible*</u> for his moral choice. The complete

   [margin: not always "No, No", but shows better way to do it]

work of the Holy Spirit in conviction is to convince man as to sin, righteousness, and the judgment, and to show man that he must choose *one* of the two alternatives. Many would like God to make this choice for them, but to do so would reduce man to a mere mechanical robot. The power to choose, which is man's greatest power, not only makes him privileged but also endows him with a great responsibility.

[margin note: man's free will]

4. *Man's Response*—*Man reacting to his moral responsibility.*

Man's response is either rejection or repentance. Man may choose to reject God's Plan of Salvation and remain in his lost condition.

Man's other choice is to repent.

> ". . . Repent, for the kingdom of heaven is near."
> Matthew 3:2, NIV

> ". . . But unless you repent, you too will all perish."
> Luke 13:3, NIV

Repentance means the turning from sin which includes a brokenness of spirit.

> It is a broken spirit you want—remorse and penitence. A broken and a contrite heart, O God, you will not ignore.
> Psalm 51:17, TLB

It also includes the confessing and forsaking of sins and the trusting in Christ as Redeemer.

> If we confess our sins, he is faithful and just and will forgive us our sins and purify us from all unrighteousness.
> I John 1:9, NIV

Forsaking of sins carries with it the thought of *restitution*. Man must turn his back on sin and also make right the wrongs which he has committed—with the guidance of the Holy Spirit.

When you deal with the subject of repentance, you will see man turning from his sins.

> "... But if the wicked turns from his wickedness and does what's fair and just, he shall live."
> Ezekiel 33:19, TLB

> "... then if my people will humble themselves and pray, and search for me, and turn from their wicked ways, I will hear them from heaven and forgive their sins and heal their land."
> II Chronicles 7:14, TLB

Not only does repentance carry with it the idea of man turning from his acts of sin, but it also includes the necessity of trusting Christ alone.

> ... for God's way of making us right with himself depends on faith—counting on Christ alone.
> Philippians 3:9b, TLB

> This righteousness from God comes through faith in Jesus Christ to all who believe.
> Romans 3:22a, NIV

Without turning back in your material, please fill in the four areas of response in the box below.

AREAS OF RESPONSE REGARDING THE CRISIS OF THE BORN-AGAIN LIFE
1. *God's initiative – God reaching out to man*
2. *being aware of need – Man recognizing His sinful condition*
3. *Man realizing his moral responsibility*
4. *Man's response – man reacting to his moral responsibility*

B. Crisis Culminates with a Result

The terms *saved* and *converted* are, many times, used interchangeably with the phrase "born again" to describe what happens when man turns from sin and trusts Christ as his Redeemer.

When a sinner (1) responds to Divine initiative, (2) becomes aware of his sinful condition of separation, (3) becomes aware that he must choose either evil or righteousness, and (4) repents—turns and trusts—then something happens on the Divine side. God, through the Holy Spirit:

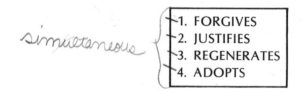

simultaneous
1. FORGIVES
2. JUSTIFIES
3. REGENERATES
4. ADOPTS

1. Forgiveness

God's *forgiveness* is the pardon given to man to free him from the penalty of his sinful acts.

> If we confess our sins, he is faithful and just and will forgive us our sins and purify us from all unrighteousness.
>
> I John 1:9, NIV

> "All the prophets testify about him that everyone who believes in him receives forgiveness of sins through his name."
>
> Acts 10:43, NIV

> ... And let him return to the Lord, And He will have compassion on him; And to our God, For He will abundantly pardon.
>
> Isaiah 55:7, NASB

2. Justification

Justification is *God's act*. It is the legal act of satisfying the demands of the *Law*. The Law had required <u>a blood sacrifice for committed sins</u>. Jesus Christ, having been put to death on the Cross, became that Blood Sacrifice—the Atonement (Leviticus 5:10, NASB)—allowing you to be fully justified. An easy way to remember *justification* is . . . you are *just as if* you had never sinned.

> But now a righteousness from God, apart from law, has been made known, to which the Law and the Prophets testify. This righteousness from God comes through faith in Jesus Christ to all who believe. There is no difference, for all have sinned and fall short of the glory of God, and are justified freely by his grace through the redemption that came by Christ Jesus. God presented him as a sacrifice of atonement, through faith in his blood. He did this to demonstrate his justice . . .
> Romans 3:21-25, NIV

> But now he has reconciled you by Christ's physical body through death to present you holy in his sight, without blemish and free from accusation—
> Colossians 1:22, NIV

NOTES 98

[margin note: believer is freed from all things, from which you could not be freed through the Law of Moses]

> Look up the following Scriptures and write them out in the blanks provided.
>
> Acts 13:38-39 *NASB* Therefore let it be known to you, brethren, that through Him forgiveness of sins is proclaimed to you, and through Him everyone who
>
> Titus 3:7 that being justified by His grace we might be made heirs according to the hope of eternal life

Man's forgiveness is justified by God's having met all of His own requirements by providing the sinless Son of God as the Atoning Sacrifice for human sins. In the New Testament, justification is the <u>*act of God* which *declares* this new relationship, while forgiveness *establishes* that relationship</u>. Thus, man is accepted and restored to God's favor.

3. *Regeneration*

Regeneration is the work of the Holy Spirit which gives *new life* through Christ to the person who was dead in sins and trespasses. Sin is death. Death means separation. *Regeneration* literally means "to be again." Therefore, regeneration is a restoration to the Image of God in the heart of the penitent believer.

> Therefore, if anyone is in Christ, he is a new creation; the old has gone, the new has come!
> II Corinthians 5:17, NIV

> He saved us, not on the basis of deeds which we have done in righteousness, but according to His mercy, by the washing of regeneration and renewing by the Holy Spirit.
> Titus 3:5, NASB

4. *Adoption*

Adoption is the *act of God* declaring that man, being justified by faith in Jesus Christ, is now received into the Family of God and reinstated in the privilege of sonship. Adoption occurs at the same moment as forgiveness, justification, and regeneration; but in the order of thought, logically follows them.

> ... to redeem those under law, that we might receive the full rights of sons. Because you are sons, God sent the Spirit of his Son into our hearts, the Spirit who calls out, "Abba, Father." So you are no longer a slave, but a son; and since you are a son, God has made you also an heir.
> Galatians 4:5-7, NIV

> For you did not receive a spirit that makes you a slave again to fear, but you received the Spirit who makes you sons. And by him we cry, "Abba, Father." The Spirit himself testifies with our spirit that we are God's children. Now if we are children, then we are heirs—heirs of God and co-heirs with Christ...
> Romans 8:15-17, NIV

> 1. FORGIVENESS gives pardon from the penalty.
> 2. JUSTIFICATION gives fulfillment of the demands of the Law.
> 3. REGENERATION gives new life through Christ.
> 4. ADOPTION gives reception into the Family of God.

In the born-again experience (which includes forgiveness, justification, regeneration, and adoption), two choices are involved: God's choice and man's choice. This born-again relationship does not, in any way, destroy man's power to choose. The condition of the born-again man is secure only as long as man chooses to remain an adopted child. If man subsequently chooses to commit a sin (a willful transgression against the known law of God), then he is once again separated from God. However, if man chooses to walk in the light as God is in the light, then man has fellowship with God and his condition is secure, and *nothing* can move him from that position except <u>his own choice</u>.

Romans 8:14 (NIV) states, "Those who are led by the Spirit of God are sons of God," and, as a consequence, the born-again man can say with St. Paul:

> For I am convinced that neither death nor life, neither angels nor demons, neither the present nor the future, nor any powers, neither height nor depth, nor anything else in all creation, will be able to separate us from the love of God that is in Christ Jesus our Lord.
>
> Romans 8:38-39, NIV

NOTES

In the space provided below, list and give a brief explanation of the four responses included in the crisis of the born-again life.

Result
RESPONSE	EXPLANATION
1. forgiveness	we are pardoned from our sinful being
2. justification	Christs' shed blood paid our penalty
3. regeneration	we are restored to God's image of heart
4. adoption	are heir to God's glory

List below and give a brief explanation of the four results of the born-again crisis.

Response
RESULT	EXPLANATION
1. Divine initiative	God desires us + forgives first
2. awareness of need	man recognizes sinful condition
3. awareness of moral choice	man realizes moral responsibility
4. man's response	man reacting to his moral responsibility

II. The Continuation of the Born-Again Life

What happens in the interim between the crisis of the new birth and the Spirit-filled life? As a new convert, you are faced with moral confrontation in the continuation of the born-again experience. However, the new life must be continued in spite of the confrontations that arise from within and from without.

The distinction between the words *confrontation* and *conflict,* in this study, is:

> CONFRONTATION the act of facing or presenting moral alternatives for comparison;
>
> CONFLICT fight, clash, or struggle for moral mastery.

It is vitally important for you, as a new convert, to discover your spiritual potential and your impending problems. You must make adjustments. You must discipline yourself and grow. Your internal adjustments will lead to spiritual conquests which will be *externalized* in observable behavior.

Consider now the *internal adjustments* needed for a successful continuation of the born-again life.

A. Internal Adjustments Necessary to this Continuation

There are a number of simple but essential steps that will help establish you as a new Christian and keep you from falling away.

1. The attitude of *steadfastness* is the key to conquest. Your decision for Christ must be reinforced by a continuing determination to be victorious.

2. Your attitude will show the *open-mindedness* of the "learner's heart." Your heart will be filled with a burning desire to take advantage of every God-given opportunity to advance, to progress, to serve, and to grow.

3. *Reverence* and *Godly fear* will produce a desire for *immediate obedience*. These attitudes will be developed under the guidance of the Holy Spirit through the written, the declared, and the Living Word of God!

4. Your attitude of *thankfulness,* when counting your blessings in times of discouragement, will bring God's Presence very near. It will develop your *power of praise* and *growth in gratitude.*

5. The testimony or witness of your Christian experience will strengthen your own faith. It may bring inspiration or conviction to the lives of others.

6. The attitude of *faithfulness in your prayer life* will solve problems, salvage situations, and build an inner strength for continued growth.

7. Your attitude of *forgiveness,* even as God has forgiven you, will protect you from the pitfalls of resentment, injured feelings, bitterness, and criticalness.

8. With the help of God, you must develop an attitude of *self-discipline* and a *willingness* to change any undesirable mental habit patterns that may persist as a hindrance to your new way of life. You will be confronted with the need to reorganize the priorities of your ambitions, life-purposes, and goals.

9. It will be necessary to develop an attitude of Christian *optimism* that arises from the God-confidence of a courageous faith.

There are, no doubt, many other *internal* attitudinal adjustments that will help you in your victorious *continuation* of the born-again life. However, please direct your attention now to some *external adjustments* which are a result of your *internal* attitudes.

B. External Adjustments Necessary to this Continuation

External adjustments are those observable responses which are based upon the attitudinal adjustments.

1. An adjustment to *regular church attendance* may be necessary if you are not already in the habit of attending. The influence and inspiration of fellow Christians must replace old, sinful associations. The Church is composed of the believers and is the Body of Christ. It is the Family of God. It is where new Christians find strength and direction. Maturity takes place best within the environment and spiritual influence of the Church.

2. Adjustment must be made to *cultivate new friendships* and associations which are in harmony with your new ideals and concerns. Your new direction as a born-again Christian will separate you from the fellowship of those who are truly adverse to your newfound faith. Others, however, will be a part of your circle of influence from which new converts will be won.

In the following blanks, please indicate the necessary adjustments in each of the areas listed.

3. Recreation _____
   _____
   _____

4. Physical habits _____
   _____
   _____

5. Stewardship:

   a. Time _____
      _____
      _____

   b. Money _____
      _____
      _____

   c. Talent _____
      _____
      _____

6. Other _____
   _____
   _____

7. Other _____
   _____
   _____

These and other *internal* and *external* adjustments must be made in your new life. Christ's Plan for you as a born-again Christian is to grow and triumph through many confrontations that follow your change of direction. These adjustments need to be purposely nurtured, carefully cultivated, and zealously guarded. They must be maintained in spite of all internal or external influences or opposition.

> Then said Jesus to those Jews which believed on him, If ye continue in my word, *then* are ye my disciples indeed; And ye shall know the truth, and the truth shall make you free.
>
> John 8:31-32, KJV

> "We must go through many hardships to enter the kingdom of God," they said.
>
> Acts 14:22b, NIV

III. The Moral Conflict in the Born-Again Life

Review the experience of the born-again life using the diagram below.

Born-Again Life

CRISIS

1. Divine Initiative
2. Awareness of Need
3. Awareness of Moral Choice
4. Man's Response

1. Forgiveness
2. Justification
3. Regeneration
4. Adoption

CONTINUATION

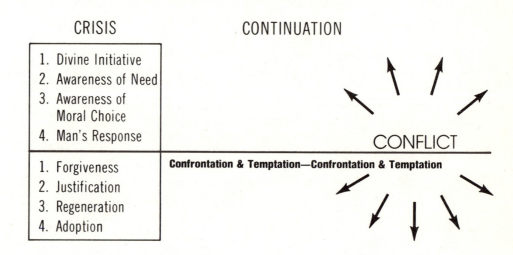

CONFLICT

Confrontation & Temptation—Confrontation & Temptation

You have looked at the *crisis* of the born-again life in the light of the change of direction. You have also considered the *continuation* of the born-again life. You noted the necessity for positive adjustments in the light of attitude and action in the internal and external confrontations of this new life. A conflict is sure to arise, sooner or later, in the struggle for moral mastery in the heart of every born-again believer. Examine now the basic cause for this conflict.

A. Original Sin is the Basis for Moral Conflict from Within

John Wesley wrote, "Original sin is the corruption of the nature of every man, whereby man is in his own nature inclined to evil, so that the flesh lusteth contrary to the Spirit."[13]

Paul described original sin:

> Therefore, just as sin entered the world through one man, and death through sin, and in this way death came to all men, because all sinned—for before the law was given, sin was in the world. But sin is not taken into account when there is no law. Nevertheless, death reigned from the time of Adam to the time of Moses, even over those who did not sin by breaking a command, as did Adam, who was a pattern of the one to come.
>
> But the gift is not like the trespass. For if the many died by the trespass of the one man, how many more did God's grace and the gift that came by the grace of the one man, Jesus Christ, overflow to the many! Again, the gift of God is not like the result of the one man's sin: The judgment followed one sin and brought condemnation, but the gift followed many trespasses and brought justification. For if, by the trespass of the one man, death reigned through that one man, how much more will those who receive God's abundant provision of grace and of the gift of righteousness reign in life through the one man, Jesus Christ.
>
> Consequently, just as the result of one trespass was condemnation for all men, so also the result of one act of righteousness was justification that brings life for all men.
>
> Romans 5:12-18, NIV

---

[13]John Wesley, *Works*, Volume V (Kansas City, Mo.: Nazarene Publishing House, reprint, 1958), p. 144.

Therefore you can see that *original sin* and *inherited depravity* are identical terms.

Original sin, which is often referred to as *inherited depravity,* is the moral corruption of fallen mankind. It is the ever-present evil nature, an inherited tendency toward perverted self-will in opposition to the Nature, Purpose, and Will of God. It manifests itself not only in a state of rebellion against God and a tendency toward evil but also an inner inclination to yield to temptation. Depravity is the perversion of natural desires and appetites and has a blighting effect on the mind, emotions, and will. This condition must be cleansed by the presence and power of the Holy Spirit.

1. There are many *general terms* used to describe the condition of *original sin.*

inbred sin	infection of the moral nature
indwelling sin	sinful nature
inward pollution	depraved nature
enmity against God	sinful propensity
moral corruption	root of bitterness
carnality	tendency to sin
the old man	the old Adam
the sin principle	the sin in believers
the law of sin	war against the Spirit
a bent toward sinning	uncleanness
rebellion	an impure heart
the carnal mind	fallen nature
double-mindedness	

In the above list of descriptive terms for *original sin* are either Scriptural or theological terms that refer to the basis of moral conflict which remains in the heart of the born-again believer.

2. *Original sin is displayed* through contrary choices of a perverted will.

The contrary will chooses its own way rather than the way of God. Original sin results in man's enmity against God's sovereignty. Man's depravity is not totally evil, without any trace of good remaining in him, but it is "total" in the sense that this depravity has affected man in his entirety, i.e., body, soul, and spirit. This original sin in man is the cause of the *inner conflict.* The carnal nature is the virus of sin which spreads its invisible tentacles over every power and function of man.

It is a defacing of the original Image of God on the moral nature of man. Man's depravity is an egotistical, self-willed deviation from God-likeness. Man's fascination and enchantment with evil reflects his propensity or bent toward sin. The forgiven, but unclean, moral nature of man is the cause of his conflict. He sees the potential of becoming all that God wants him to become . . . but yet, "finds another law warring in his members." The born-again life takes care of one of the aspects of the twofold problem of sin, i.e., the accumulated acts of sin; however, it takes a subsequent work of the Holy Spirit to deal with the problem of original sin. The "conflict" in the continuation of the born-again life is the Holy Spirit's way of letting man know that there is a deeper problem that needs to be met by the cleansing power of the Holy Spirit.

B. Diagrams of the Three Conditions of Man's Heart

The three possible conditions of the heart are described by the diagrams above. You should be aware that there is no way to adequately diagram man's heart or spirit, but these will help you to understand man's heart from a functional point of view.

 The *"dark heart"* is descriptive of the sinner whose life is controlled by original sin and his life is plagued by accumulated acts of sin.

 The *"mixed heart"* is descriptive of the born-again life into which Christ has come to reside; however, original sin or depravity is still present and thereby has created a conflict. It is the co-existence of *all of Christ* and *all of sinful-self* which creates a conflict of purpose and plan that finds its way, sooner or later, into the attitudes and, too often, into the actions of every born-again believer.

 The *"clear heart"* represents the consecrated and cleansed heart. This is the heart which is filled and controlled by the indwelling Presence of God.

The Spirit-Filled Life
(outline)

I. The Crisis of the Spirit-Filled Life

  A. The Spirit-Filled Life Commences with a Response

    1. Divine Initiative
    2. Awareness of Need
    3. Awareness of Moral Choice
    4. Man's Response
      a. Acknowledge
      b. Confess
      c. Commit
      d. Believe

  B. The Spirit-Filled Crisis Culminates with a Result

    1. Heart Purity
    2. Heart Perfection
      a. The heart of every Spirit-filled Christian reflects the Love of God.
      b. Man's motive is his inner drive, the cause for his action.
    3. The Infilling of the Holy Spirit
    4. The Empowering of the Holy Spirit

II. The Continuation of the Spirit-Filled Life

  A. Growth

    1. A more intense love for His Word
    2. A more intense love for others
    3. An eager adjustment to new light revealed
    4. Influence and effect on the amoral functions

B. Confrontation and Temptation But No Conflict
      1. Confrontation
      2. Temptation
      3. No Conflict

III. The Concerns Regarding the Spirit-Filled Life

The sanctifying Spirit pour,
  To quench my thirst and wash me clean,
Now, Saviour, let the gracious shower
  Descend, and make me pure from sin.
                              —John Wesley

The Spirit-Filled Life

The Spirit-filled life, like the born-again life, is described in different ways by different people. It has been referred to as:

> Christian Perfection,
> Sanctification,
> Baptism with the Holy Spirit,
> Christian Holiness,
> Perfect Love,
> Heart Purity, and
> Fullness of the Blessing.

This experience may well be defined as:

> . . . that act of God, subsequent to regeneration, by which believers are made free from original sin, or depravity, and brought into a state of entire devotement to God, and the holy obedience of love made perfect.

> It is wrought by the baptism with the Holy Spirit, and comprehends in one experience the cleansing of the heart from sin and the abiding indwelling presence of the Holy Spirit, empowering the believer for life and service. Entire sanctification is provided by the blood of Jesus, is wrought instantaneously by faith, preceded by entire consecration; and to this work and state of grace the Holy Spirit bears witness.[14]

---

[14] *Manual/1976 Church of the Nazarene* (Kansas City, Mo.: Nazarene Publishing House, 1976), p. 29.

...entirely with ...our interest in other men."¹⁵

J. A. Wood quotes the German United Brethren Church as saying:

> By perfect holiness we understand the separation and purification from all inhering sin, after regeneration, by the blood of Jesus Christ, the Son of God; and the filling of the heart with the love of God by the Holy Ghost.¹⁶

He also states:

> Charles Wesley put it into his hymns, and without caviling over it, millions have sung for a century:
>
>> "Give us, Lord, this second rest."
>> "Speak the second time, be clean."
>> "Let me gain that second rest."
>
> Even the Calvinistic Augustus Toplady wrote:
>
>> "Let the water and the blood,
>> From thy wounded side which flowed.
>> Be of sin the double cure,
>> Save from wrath, and make me pure."¹⁷

---

[15] Oswald Chambers, *My Utmost for His Highest* (New York, N.Y.: Dodd, Mead, & Company, 1965), p. 10.

[16] J. A. Wood, abridged by John Paul, *Perfect Love* (Beacon Hill Press, Kansas City, Mo.: 1954), pp. 20-21.

[17] *Ibid.*, p. 94.

I. The Crisis of the Spirit-Filled Life

A. The Spirit-Filled Life Commences with a Response

Look again at the diagram which was partially presented on page 106. As you recall, the diagram took you only to the point of conflict. This conflict revealed itself initially in the confrontations of your born-again experience. You became aware of a spirit of rebellion as you began to identify with both the positive and negative alternatives. This was moral conflict.

The crisis includes the following four areas of response.

> 1. Divine Initiative
> 2. Awareness of Need
> 3. Awareness of Moral Choice
> 4. Man's Response

1. *Divine Initiative—God reaching out to deliver man from indwelling sin.*

> "No one can come to me unless the Father who sent me draws him, and I will raise him up at the last day."
> John 6:44, NIV

> And so Jesus also suffered outside the city gate to make *his people holy* through his own blood.
> Hebrews 13:12, NIV

God continues to reach out to man by means of the ever-active presence of the Holy Spirit in the heart of the believer. God, in His holiness, cannot look with favor on the inward pollution of the uncleansed heart, even though it is the heart of a believer. God longs to deliver His adopted and born-again children from the dilemma of their inner conflict. He does not want anything to separate them in the least degree from His intimate fellowship and favor. He desires to remove all inner hindrance so that perfect conformity to His Divine Will may be experienced in their lives.

He has, through the Atonement, initiated a twofold Plan of Salvation which effectively remedies the divided allegiance of the double-minded condition.

> God made him who had no sin to be sin for us, so that in him we might become the righteousness of God.
>
> II Corinthians 5:21, NIV

> For what the law was powerless to do in that it was weakened by our sinful nature, God did by sending his own Son in the likeness of sinful man to be a sin offering. And so he condemned sin in sinful man, in order that the righteous requirements of the law might be fully met in us, who do not live according to our sinful nature but according to the Spirit.
>
> Romans 8:3-4, NIV

2. *Awareness of Need—Man recognizing his deeper spiritual need.*

The awareness of your moral *conflict* will lead you to a sense of your own desperate need for Divine assistance. The Apostle Paul graphically portrays this desperate need:

> What a wretched man I am! Who will rescue me from this body of death?
>
> Romans 7:24, NIV

It is the work of the Holy Spirit that brings you to the awareness of your need and quickens your heart with the hope that there is a solution for your conflict.

The Holy Spirit drawing, illuminating, and convicting is at work constantly through the Word of God, either written, declared, or Living. He works just as He did in convicting and awakening your conscience in the born-again experience.

You are faced now with the need to admit to yourself and to God your inner conflict with the carnal mind and its debilitating double-mindedness.

The Holy Spirit will help you see how the condition of your divided heart has caused you to fall short of the perfect Will of God. You will realize that your influence and example have not measured up to your own expectancy . . . or God's. This will produce, under God, a great hungering and thirsting, an insatiable longing and searching for a higher spiritual level of deliverance and victorious living.

> Blessed are they which do hunger and thirst after righteousness: for they shall be filled.
> Matthew 5:6, KJV

3. *Awareness of Moral Choice—Man recognizing his responsibility to seek deliverance from indwelling sin.*

The Holy Spirit throws the searchlight of revealed truth into your heart so that you can clearly see the ugly nature of the inner pollution which was inherited through the Fall. As you see the problem of inner conflict and the possibility of its solution, through the experience of heart purity, you are brought face-to-face with the necessity of moral choice.

> "Oh, that you would choose life; that you and your children might live! Choose to love the Lord your God and to obey him and to cling to him, for he is your life and the length of your days."
>
> Deuteronomy 30:19b-20a, TLB

The power of *choice*, the exercise of free-moral agency, is an awesome responsibility. The stakes are high. The consequences are eternal, and you can *choose* either to have your life controlled by the carnal self or by the Holy Spirit. You can *choose* your own selfish way or you can *choose* "The Holy Highway."

> And a main road will go through that once-deserted land; it will be named "The Holy Highway." No evil-hearted men may walk upon it. God will walk there with you, even the most stupid cannot miss the way.
>
> Isaiah 35:8, TLB

There must be a "crucifixion" of the principle of lawlessness within.

> I have been crucified with Christ and I no longer live, but Christ lives in me. The life I live in the body, I live by faith in the Son of God, who loved me and gave himself for me.
>
> Galatians 2:20, NIV

There must be a "dying out to self and to sin." This choice may be more difficult for some than others, but the sooner you let go of all perverted self-centeredness, the sooner you will receive complete deliverance. You must *choose* the whole Will of God.

> But just as he who called you is holy, so be holy in all you do, for it is written: "Be holy, because I am holy."
>
> I Peter 1:15-16, NIV

> **DEFINE ORIGINAL SIN**

> **LIST OTHER DESCRIPTIVE TERMS FOR ORIGINAL SIN**

> **RECALL AN EXAMPLE OF WHAT HELPED YOU BECOME AWARE OF YOUR *NEED* FOR THE SPIRIT-FILLED LIFE. LIST THREE.**

4. *Man's Response—Man reacting to his need for the Spirit-filled life.*

    Man has the alternative to accept or reject the provisions of the Spirit-filled life. If you *choose* to accept the Spirit-filled life, it is your *responsibility* to:

    a. *Acknowledge*, through the help of the Holy Spirit, the extent of your need as it has been shown to you. (The basic cause of your moral conflict was the inherited, depraved nature.)

    b. *Confess* this need to God. You are not responsible for having inherited this plague of moral infection, but <u>you are responsible to avail yourself of God's cleansing cure</u>.

    As you are led to realize the importance of this new light, which reveals your deepest needs, you may be brought to a point of obedience to all you know of the Will of God.

(c.) ***Commit*** all you have, are, or ever expect to be. At this time, you lay down your arms of inner rebellion and self-serving as you make a complete *commitment* and a full consecration of *all* of self.

> I beseech you therefore, brethren by the mercies of God, that ye present your bodies a living sacrifice, holy, acceptable unto God, <u>which is your reasonable service.</u>
>
> Romans 12:1, KJV

WRITE IN THE SPACE PROVIDED, WHAT IS YOUR PRESENT LEVEL OF COMMITMENT NOW.

(d.) ***Believe*** God to accept you and to cleanse you from all indwelling sin. At this time, you must come to the point of total commitment and full consecration where you *trust* God with all of your life.

> We are saved from sin by faith, we are made holy by faith. This I testified in private, in public and in print, and God confirmed it by a thousand witnesses.[18]

---

[18]*Op. cit.,* Wesley, *Works,* Volume VII, p. 3.

Wesley declares that the experience of heart purity is attained by faith.

> Exactly as we are justified by faith, so are we sanctified by faith. Faith is the condition, and the only condition, of sanctification (the cleansed and Spirit-filled life), exactly as it is of justification.[19]

You are now ready (by faith and faith alone) to step out on the unfailing promises of God. You must trust that He, at this very instant of believing, *accepts* your commitment, *cleanses* your heart, and *fills* it with the presence and power of His Holy Spirit. Here . . . you rest your case in the *full assurance of faith,* the unfailing dependability of God.

> LIST THE AREAS OF MAN'S RESPONSE IN RECEIVING THE SPIRIT-FILLED LIFE.
> 1. *Divine Initiative*
> 2. *Awareness of Need*
> 3. *Awareness of Moral Choice*
> 4. *Man's Response*

Acknowledge
Confess
Commit all
Believe — faith

B. The Spirit-Filled Crisis Culminates with a Result

You observed in the previous section how the Spirit-filled crisis begins with a response: (1) God's response—Divine Initiative, (2) man's awareness of his need, (3) the necessity of a moral choice, and (4) how man responds in consecration, dedication, and faith. Upon man's response God does the following works.

---

[19]John Wesley, *Sermons, Volume 1* (New York: Lane and Scott, 1852), p. 388.

> 1. Heart Purity is cleansing.
> 2. Heart Perfection is restoration.
> 3. Infilling of Holy Spirit is His uncontested indwelling.
> 4. Empowering of Holy Spirit is Divine energizing.

1. *Heart Purity*

To purify or to cleanse is to make free from adulterating matter, impurities, pollution, or corruption. The Greek word, *katharidzo,* means "to cleanse or purify," and is the word that Peter used in referring to what happened on the Day of Pentecost. These two words mean the purging of the moral nature of man from the carnal corruption of original sin or depravity.

> "God, who knows the heart, showed that he accepted them by giving the Holy Spirit to them, just as he did to us. He made no distinction between us and them, for he purified their hearts by faith."
>
> Acts 15:8-9, NIV

The following Scriptures should also prove helpful:

> Cleanse your hands, ye sinners; and purify your hearts, ye double minded.
>
> James 4:8b, KJV

> And the very God of peace sanctify (cleanse) you wholly; and I pray God your whole *spirit* and *soul* and *body* be preserved blameless unto the coming of our Lord Jesus Christ. Faithful is he that calleth you, who also will do it.
>
> I Thessalonians 5:23-24, KJV

The Spirit-filled life makes possible freedom *from* sin, not *in* sin. It is a beautiful experience to be cleansed from *all original sin.*

> But if we walk in the light, as he is in the light, we have fellowship one with another, and the blood of Jesus Christ his Son cleanseth us from all sin.
> I John 1:7, KJV

It is the blood of Jesus Christ that pardons you from the *acts of sin*. It is also the blood of Jesus Christ that cleanses you from all *indwelling sin*.

> Wherefore Jesus also, that he might sanctify (cleanse) the people with his own blood, suffered without the gate.
> Hebrews 13:12, KJV

> What a wretched man I am! Who will rescue me from this body of death?
> Romans 7:24, NIV

For the *double* necessity . . . Jesus provided the *double* cure.

2. *Heart Perfection*

Heart perfection is the *restoration of God's moral nature* in man's perfected affections (love) and perfected motives (intent). It includes such *spiritual* qualities and elements of excellence as are in keeping with God's expectations and requirements *for man*.

a. The heart of every Spirit-filled Christian reflects the Love of God.

Heart perfection is the restoring of the affectional nature of man from its inner hostilities, i.e., hate, pride, greed, carnal jealousies, to a condition of Divine Love. John Wesley reaffirms this position.

> Both my brother (Charles Wesley) and I maintain, that Christian Perfection is that love of God and our neighbor which implies deliverance from all sin. It is the loving God with all our heart, mind, soul, and strength.[20]
>
> It is nothing higher, and nothing lower than this—pure love of God and man. It is love governing the heart and life, running through all our tempers, words, and actions.[21]

The conclusion of this matter is the commandment of love as stated by the Master when He said:

> ... Thou shalt love the Lord thy God with all thy heart, and with all thy soul, and with all thy mind. This is the first and great commandment. And the second is like unto it, Thou shalt love thy neighbor as thyself. On these two commandments hang all the law and the prophets.
>
> Matthew 22:37-40, KJV

b. Man's motive is his inner drive, the cause for his action. It is the fixation of his attention and purpose. It is his controlling fascination with the desired ends toward which he strives.

You learned in a previous chapter that perfect motive does not mean perfect judgment. As long as the mind, emotions, and will (soul functions) are imperfectible, you will have imperfect judgment. However, the Apostle Paul in I Thessalonians made this very clear when he prayed...

> May God himself, the God of peace, sanctify you through and through. May your whole spirit, soul and body be kept *blameless* (not faultless) at the coming of our Lord Jesus Christ.
>
> I Thessalonians 5:23, NIV

---

[20] *Op. cit.*, Wesley, *Works*, Volume VI, p. 500.
[21] *Ibid*, p. 502.

The Spirit-filled Christian must follow the example of Christ in the Garden as He prayed, "Not my will, but thine, be done" (Luke 22:42, KJV). In the cleansed and Spirit-filled life, it is not your selfish will but God's Will which should be the controlling motive of every confrontation.

3. *The Infilling of the Holy Spirit*

   This gift of infilling is only possible in the absence of original sin. The Holy Spirit is more than an influence. He is more than a blessing. He is the third Person of the Trinity. The Holy Spirit feels, thinks, wills, and, as the Comforter, speaks to your heart. He guides you into all truth, and assists you in prayer. He intercedes, inspires, instructs, and warns you. He can be resisted, or rejected, and thus grieved by your negative reactions to His directions. He is God's greatest Gift to you.

   Perfect relationship is established in the Spirit-filled life between the Holy Spirit and you.

   > "If you then, though you are evil, know how to give good gifts to your children, how much more will your Father in heaven give the Holy Spirit to those who ask him!"
   >
   > Luke 11:13, NIV

   > If ye love me, keep my commandments. And I will pray the Father, and he shall give you another Comforter, that he may abide with you for ever; *Even the Spirit of truth; whom the world cannot receive, because it seeth him not, neither knoweth him: but ye know him; for he dwelleth with you, and shall be in you.* I will not leave you comfortless: I will come to you.
   >
   > John 14:15-18, KJV

   > But the Comforter, which is the Holy Ghost, whom the Father will send in my name, he shall teach you all things, and bring all things to your remembrance, whatsoever I have said unto you.
   >
   > John 14:26, KJV

4. The Empowering of the Holy Spirit

This gift gives strength to maintain purity and to do God's Will. It is power to pray. It is power to testify. It is power to meet the inner spiritual confrontations... and overcome victoriously. It is the quickening energy for service, resulting from the presence of the Holy Spirit.

> "But you will receive power when the Holy Spirit comes on you; and you will be my witnesses in Jerusalem, and in all Judea and Samaria, and to the ends of the earth."
>
> Acts 1:8, NIV

This spiritual power is the result of both (1) an absence of moral conflict, or a cleansed heart, and (2) the indwelling presence of the Holy Spirit, the Power-Source.

The Holy Spirit is now at the control-center of the Spirit-filled heart. He empowers it, motivates it, directs it, anoints it, and blesses it.

This power is with a purpose. That purpose is for righteous living and Christian witnessing. It is not for selfish use or for personal advancement and honor. It is for the glory of God.

> And, behold, I send the promise of my Father upon you: but tarry ye in the city of Jerusalem, until ye be endued with power from on high.
>
> Luke 24:49, KJV

Observe the experience of the born-again and Spirit-filled life using the following diagram.

CRISIS	CONTINUATION	CRISIS
1. Divine Initiative 2. Awareness of Need 3. Awareness of Moral Choice 4. Man's Response	CONFLICT Confrontation & Temptation—Confrontation & Temptation	1. Divine Initiative 2. Awareness of Need 3. Awareness of Moral Choice 4. Man's Response
1. Forgiveness 2. Justification 3. Regeneration 4. Adoption		1. Heart Purity 2. Heart Perfection 3. Infilling of the Holy Spirit 4. Empowering of the Holy Spirit
BORN-AGAIN		SPIRIT-FILLED

In the conclusion of this section dealing with the crisis of the Spirit-filled life, you should consider the witness of the Spirit. Just as you experienced the witness of the Holy Spirit in the born-again life, so it is experienced in the Spirit-filled life.

In relation to the Holy Spirit and His witness, the Scripture teaches the witness is assured. It may be immediate or, in some cases, delayed.

> Those who obey his commands live in him, and he in them. And this is how we know that he lives in us: We know it by the Spirit he gave us.
> I John 3:24, NIV

> We know that we live in him and he in us, because he has given us of his Spirit.
> I John 4:13, NIV

> This is the one who came by water and blood—Jesus Christ. He did not come by water only, but by water and blood. And it is the Spirit who testifies, because the Spirit is the truth. Anyone who believes in the Son of God has this testimony in his heart. Anyone who does not believe God has made him out to be a liar, because he has not believed the testimony God has given about his Son.
> I John 5:6, 10, NIV

Once the Spirit-filled life has been experienced, the fruit of the Spirit becomes observable as both an internal and external evidence of the infilling of the Holy Spirit.

> But the fruit of the Spirit is love, joy, peace, patience, kindness, goodness, faithfulness, gentleness and self-control. Against such things there is no law. Those who belong to Christ Jesus have crucified their sinful nature with its passions and desires. Since we live by the Spirit, let us keep in step with the Spirit.
>
> Galatians 5:22-23, NIV

Although this is an internal and external evidence, these qualities must be further developed.

II. The Continuation of the Spirit-Filled Life

Just as there was spiritual growth following the crisis of the born-again life, so there must be spiritual growth following the crisis of the Spirit-filled life. Examine the diagram on the following page.

The Christian Experience

CRISIS

1. Divine Initiative
2. Awareness of Need
3. Awareness of Moral Choice
4. Man's Response

1. Forgiveness
2. Justification
3. Regeneration
4. Adoption

BORN-AGAIN

CONTINUATION

Confrontation & Temptation—Confrontation & Temptation

CONFLICT

CRISIS

1. Divine Initiative
2. Awareness of Need
3. Awareness of Moral Choice
4. Man's Response

1. Heart Purity
2. Heart Perfection
3. Infilling of the Holy Spirit
4. Empowering of the Holy Spirit

SPIRIT-FILLED

CONTINUATION

Confrontation & Temptation—etc.—etc.

ABSENCE OF CONFLICT

At the conclusion of the previous section, you noted that the fruit of the Spirit was an evidence of the Spirit-filled life. Two of the evidences of the Spirit-filled life are cited here.

A. *Growth:* The way that the fruit of the Spirit is developed is through growth in the following areas.

1. A more intense *love for His Word*

    As a Spirit-filled Christian, you will continue to mature as you develop an increased love for and application of the Word in your life.

    > Nothing is perfect except your words. Oh, how I love them. I think about them all day long.
    > Psalms 119:96-97, TLB

2. A more intense *love for others*

    Although this imparted love is Divine in its nature and quality, it may be increased in its capacity and expression.

    a. You will find an increased love for those in the Body of the Believers.

    b. You will find an increased love for those in your world who so desperately need a personal experience with Christ.

    > This is the message you heard from the beginning: We should love one another.
    > I John 3:11, NIV

    > No one has ever seen God; but if we love each other, God lives in us and his love is made complete in us.
    > I John 4:12, NIV

    > And he has given us this command: Whoever loves God must also love his brother.
    > I John 4:21, NIV

3. An eager *adjustment to new light* revealed

    Your attitude toward growth will be revealed in your eagerness to respond to the slightest revelation of God to you.

    It requires a disciplined effort not to rationalize yourself into a position that is less than God's very best. This sensitivity is not something that is always conscious nor is it easily maintained. Rather, it involves your intuitive sense that what God wants is best.

> But if we walk in the light, as he is in the light, we have fellowship with one another, and the blood of Jesus, his Son, purifies us from every sin.
> I John 1:7, NIV

4. *Influence and effect* on the *amoral functions*

> But speaking the truth in love, we are to grow up in *all aspects* into Him, who is the head, even Christ.
> Ephesians 4:15, NASB

The Holy Spirit wants to not only change the condition of your heart, but He also wants that change to be *worked out* in your everyday existence as it *affects every aspect* of your life.

a. The Spirit-filled life will have a "leveling out" or "balancing" effect on your psychical functions. The Spirit's influence will be observed as the extreme "highs" and "lows" of your psyche tend to find a balance.

b. The influence and effect of the Holy Spirit in *some cases* will even be felt in the physical area of your life. With the lack of inner moral conflict comes strength and beauty for life.

B. **Confrontation and Temptation But No Conflict:** The way that the fruit of the Spirit is developed through confrontation and temptation is discussed below.

1. In the continuation of the Spirit-filled life, there will always be the need for *confrontation*, i.e., the facing of alternatives. Moral growth and motivation come by choice and experience. These confrontations will be accompanied by varying degrees of *temptation*. (Temptation is an endeavor to persuade you to select one of the alternatives.)

There is an entire subsequent chapter devoted to the subject of "Temptation." As you can see, there is no temptation without confrontation. In the Spirit-filled life, there will always be *confrontation* and *temptation* but without conflict. Conflict is a problem that stems from the sinful carnal nature.

2. The question is sometimes raised as to the difference between the *temptations* of those who are Spirit-filled and those who are not. The difference lies in the fact that, in the carnal Christian, temptation stirs up the natural corruption of the heart with its bias and bent toward sin. However, in the Spirit-filled life, the Tempter finds no responsive ally within the heart.
This does not mean that the Spirit-filled Christian cannot yield to temptation and sin. But, freedom from indwelling sin serves to strengthen you in the hour of temptation. You can see now why the Spirit-filled life is an indispensable requisite to the life of constant victory over sin.

> Blessed is the man that endureth temptation: for when he is tried, he shall receive the crown of life which the Lord hath promised to them that love him.
> James 1:12, KJV

3. As you have noted, there will be confrontations and temptations in the Spirit-filled life. It must be pointed out, however, that since the carnal sinful self no longer resides in the heart, there can be *no conflict.*

Bill Gaither, in his powerful song entitled "It Is Finished," graphically portrays the *conflict* within the person whose heart is not totally yielded to the Lordship of the Holy Spirit. However, he does not leave the condition as an unsolved problem but announces that victory is possible for the asking, and Jesus can be not only *Savior* but also *Lord.*

Yet in my heart a battle was raging,
Not all pris'ners of war had come home.
They were battlefields of my own making,
I didn't know that the war had been won.

Then I heard that the King of the ages
Had fought all the battles for me.
And vict'ry was mine for the asking,
And now, praise His name, I am free!

It is finished, the battle is over.
It is finished, there'll be no more war.
It is finished, the end of the conflict.
It is finished, and Jesus is Lord.

He is Lord!
   He is Lord!
      He is Lord![22]

III. The Concerns Regarding the Spirit-Filled Life

Consider some of the most prevalent questions concerning the Spirit-filled life.

A. What are the differences between the amoral and moral natures of man?

It must be clearly understood that the Spirit-filled crisis changes the moral condition of the heart. The body and the soul are *only affected indirectly* from the heart. There is no morality in either the body or soul, but these body and soul functions are affected by a *changed heart*.

The heart or spirit function of man is his moral nature for which he is accountable to God. This spirit or moral nature must be dealt with and distinguished from the amoral function.

B. How can one know that he is Spirit-filled?

In the previous chapter, you established the fact that sin is twofold. There are the *acts* of sin and the *nature or condition*

---

[22] Copyright 1976 by William J. Gaither. International Copyright Secured. All Rights Reserved. Used by Special Permission of the Publisher.

of sin. The acts of sin are those choices that you have made against the Will of God. The sin nature or condition is the original sin *principle or tendency* with which you were born. When you are born-again, you confess your sins (the acts) and, by faith, Christ forgives you of your sins.

> If we confess our sins, he is faithful and just and will forgive us our sins and purify us from all unrighteousness.
> I John 1:9, NIV

The Spirit-filled crisis follows essentially the same steps as the born-again life. You consecrate or surrender your heart to God, and He cleanses or purifies it by faith. Just as you know Christ *forgives* you by faith, so you know Christ *cleanses* your heart by faith.

> "God, who knows the heart, showed that he accepted them by giving the Holy Spirit to them, just as he did to us. He made no distinction between us and them, for he purified their hearts by faith."
> Acts 15:8-9, NIV

C. When can one be filled with the Spirit?

There are occasions when people have been filled with the Spirit soon after conversion, while, with others, the interval may have been longer.

The Apostle Paul was converted on the road to Damascus (Acts 9:1-16). Then, in the same chapter, verse 17, Paul was filled with the Holy Spirit. This occurred only a short time after his conversion.

There is no required time interval for this experience. You not only can, but should, be filled with the Holy Spirit. Once you realize the need, the experience is for you.

D. What are the major theories for dealing with man's carnal conflicts taught by most evangelicals?

Most evangelicals accept one of the following three theories:
- Suppression
- Counteraction
- Eradication

1. Suppression

The Suppressionist's position is that as long as you live in this mortal body, you will have to "hold down" your sinful nature with the help of the Holy Spirit. They hold that the infilling of the Holy Spirit does not remove the sinful nature.

Those who hold to this theory believe that man's human nature (body and soul) *is so inseparably and unalterably a part of his sinful moral nature that only death can release him* from its effects and control. The Suppressionists do not distinguish between the amoral nature (the body and soul) and the moral nature (the heart or spirit) which either Christ or self controls.

The inconsistencies of this theory are at least twofold:

a. If the human nature (body and soul) is sinful, then one can only conclude that Jesus was sinful.

b. If the human nature (body and soul) is sinful, Jesus' coming and dying on the Cross accomplished nothing.

> But you know that he appeared so that he might *take away our sins* . . . No one who lives in him keeps on sinning. No one who continues to sin has either seen him or known him.
> I John 3:5-6, NIV

2. Counteraction

Counteractionists believe there is the inborn tendency to sin. In every individual it is counteracted, not eradicated, by the indwelling of the Holy Spirit. If you were to take a piece of lead and place it on a lifeboat and then place the boat in the water, the lead would not sink.

That is, *the tendency for the lead to sink is counteracted by the capacity of the lifeboat not to sink.*

It is an untenable and unscriptural position to believe that the sin principle is a dormant, passive potentiality, just lying there on a boat. Rather, the sinful nature is an inner, active, dynamic disposition that rebels against God's Will for your life.

The following Scriptures indicate the weaknesses of the counteractionist theory:

> The heart is the most deceitful thing there is, and desperately wicked. No one can really know how bad it is! Only the Lord knows! He searches all hearts and *examines deepest motives* so he can give to each person his right reward, according to his deeds—how he has lived.
>
> Jeremiah 17:9-10, TLB

> ... because the sinful mind is hostile to God. It does not submit to God's law, nor can it do so.
>
> Romans 8:7, NIV

> So I say, live by the Spirit, and you will not gratify the desires of your sinful nature. For the sinful nature desires what is contrary to the Spirit, and the Spirit what is contrary to the sinful nature. They are in conflict with each other, so that you do not do what you want.
>
> Galatians 5:16-17, NIV

3. *Eradication*

The Eradicationists believe that the human nature (body and soul) is amoral and that only the heart of man is moral. To eradicate means to "root out" or remove the carnal sinful nature, which is called original sin.

All orthodox Christian theologians agree that Adam and Eve were created *without this original sin or carnal nature.*

Yet, when they chose to turn their backs on God's Will, they fell from grace, and they and all their children experienced this sinful selfish condition.

It is clear that to root out sin only means that sin is no longer in the heart, but the *possibility* for the sinful moral condition to return is always present as long as you have the capacity to choose. As long as there is choice, there is the possibility to sin, but this possibility does not mean the presence of sin.

In the heart that is cleansed, sin (this moral sinful condition) is now non-existent. *It is not suppressed or counteracted, it is gone!*

E. Is there a different standard of living for the carnal Christian?

There are many born-again Christians who have the misconception that because they are not filled with the Holy Spirit—i.e., not sanctified—the level of their Christian lives, *as far as obedience to God* is concerned, is different and not so demanding as the life of the Spirit-filled Christian.

This is a nonbiblical position and from a practical point of view very dangerous both personally and influentially.

I John 3:9 declares:

> No one who is born of God will continue to sin . . .
> I John 3:9a, NIV

The act of disobedience is sin, and "sin separates a man from God" (Isaiah 59:2).

F. Is it possible that restitution may be a requirement of the Spirit-filled life?

The answer is "yes." This is a very subtle problem. As a sincere Christian, you should be concerned about living up to the claims of the Lordship of Christ in your life.

From a practical point of view, in the carnal Christian's life, several problems are posed.

1. The heart is diseased, selfish, and contrary to Christ's best. Your attitudes toward God's Will and the people around you aren't always as they ought to be.

2. Just simply to recognize these bad attitudes and condition and say, "God, please cleanse me of all this pollution," is not always adequate.

    a. What about the sorrow you've caused God?
    b. What about the problem you've created for others?

The *willingness* to make restitution, both to God and your fellowman, *as light is revealed,* is a *must* if you are to enjoy a life filled with God's Spirit.

> "Therefore, if you are offering your gift at the altar and there remember that your brother has something against you, leave your gift there in front of the altar. First go and be reconciled to your brother; then come and offer your gift."
>
> Matthew 5:23-24, NIV

G. Can one sin after he is filled with the Spirit?

There is the misconception among many evangelicals that the teachings of the Spirit-filled or the sanctified life include the idea that you can no longer sin.

In both the born-again and Spirit-filled life, you have the capacity to choose; therefore, you have the capacity to sin. However, it must be noted that in the Spirit-filled life, there is a significant difference, for there is no longer the inner conflict but the added power to live the victorious Spirit-filled life.

H. What is the solution to the apparent problem of total surrender and personal ambition in the Spirit-filled life?

One of the most thrilling things about the totally surrendered life is the fact that you are so excited about doing God's Will that once you *know* what His Will is, there should be neither lack of ambition nor settling for mediocrity.

Personal ambition is never at a higher pitch than when your will is surrendered to God. The only conflict or problem that can be experienced is when you want your own way instead of God's way. You can be assured that God wants that which is best for you.

I. How does one lose and/or regain the Spirit-filled life?

1. In the beginning Adam and Eve possessed moral perfection. How did they lose this condition? By sinning against the known Will of God. Therefore, the way by which *you lose* this moral perfection is *by sinning against* the known Will of God.

   > Remember, too, that knowing what is right to do and then not doing it is sin.
   > James 4:17, TLB

2. You regain this Spirit-filled life by first repenting of your sins and, when necessary, making restitution. Secondly, you must consecrate your heart to God.

Both of these experience are consummated or completed by faith in what Christ did for you on the Cross.

> For it is by grace you have been saved, through faith—and this not from yourselves, it is the gift of God.
> Ephesians 2:8, NIV

> And so Jesus also suffered outside the city gate to make his people holy through his own blood.
> Hebrews 13:12, NIV

J. Can the Holy Spirit leave you?

The answer is "yes." The Holy Spirit *can* leave you *if* you turn your back on Him. However, He *will not* leave you *if* you are obedient to Him.

K. How much does one's personality change when he is Spirit-filled?

The personality of the individual involves the abilities, interests, and attributes that makes one person different from another. *This includes the total physical, intellectual, emotional, volitional, and spiritual capacities of the individual.* The essential change is that the seat of the affections or heart of a person is purified, and the decisions and directions will *no longer be self-centered but Christ-centered.*

This basic change will only affect these abilities, interests, and attributes in the way they relate to God's Will.

L. What does total commitment mean?

Total commitment is when your body, soul, and spirit are completely given to God's ownership. The will of your life has been voluntarily and completely surrendered in favor of God's Will.

In a later chapter on "Commitment," you will deal further with this subject.

M. Can one experience depression if he is Spirit-filled?

The spirit of man is housed in an imperfect body and soul. The body and soul may be a source of amoral depression which is not spiritual in nature. For example, you are told that colors in a room may affect your disposition. Weather changes may cause you to have feelings of depression. Depression may be a result of chemical changes or cycles which occur in the bodies of both men and women. And there are many other factors that may affect physical, mental, and emotional depression.

There is no reason to feel any guilt about this amoral depression. However, this type of depression which stems from a body or soul function must be distinguished from spiritual depression, which can be a result of a sinful response in one's life.

This is a result of an act of disobedience or the failing to respond, in a timely manner, to what God has shown you. This moral, spiritual depression comes as a result of guilt in one's life and may be evidenced by self-pity.

Depression experienced in the body or soul functions, if not dealt with, may have a detrimental effect on one's spiritual life. The important fact that must be understood at this point, is that the more control the Holy Spirit has of your heart or spirit, the more readily the soul function of man can be improved and depression lessened.

N. What is the problem when one has a bad spirit?

Generally speaking, a bad spirit is a spiritual condition—where the Holy Spirit is not in complete control. In this condition, self is the most important and is usually evidenced by attitudes of self-defense, negative responses, or other carnal behavior.

O. Is it possible to be born-again and Spirit-filled simultaneously?

Simultaneous means "two or more events happening at the same instant." With this definition, the answer would be "no." One must first be born-again before he is eligible for the infilling of the Holy Spirit.

P. What is the difference between *initial sanctification* and *entire sanctification*?

Both initial and entire sanctification are acts of the Holy Spirit. You will find both of these terms used repeatedly in the writings of John Wesley.

Quite simply, *initial sanctification* refers to the *born-again* experience where the *Holy Spirit* comes into the heart of the person in forgiveness, justification, regeneration, and adoption. But the carnal nature is also present. So entire sanctification refers to the work of the Holy Spirit in the *Spirit-filled life* where He cleanses the carnal pollution and restores the diseased nature, perfects the moral motivation, entirely fulfills and controls the heart, and empowers the believer for service.

> Initial or partial sanctification includes in its scope all that acquired pollution which attaches to the sinner's own act; while entire sanctification includes the cleansing from original sin or inherited depravity.
> (*Introduction to Christian Theology*, Wiley and Culbertson, Volume 2, p. 481)

Q. Is it true that only Jesus comes into your heart in the born-again experience, then the Holy Spirit comes in at the time of sanctification or the Spirit-filled experience?

The answer is "no." If you only receive *Jesus* into your heart at the time of the born-again experience and the *Holy Spirit* at the time of sanctification, then when do you receive *God the Father?* As Paul states:

> For in Christ all the fullness of the Deity lives in bodily form, and you have this fullness in Christ, who is the head over every power and authority.
> Colossians 2:9-10, NIV

Or, another way of expressing it:

> For in Christ there is all of God in a human body, *so you have everything when you have Christ,* and you are filled with God through your union with Christ.
> Colossians 2:9-10, TLB

When Christ comes into your heart, all of the Godhead is there, not just part of Him. The born-again experience, as well as the Spirit-filled experience, is a work of the Holy Spirit. Sanctification begins in conversion. The problem of the converted life stems from the fact that after the born-again experience all of the selfish, carnal nature also remains in the heart. As was once stated, "The Holy Spirit is 'resident' but not president'." All orthodox Christianity believes that after the born-again experience, there still remains the presence of original sin. The real question centers around the idea of *when* can man be freed from this internal civil war caused by the co-existence of the two natures. The "Good News" is that the believer does not have to wait until physical death frees him, but rather, he can know the cleansing, empowering fullness of the Holy Spirit in this present life.

Without the presence of the Holy Spirit in your born-again life, you would never have the power to appropriate the Lordship of the Holy Spirit through the Spirit-filled experience.

> . . . no one can say, "Jesus is Lord," except by the Holy Spirit.   1 Corinthians 12:3, NIV

In the born-again life you have *all* of the Godhead in you. But when you realize the warring and the possibilities of peace, and as you acknowledge, confess, commit, and believe, you then have Him in His fullness because He then finally has *all* of you.

In this chapter on the Spirit-filled life you have examined *Crisis, Continuation,* and *Concerns.* You are now ready to turn to the inspirational concept of "FAITH."

REVIEW EXERCISE

Divide your group into pairs and have each couple draw the diagram of *THE CHRISTIAN EXPERIENCE*. Be sure to include:

1. Crisis of the Born-Again Life
    a. Four areas of response
    b. Four areas of result

2. Continuation
    a. Confrontation
    b. Temptation

3. Conflict

4. Crisis of the Spirit-Filled Life
    a. Four areas of response
    b. Four areas of result

5. Continuation
    a. Confrontation
    b. Temptation

Now have each person, on a "one-to-one" situation, explain the process of the Christian experience.

Faith
(outline)

I. Introduction

    A. Some Confusion Concerning Faith

    B. The Neutrality of Faith

II. The Gift of Faith

    A. Man Was Created in God's Image

    B. A Practical Application

    C. James Speaks to the Problem

    D. Faith in Relation to Good and Evil

III. Saving Faith

    A. The Scope of Faith

    B. The Singularity of Faith

    C. God Gives Faith

    D. Man's Response of Faith

    E. The Process of Saving Faith

IV. Achieving Faith

    A. Obtaining God's Provisions Through Achieving Faith

    B. Satan Tries to Pervert Our Faith

    C. Achieving Faith as it Relates to God's Will

    D. A Functional Definition of Faith

I do beg of you to recognize, then, the extreme simplicity of faith; namely, that it is nothing more nor less than just believing God when He says He either has done something for us, or will do it; and then trusting Him to keep His word.

—Hannah Whitall Smith

Faith

> Faith is the capacity to believe and to act upon that belief.

I. Introduction

A. Some Confusion Concerning Faith

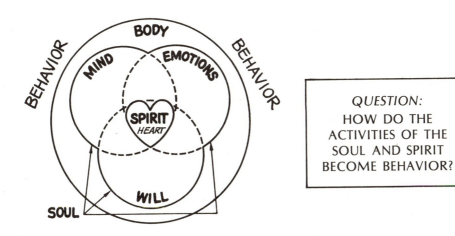

> QUESTION: HOW DO THE ACTIVITIES OF THE SOUL AND SPIRIT BECOME BEHAVIOR?

Perhaps one of the most misunderstood subjects relating to our Christian experience is that of faith. You have learned that *without faith we can't please God* (Hebrews 11:6), and you have read that *faith is the measure of your blessing* (Romans 12:3). You have also sung songs and heard sermons on the

149

"Faith of Our Fathers," and somehow, in your mind's eye, you have pictured a package all neatly wrapped up with ribbons on the top and a sign stamped on the side which said:

HANDLE WITH CARE AND PRESERVE FOREVER.
CONTENTS ARE FRAGILE AND MYSTERIOUS.
PACKAGE MUST NOT BE OPENED UNTIL THE JUDGMENT.

However, the tragedy is that without a clear understanding of faith, there is a strong possibility that you will miss God's "best" for your life.

To some degree the confusion which surrounds the subject of faith is the same as the confusion with which you wrestled in dealing with the subjects of "The Born-Again Life" and "The Spirit-Filled Life" in the previous sessions. You are inclined to think: There is *flesh* and there is *spirit;* there is *good* and there is *bad;* there is *religious* and there is *non-religious.* Then you conclude that this thing called "faith" has something *only* to do with *religious.* You learn that it is a "gift of God," and you begin to pray for it, wait for it, beg to have it increased—and, then, if something "magic" doesn't happen, you get discouraged, quit, and become the object of Satan's ridicule.

B. The Neutrality of Faith

At the outset, you must see that *faith is a neutral capability available to be controlled either by the Spirit of Good or the Spirit of Evil.* What you must understand is that man was created in God's own Image—that is: you think, you act, you feel, you desire, you will, etc. But these neutral abilities, without outside influence, are neither good nor evil. They were originally created as raw material that is to be directed by the Spirit that is within you. And that Spirit within you can be *either* Good or Evil. To love, to hate, to admire, to despise, to boast, to be humble, to be upset, to be calm, to have fear, to be bold, to be stern, to be gentle—any of these can be right and any can be wrong.

In this session you will be dealing with three main aspects of the subject of faith:

THE GIFT OF FAITH   Faith is a gift from a loving God
SAVING FAITH   How faith is related to the Plan of Salvation
ACHIEVING FAITH   How faith works in the everyday Christian life

II. The Gift of Faith

A. Man Was Created in God's Image

> THE VERY ESSENCE OR QUALITY OF THE SPIRIT IS LOVE, EITHER PURE OR PERVERTED.
> "AS A MAN THINKETH IN HIS HEART—SO IS HE."
> (Pure or perverted in his love.)

God is Love, and as man was created in God's Image, so man was given the capacity for love, either purified or perverted. The object of man's love possesses him. Love of the world *or* love of the Father *must* dominate the human heart or spirit.

> Don't you realize that you can choose your own master? You can choose sin (with death) or else obedience (with acquittal). The one to whom you offer yourself—he will take you and be your master and you will be his slave.
> Romans 6:16, TLB

> "You cannot serve two masters: God and money. For you will hate one and love the other, or else the other way around."
>
> Matthew 6:24, TLB

Man *must* love, because he was created with the *necessity* to love. Love is the quality and the very essence of the SPIRIT that you learned about in the previous sessions. The Spirit of Love (either love of Good *or* love of Evil) is the driving force of your activities. This love (pure or perverted) controls and creates all that ever comes to pass. That is what the Scriptures refer to when they declare that GOD IS LOVE. He is that creative, dynamic Force and Personality that brought everything into existence. *Love motivates, but faith carries out the urges of the Spirit of Love.*

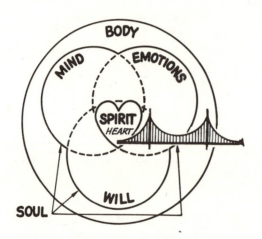

THE VERY ESSENCE OR QUALITY OF THE SPIRIT IS LOVE, EITHER PURE OR PERVERTED.
"AS A MAN THINKETH IN HIS HEART—SO IS HE."
(Pure or perverted in his love.)

B. A Practical Application

Let's apply this, then, to the diagram explaining the spirit, the soul, and the body. The Spirit of Love motivates you to send your special friend a greeting card through the mail to tell him/her of your appreciation. (1) This passes through the *intellect,* and you construct and weigh all the reasons and merits of such an action. (2) While this process is going on, the very thought of this person gives you a warm *emotional* feeling, and, in fact, you even catch yourself getting excited about sending this card of appreciation. Thereupon, your *will,* or volition, goes into action, and you say to yourself, "That's a great idea—I'll do it!" Now, the question is, "How does this intention move from the soul into actual accomplishment?" *By faith!* By the activities of your soul—i.e., mind, emotions, and will—you become convinced of the value of this project. It is at this point that faith takes over and actually becomes the *bridge* that connects the function of the soul to actual behavior.

C. James Speaks to the Problem

Throughout his writings, James diligently tries to emphasize the fact that *without this bridge called "faith,"* which links the function of the soul to actual behavior, *you are left with only intentions.* The actions which should have resulted from these good intentions, therefore, died before they were even born.

> Are there still some among you who hold that "only believing" is enough? Believing in one God? Well, remember that the demons believe this too—so strongly that they tremble in terror! Fool! When will you ever learn that "believing" is useless without *doing* what God wants you to? Faith that does not result in good deeds is not real faith.

> Don't you remember that even our Father Abraham was declared good because of what he *did* when he was willing to obey God even if it meant offering his son Isaac to die on the altar? You see, he was trusting God so much that he was willing to do whatever God told him to; his faith was made complete by what he did, by his actions, his good deeds.
>
> James 2:19-22, TLB

James is saying here that it is possible to use the function of your intellect and become convinced of the merits of something, but without this *bridge* of faith, it never has a chance of moving from the soul or heart to the actual behavior. As you will recall from the diagram, faith is the bridge over which desires travel to bring about activity.

D. Faith in Relation to Good and Evil

You may ask, then, "Does the function of this faith only work in relation to the pure Love or the Spirit of Good as seen in the diagram?" *Or* is it necessary that this faith also goes into action in connection with the Evil Spirit?

To answer this, let's look at what happened to Adam and Eve. They were created without darkness in their hearts; they were morally pure; they were without a sinful nature or inborn tendencies to do wrong. Yet, *they had the power to choose.*

Satan approached Eve through her intellect and asked, ". . . None of the fruit in the garden? God said you mustn't eat any of it?"

"Of course we may eat it," the woman told him. "It's only the fruit from the tree at the center of the garden that we are not to eat. God says we mustn't eat it or even touch it, or we will die."

"That's a lie!" the serpent hissed. "You will not die!" (Genesis 3:1-4, TLB)

At this point Satan has fully engaged the woman's emotions as well as her intellect. Those things on which she had previously counted, she begins to doubt. This shakes her intellect and her emotions.

Satan continues: "God knows very well that the instant you eat it, you will become like Him, for your eyes will be opened —you will be able to distinguish good from evil."

The woman is convinced in her heart. How lovely and fresh looking the fruit is! And it will make her so wise! So she eats some of the fruit and gives some to her husband.

Eve dramatically demonstrates that faith is also active when moving an intention into actual behavior, even if it is an evil intention resulting in evil behavior.

Thus, we see that faith, which is a God-given faculty, is the only way by which a person can go through all the processes of doing or obtaining the things he desires.

NOTES   156

FAITH IS NECESSARY IN MOVING A PURE INTENTION INTO AN ACT OF GOOD OR RIGHT BEHAVIOR.
EXAMPLE: ABRAHAM BEING CONVINCED OF WHAT WAS RIGHT . . . THEN ACTUALLY *WALKING* OUT INTO THE DESERT.   (Genesis 12)

FAITH WAS ALSO NECESSARY IN MOVING EVE'S PERVERTED INTENTION INTO AN EVIL ACT OF BEHAVIOR.
(Genesis 3)

You will get into this part of the study of faith later, but it is interesting to note, at this point, that if man is made in the Image of God, and if man's fundamental, God-given faculties are those of love and faith, then they are also God's ways of action—even of creation—and even with His continual dealings with man today!

God had faith in man that man would take advantage of His Plan of Redemption. If He had not had faith in man, as well as love for man, His Son, Christ, would never have been sent.

At this point, however, it is only important to see that as long as a person lives and breathes, he will always be exercising faith, and that faith, in and of its unaffected self, is neither good nor bad, but it is capable of being influenced and controlled by either the Spirit of Good or Evil. Faith fulfills the function of moving the intellectual, emotional, and volitional activities of the soul and heart into the area of man's actual behavior.

As long as man lives and breathes, he can never quit exercising faith. Seeking faith would be like asking for a mouth with which to eat or asking for lungs with which to breathe... you already have it. It is a marvelous gift, given to every man by a loving God.

How will you use this gift?

What Spirit will you allow to influence and control this gift?

III. Saving Faith

A. The Scope of Faith

You have now seen that faith is a very normal activity in your everyday life. God created you with this faculty, knowing that you would use it every single day of your existence. It is a gift from God. You didn't order it from a Sears catalog or construct it from an electronics "do-it-yourself" kit. You were born with this capacity. In the normal functions of life, the process of this living faith is so unalterably a part of your life that it sometimes goes unnoticed. This faith is so continual that it is tough for you to even dream of calling it "faith"... but it is!

The writer to the Hebrews was talking about that when he stated that faith, quite simply, is . . .

> . . . the confident assurance that something we want is going to happen. It is the certainty that what we hope for is waiting for us, even though we cannot see it up ahead.
> Hebrews 11:1, TLB

You also have seen that faith must have a motivation from the Spirit to activate it as well as the object (behavior) that it "sees."

B. The Singularity of Faith

It is the familiarity with these normal, everyday functions of faith that sometimes causes you to think, "Surely there must be two kinds of faith; this natural kind of faith can't be the same kind of faith I am called upon to exercise when dealing with the born-again life or the Spirit-filled life or the process of everyday Christian maturity" . . . but it is! *It is the same faith, the activating of this same God-given faculty, that God honors when He forgives us, justifies us, regenerates us, and adopts us into His Family as His very own Children.*

> He has done this through the death on the cross of his own human body, and now as a result Christ has brought you into the very presence of God, and you are standing there before him with nothing left against you—nothing left that he could even chide you for; the only condition is that you fully believe the Truth, standing in it steadfast and firm, strong in the Lord, convinced of the Good News that Jesus died for you, and never shifting from trusting him to save you.
> Colossians 1:22-23a, TLB

> For God sent Christ Jesus to take the punishment for our sins and to end all God's anger against us. He used Christ's blood and our faith as the means of saving us from his wrath.
> Romans 3:25a, TLB

> Then what can we boast about doing, to earn our salvation? Nothing at all. Why? Because our acquittal is not based on our good deeds; it is based on what Christ has done and our faith in him. So it is that we are saved by faith in Christ and not by the good things we do.
> Romans 3:27-28, TLB

> For it is by grace you have been saved, through faith—and this not from yourselves, it is the gift of God...
> Ephesians 2:8, NIV

> For it is with your heart that you believe and are justified, and it is with your mouth that you confess and are saved. As the Scripture says, "he who believes in him will not be put to shame."
> Romans 10:10-11, NIV

It is the activating of this same faith that God honors when filling you with the Holy Spirit, thereby allowing you to begin to function as you were intended to function rather than living out the frustrations of a perverted life.

> "'... to open their eyes and turn them from darkness to light, and from the power of Satan to God, so that they may receive forgiveness of sins and a place among those who are sanctified by faith in me.'"
> Acts 26:18, NIV

> "He made no distinction between us and them, for he purified their hearts by faith."
> Acts 15:9, NIV

C. God Gives Faith

One of the most beautiful things about God's Plan of Salvation is the fact that He has taken every possible means that could be taken to help stimulate faith in Himself. God is eager that the "gulf of separation" be bridged and that man be redeemed and restored back to Him. This is the reason for God Himself entering the human arena in sending His beloved Son to become very much man. God knew when He sent Christ that He was to become the Sin Sacrifice that God Himself had demanded. Yet, Christ came to earth so that you could perceive Him with your own soul functions, i.e., mind, emotions, and will (I John 1:1-3, TLB).

Yes, He came so you could listen to Him with your ears, reason with Him with your intellect, cry with Him when His friend Lazarus died, be excited with Him when the lame man picked up his bed and walked, and rejoice with Him when Peter, with the eye of faith, finally "saw" that Christ was the Son of God in the flesh.

Why would God do this?

Why would Christ go to the bother?

> If faith needs motivation to activate it, then His touchable love would become the motivation. If faith requires an object, then *He* would become the object so that it would be easier for your eye of faith to "see" the possibilities of restoration.

For God is at work within you, helping you want to obey him, and then helping you do what he wants.
    Philippians 2:13, TLB

Down through history God has tried to make it easy for man's faith to bridge the activities of his soul and heart to bring about actual restoration. His dealings with the Children of Israel (His chosen people from the time of Abraham) and His mighty works of deliverance and provision foretell the extent to which He will go to help you.

> "O Lord God of our fathers: Abraham, Isaac, and Israel! Make your people always want to obey you, and see to it that their love for you never changes. Give my son Solomon a good heart toward God, so that he will *want to obey you* in the smallest detail, and will look forward eagerly to finishing the building of your temple, for which I have made all of these preparations."
>
> I Chronicles 29:18-19, TLB

> Restore to me again the joy of your salvation, and make me *willing to obey you.*
>
> Psalm 51:12, TLB

Then, as the Bible says, in the fullness of time, the ultimate, convincing, persuasive Plan was put into action. The True Light shown out in the darkness; the Word was made Flesh and dwelt among us, full of grace and truth (John 1:1-3).

Here are some visible, tangible testimonies which show the extent to which God will go in order to help us activate our faith in His promised restoration:

1. Christ's wisdom and instruction (Matthew 5, 6, 7).

2. Christ's activities of ministry, including miracles and many symbolic teachings (John 14:11).

3. Christ's prophetically foretold death and resurrection (Psalm 22; Isaiah 9, 11, 42, 46, 53).

4. Christ's witnessed appearances after His resurrection (John 20, 21; I Corinthians 15:5-8).

5. Christ's attested ascension back into Heaven (Luke 24; Acts 1:9-11).

6. The coming of the Holy Spirit which Christ had specifically promised (Luke 24:49; Acts 1:8).

7. The transformed lives of His followers (Book of Acts).

8. The written records of and by these transformed followers (Gospels and Epistles).

9. The miracles which you have seen with your own eyes in your lifetime.

10. The changed lives to which you can point.

> He wants your faith to operate as freely in *spiritual matters* as it does in the *normal everyday life processes.*

D. Man's Response of Faith

The strange phenomenon is that even with God fulfilling what would appear to be 99% of the deal, yet it still takes your 1%, which is your *Accepting Faith,* to make the transaction complete. No wonder it is stated that *without faith no man can please God* (Hebrews 11:6).

> If man does not exercise his faith in *accepting,* he can never *receive* God's promised provision.

E. The Process of Saving Faith

When a person is convicted of sin, the Holy Spirit penetrates that person's self-righteousness and allows him to see his condition as it really is. Pressure is brought to bear, not only directly upon the heart, but also through the functions of the soul. For example, a near-accident may cause you to think about your spiritual need. The emotional experience of losing a loved one may cause you to examine your own spiritual condition. For, you see, every person has built around himself some working philosophy of life:

1. You are as good as anyone else.

2. You don't rob banks.

3. You don't beat your wife.

4. You don't even kick your dog too often.

5. You believe in a Creator who must look something like Santa Claus, who is jolly and full of love; therefore, hell is unthinkable.

6. Everything is going to be all right.

You, like every other person, must have some basis for life—a working self-chosen philosophy—however flimsy, however unsatisfactory, or however unfulfilling it may be. And to that basis, to that philosophy, your *faith* is attached.

It is not that you *don't* have faith; you *have* faith!

Now conviction of sin, whatever method the Holy Spirit uses to activate it, knocks out the flimsy props from under you. Your selfish basis for life can no longer satisfy.

> . . . When we put on our prized robes of righteousness, we find they are but filthy rags . . .
> Isaiah 64:6, TLB

Then you realize that you have built for yourself "broken cisterns that can't hold water" (Jeremiah 2:13, TLB). At this point the foundations of your bridge of faith begin to crumble.

What will you do?

How can you rebuild them?

Now the Holy Spirit points to Jesus, the Author and Finisher of faith.

> "Whoever puts his faith in the Son has eternal life..."
> John 3:36, NIV

> "The Spirit and the bride say, 'Come!' And let him who hears say, 'Come!' Whoever is thirsty, let him come, and whoever wishes, let him take the free gift of the water of life."
> Revelation 22:17, NIV

There is a positive response of the sin-sick spirit to the gentle but persuasive pressure of the Holy Spirit. All systems of the soul are "go." In an instant your faith transcends all human reason and emotion and bridges your spirit with the glorious ideal of restoration and the born-again life. This experience demands the "leap of faith."

At that very same split-second, with angel choirs singing and saints who have gone on before in the grandstands cheering (Hebrews 12:1), God wonderfully forgives, justifies, and declares you "not guilty." God regenerates and imparts a new nature, and lovingly adopts you as a full-fledged member into the Family of God.

As strange and wonderful as it may seem, that even with God fulfilling what would appear to be 99% of the deal, yet it still takes your simple and active faith in accepting Christ's provision to complete your restoration. Without this, there isn't enough conviction, or sorrow, or tears, or prayers, or resolutions in the whole world to bring the seeker into the enjoyment of receiving God's grace. That faculty of faith has to be exercised.

It is important to see that faith cannot save; only God's grace can do that (Ephesians 2:8-9). Faith is the decisive action of the free spirit which actually allows the Holy Spirit to live the life of Jesus Christ through you to the glory of the Father.

IV. Achieving Faith

A. Obtaining God's Provisions through Achieving Faith

> And now just as you trusted Christ to save you, trust him, too, for each day's problems...
> Colossians 2:6, TLB

Achieving Faith, or the "daily living faith," is the dimension of faith that gives the Christian the most difficulty.

How do you use faith in your everyday life in order to receive the provisions God has in store for you?

You have now learned that you continually use faith in your everyday life activities such as getting in an elevator and counting on it to safely take you to the 20th floor, or setting your alarm clock and counting on it to awaken you at the proper time, etc. You can understand these examples quite simply.

In reality, Saving Faith is also quite simple:

1. You see your need.
2. You see the solution.
3. You take Christ at His Word.
4. You confess Him.
5. Suddenly Christ is your own.
6. You know it and have a first-hand chance to witness as to the changes that have taken place in your life.

This simplicity is largely due to the fact that Saving Faith, in the mind of the believer, has more to do with the past and the future than it does with the present.

> When a person comes to Christ as a sinner, his main concern is usually his past sins and their consequences, and his future destiny, rather than the present.

And when that *Saving Faith* is activated, the past is blotted out, and the future is assured by the gift of eternal life (John 3:16, NIV). But the problem with everyday, present-tense *Achieving Faith* can be very knotty. Take some of the present-tense experiences of Peter for example. Peter was the pioneer in matters of faith among the disciples. It is interesting to watch him develop, and it is easy to identify with him in his "water-walking" episode (Matthew 14:28).

Christ allowed Peter to "see" some undreamed-of possibilities through faith and then encouraged him into the test. Christ told Peter to launch on out where the water was deeper and let down his nets. He assured Peter that if he did, he would bring in a real "haul" even though they had not caught a single fish all night. Peter struggled as he sifted this proposition . . .

- . . . through his *intellect* (he had been fishing right there all night) . . .

- . . . through his *emotions* (what would his partners think of this action?—after all they were "professional" fishermen) . . .

- . . . and through his *will* (is he going to follow through or not?).

He hesitated, then plunged:

> "Sir . . . we worked hard all night and didn't catch a thing. But if you say so, we'll try it again." And this time their nets were so full that they began to tear! . . . and soon both boats were filled with fish and on the verge of sinking.
>
> Luke 5:5-7, TLB

Peter learned a great lesson here for everyday living: *there are resources in God which counteract nature, and, by faith, man can use them.*

The next time Peter needed no invitation. In the middle of the storm, he saw Christ walking on water toward their boat. Peter called out to Him, "Lord, if it's you . . . tell me to come to you on the water" (Matthew 14:28, NIV).

You can imagine Christ's inner response to this display of faith. "Come," He said to Peter, and Peter got out and walked. For the only time in recorded history, the laws of gravity which govern the sinking of a body in water were altered.

How?

By Peter's faith which actually affected his behavior.

Now it's true that when faced by a huge wave, Peter transferred his faith back to the already-known fact that man sinks in water. It is also true that he got a dunking for his daring, but he gained something more priceless than any of his more cautious stay-in-the-boat buddies. He gained an *experiential* knowledge of *Achieving Faith.* He was able to grasp this amazing truth in the only way truth can really be known . . . by trying it out.

B. Satan Tries to Pervert Our Faith

How many people have fallen prey to Satan's subtle trickery in the areas of perverted faith? He will come to you along these lines.

> "Hey, Pal, you know you've been working overtime at this involvement and commitment thing; think of all the hours you've spent in Discipling class alone. It's about time God gives you something nice as a reward. How about that new tri-level house on the corner? It's for sale, you know . . . and the family certainly would be more comfortable there. Remember the Scriptures? 'Ask with faith and you shall receive,' or 'Whatsoever you ask in faith, it shall be given you,' or 'If you have faith, and doubt not, it shall be yours.' So, Pal, it looks like the only thing standing between you and your new house is your ability to muster up enough faith. In fact, you deserve that house so much, let's put a time limit on God. Let's have faith that you'll be moved in by the last of next month.
>
> "Oh, you say the time limit has come and gone and nothing happened? Well, join the crowd! Oh now, don't use that 'If it's Your Will' stuff. That's a cop-out. Your problem is you didn't have enough faith. Why don't you go to the altar and pray for more faith; then we'll try the whole thing again next month. In fact, you ought to put God in a corner and sell your old house, Pal; that's faith if I ever saw it.
>
> "Oh-oh, you say your time limit is up again, and God still didn't give you the house yet? You surely look stupid! You would be better off taking things back into your own hands. At least that way you can know what to count on. And remember, I told you way back at the start that this faith syndrome was a cheap hoax and can only leave you with empty disappointments. So, Pal, don't ever let me catch you using it again."

Perhaps this narrative is oversimplified, but the spiritual junkyards are full of wrecks which were promoted by Satan's encouraging a perverted understanding and use of faith.

ASSIGNMENT:

Study the following Scriptures, and do the exercise on the following page. Be prepared to discuss the questions in the next session.

I JOHN 3:21-22, TLB	But, dearly loved friends, if our consciences are clear, we can come to the Lord with perfect assurance and trust, and get whatever we ask for because we are obeying him and doing the things that please him.
I JOHN 5:14-15, TLB	And we are sure of this, that he will listen to us whenever we ask him for anything in line with his will. And if we really know he is listening when we talk to him and make our requests, then we can be sure that he will answer us.
JOHN 14:13-14, TLB	"You can ask him for *anything*, using my name, and I will do it, for this will bring praise to the Father because of what I, the Son, will do for you. Yes, ask *anything*, using my name, and I will do it!"
JOHN 15:16, TLB	"You didn't choose me! I chose you! I appointed you to go and produce lovely fruit always, so that no matter what you ask for from the Father, using my name, he will give it to you."
JOHN 16:24, TLB	"You haven't tried this before (but begin now). Ask, using my name, and you will receive, and your cup of joy will overflow."
MATTHEW 21:21-22, TLB	Then Jesus told them, "Truly, if you have faith, and don't doubt, you can do things like this and much more. You can even say to this Mount of Olives, 'Move over into the ocean,' and it will. You can get anything—*anything* you ask for in prayer—if you believe."
MATTHEW 17:20, TLB	"Because of your little faith," Jesus told them. "For if you had faith even as small as a tiny mustard seed you could say to this mountain, 'Move!' and it would go far away. Nothing would be impossible."
MATTHEW 6:31-33, TLB	"So don't worry at all about having enough food and clothing. Why be like the heathen? For they take pride in all these things and are deeply concerned about them. But your heavenly Father already knows perfectly well that you need them, and he will give them to you if you give him first place in your life and live as he wants you to."

ANSWER THESE QUESTIONS NOW!!!

Question	I John 3:21-22	I John 5:14-15	John 14:13-14	John 15:16	John 16:24	Matthew 21:21-22	Matthew 17:20	Matthew 6:31-33
1. How is Satan likely to pervert these promises?								
2. Have you ever been tempted to use these promises out of context?								
3. Can you spot the condition under which your faith in these promises will never fail?								
4. Can you think of other Scriptures that Satan perverts in order to discourage or confuse your faith?								

DO NOT PROCEED UNTIL YOU HAVE
COMPLETED THE PRECEDING EXERCISES

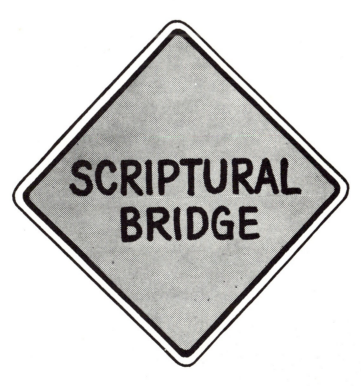

PROCEED WITH CARE

C. Achieving Faith as it Relates to God's Will

You may see *Achieving Faith*'s beginning and foundation in a discovery of the Will of God. Dr. Smiley Blanton, a noted psychiatrist, states that this whole idea of *Achieving Faith* is wrapped up in these two suggestions:

1. The practice of simple but habitual prayer and devotional meditation (see Chapter 2, "The Word of God in the Life of a Disciple").

2. The surrender of your life in an attitude of childlike trust to the Will of God.[23]

Therefore, the real key to understanding Achieving Faith is in the understanding of God's Will.

There is no way to constructively deal with the subject of Achieving Faith without first coming to grips with the subject of God's Will. There are many positive, self-help books on the market today which would promote the tragedy of the previous narrative of the perverted faith. But quite plainly, *for the Christian, there is no everyday Achieving Faith outside of the Will of God.*

John, in his letter to his friends, states:

> And we are sure of this, that he will listen to us whenever we ask him for anything in line with his will. And if we really know he is listening when we talk to him and make our requests, then we can be sure that he will answer us.
>
> I John 5:14-15, TLB

---

[23] From the book, *Faith Is The Answer* by Norman Vincent Peale and Smiley Blanton. © 1950 by Prentice-Hall, Inc., Englewood Cliffs, N.J.

John implies here that it must become the normal thing (a learned, conditioned response) for you to ask according to God's Will. Whether you live a life of frustration and continual disappointment and eventual defeat, or a victorious life of achievement *depends completely upon the motivation of your faith (your spirit) and the object of your faith (either your will or God's Will)*. Christ Himself said, "My nourishment comes from doing the will of God who sent me, and from finishing his work" (John 4:34, TLB). The Psalmist declares, "I delight to do your will, my God, for your law is written upon my heart" (Psalm 40:8, TLB).

You may feel at this point, "Well, that is a cop-out. You've just watered down the certainty of faith by saying that I have to ask for things within God's Will. Perhaps I want something for myself. Besides, how can I know God's Will?"

Paul, in I Corinthians, says:

> But the spiritual man has insight into everything, and that bothers and baffles the man of the world, who can't understand him at all. How could he? For certainly he has never been one to know the Lord's thoughts or to discuss them with him or to move the hands of God by prayer. But, strange as it seems, we Christians actually do have within us *a portion of the very thoughts and mind of Christ.*
>
> I Corinthians 2:15-16, TLB

The thrilling thing about the Spirit-filled life is that there is the certainty of actually having the spoken Word of God, the *Logos,* i.e., Jesus Christ, through the means of the Holy Spirit, dwelling inside. The reason you can know His Will is because you can know *Him,* the true motivation and object of your faith . . . a *Person!*

> For God is at work within you, helping you want to obey him, and then helping you do what he wants.
>
> Philippians 2:13, TLB

Oswald Chambers describes your *Achieving Faith* as not being based on any of God's blessings or the neat tricks you can perform; rather, it is based on a Person, Jesus Christ, and His Will, whether you ever receive any blessings or not.

The following is taken from the writings of Oswald Chambers.

> Faith is not a pathetic sentiment, but robust, vigorous confidence built on the fact that God is holy love. You cannot see Him just now, you cannot understand what He is doing, but you know *HIM*. Shipwreck occurs where there is not that mental poise which comes from being established on the eternal truth that God is holy love. Faith is the heroic effort in your life, you fling yourself in reckless confidence on God.
>
> God has ventured all in Jesus Christ to save us; now He wants us to venture our all in abandoned confidence in Him.[24]
>
> Faith by its very nature must be tried, and the real trial of faith is not that we find it difficult to trust God, but that God's character has to be cleared in our own minds.
>
> Faith in the Bible is faith in God against everything that contradicts Him—I will remain true to God's character whatever He may do. "Though He slay me, yet will I trust Him"—this is the most sublime utterance of faith in the whole of the Bible.[25]

---

[24] *Op. cit.*, Chambers, p. 129.
[25] *Ibid.*, p. 305.

Paul states to the Romans that "faith cometh by hearing, and hearing by the Word of God" (Romans 10:17, KJV). What a privilege you have to actually have the *Logos,* the Living Word of God, in your heart to help you know God's Will, and to help you know what things you should ask for in faith, believing!

Take a look at it!

No wonder Christ felt comfortable in telling His Disciples that if they would ask for anything that *He* would have asked for, they would see it come to pass!

> "In solemn truth I tell you, anyone believing in me shall do the same miracles I have done, and even greater ones, because I am going to be with the Father. You can ask him for *anything,* using my name, and I will do it, for this will bring praise to the Father because of what I, the Son, will do for you. Yes, ask *anything,* using my name, and I will do it!"
>
> John 14:12-14, TLB

This was not a *carte blanche* offer to any pagan to pick up and use out of context. It is not an invitation to engage in name-dropping. He was specifically instructing them to ask for things *within the scope of His Will,* and the Father would honor their faith by giving them the *God-centered desires* of their hearts. The same is true with Christ's words in John's Gospel:

> ". . . I appointed you to go and produce lovely fruit always, so that no matter what you ask for from the Father, using my name, he will give it to you."
>
> John 15:16, TLB

> For you to yield to Satan's temptation to pervert this basis for *Achieving Faith,* by using Jesus' name for something outside of His Will, could cause you to be charged with having uttered a forgery!

For Christ Himself said to not put God to a foolish test (Matthew 4:7). And the foolish test would certainly be the presumption of trying to apply *Achieving Faith* to something outside the scope of God's Will.

D. A Functional Definition of Faith

Now that you have explored the tremendous possibilities of actually being able to know and understand God's Will as it relates to your everyday *Achieving Faith,* take a look at an everyday functional definition of faith:

> Faith is being so convinced of God's Plan that you waive all of your own personal rights in favor of pursuing His Will.

The word *waive* simply means "to surrender one thing in favor of another."

What is meant by "personal rights"?

Do you have rights of your own?

Look at the diagram once again.

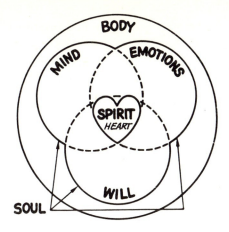

Those functions of your soul are your rights.

1. *Mind:* Your right to reason something out.
2. *Emotions:* Your right to do nothing until you feel good about it.
3. *Will:* Your right to pass judgment on a set of facts and choose.

These are God-given rights.

But to make *Achieving Faith* really become an experience of excitement, you have the privilege of waiving those rights in an on-purpose act of worship thereby allowing God to work His Plan and His Will through you as He desires. This should open your "eyes of faith" to some brand-new horizons! Just think of the possibilities of God's Will being unhindered as He works out His Plan and Ministry through your life!

Oswald Chambers states that when you are in a relationship like this, God "will tax the remotest star," or the sand on the seashore, in order to see that you have all you need to accomplish His will.[26] That is everyday, *Achieving Faith!*

---

[26] *Ibid.*, p. 336.

> So now, since we have been made right in God's sight by faith in his promises, we can have real peace with him because of what Jesus Christ our Lord has done for us. For because of our faith, he has brought us into this place of highest privilege where we now stand, and we confidently and joyfully look forward to actually becoming all that God has had in mind for us to be.
>
> We can rejoice, too, when we run into problems and trials for we know they are good for us—they help us learn to be patient. And patience develops strength of character in us and helps us trust God more each time we use it until finally our hope and faith are strong and steady. Then, when that happens, we are able to hold our heads high no matter what happens and know that all is well, for we know how dearly God loves us . . .
>
> Romans 5:1-5, TLB

This is the quality of faith that was the hallmark of the patriarchs listed in the eleventh chapter of Hebrews. *Achieving Faith* was at the center of all their attitudes and actions. Faith was the dynamic of all they did. In real life, they were so consistently convinced of God's Plan that they courageously and joyfully waived all of their personal rights in favor of pursuing God's Will.

> LEADER: Assign each of the following names to members of your group, and have them report back next session on *how these individuals were so convinced of God's Plan that they waived all of their own personal rights in favor of pursuing God's Will.*

Noah	Genesis 5:32 thru 9:39
Abraham	Genesis 11:27 thru 25:11
Sarah	Genesis 11:29 thru 17:15 and 23:1
Jacob	Genesis 25:19 thru Chapter 36
Joseph	Genesis 30:24 thru 50:26
Moses	Exodus
Hannah	I Samuel, Chapter 1 and 2
Daniel	Daniel, Chapters 1 thru 6
Mary	Luke, Chapters 1 and 2
Joseph	Matthew 1:18-24 and 2:13
Jesus	Matthew 4 and Matthew 26 and Luke 4
Paul	Acts, Chapters 7, 8, and 9

WHAT IS FAITH?

1. It is Confidence in Action.

   It is the confident assurance that something we want is going to happen. It is the certainty that what we hope for is waiting for us, even though we cannot see it up ahead. Men of God in days of old were famous for their faith.

   Hebrews 11:1-2, TLB

2. It is Obedience in Action.

   Since we have such a huge crowd of men of faith watching us from the grandstands, let us strip off anything that slows us down or holds us back . . . and let us run with patience the particular race that God has set before us.

   Hebrews 12:1, TLB

Summary: Faith is *the capacity to believe* and *to act* upon that belief.

Prayer
(outline)

I. Identification with Christ in Prayer

   A. Christ in You

   B. A Life Hid with Christ in God

II. Intimacy with Christ in Prayer

   A. God Wants You to Pray

   B. Friendship with Jesus

III. Illustrations of Prayer Forms

   A. Praise

      1. You can praise God in your own words.
      2. You can praise God through the Psalms.
      3. You can praise God through songs and music.

   B. Thanksgiving

      1. Physical Blessings
      2. Spiritual Blessings

   C. Petition

      1. Confessional Petitions
      2. Self-centered Petitions
      3. Acceptable Petitions

   D. Intercession

      1. The Ministry of Intercessory Prayer
      2. The Power of Intercessory Prayer
      3. The Security of Intercessory Prayer
      4. The Gratitude in Intercessory Prayer

IV. Interpretation of Prayer

   A. God Answers Prayer

   B. Are You Confident and Obedient Even If . . . ?

If I should neglect prayer but for a single day, I should lose a great deal of the fire of faith.
—Martin Luther

Prayer

Would you be surprised if all your prayers were answered? Have you ever had the experience of sharing with a friend some concern about which you were praying? Then your prayer was answered, and you rushed to tell him, "Guess what! My prayer has been answered!"—only to have him ask, "What did you expect?" Do you believe prayer changes God's mind? Is it possible that prayer changes you? Must long, detailed prayers always be a sign of great spirituality, or could they be an indication that you do not understand what prayer is all about? Is your relationship with God so personal that you are eager to know God better and to take time to commune with Him?

This chapter will be dealing with four main areas relating to the subject of prayer:

I.	Identification with Christ in Prayer	Christ in you
II.	Intimacy with Christ in Prayer	God is eager for a close relationship with you
III.	Illustrations of Prayer Forms	Praise, Thanksgiving, Petition, and Intercession
IV.	Interpretation of Prayer	God loves to answer your prayers—according to His Plan

There is an overlap of ideas from one area to another. For example, there may well be an overlap from one type of prayer form to another: "When do you stop praising God and start thanking Him?" On the other hand, you must attempt to define and distinguish various concepts so you can begin to refine your prayer relationship.

Prayer is an "on-purpose" effort. It is a moral, disciplined effort of the mind, emotions, and will. You must develop the habit of "on-purpose" dealing with God about everything. In looking at the diagram, remember that you will want (out of a spirit of love for God) to ". . . enter into your closet, and . . . pray to your Father which is in secret" (Matthew 6:6, TLB).

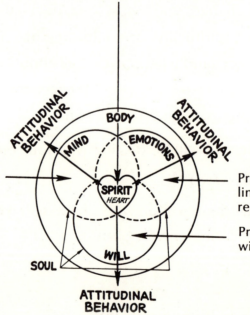

PRAYER ORIGINATES IN THE HEART

You have to discipline your mind and concentrate on purposeful prayer.

Prayer requires disciplining your motives and remembering God.

Prayer is an effort of the will.

Oswald Chambers describes it this way:

> Jesus did not say—Dream about thy Father in secret, but *pray* to thy Father in secret. Prayer is an effort of will . . . the most difficult thing to do is to pray: We cannot get our minds into working order, and the first thing that conflicts is wandering thoughts. The great battle in private prayer is the overcoming of mental wool-gathering. We have to *discipline our minds* and concentrate on wilful prayer.[27]

Prayer takes effort and must be activated no matter where you find yourself or how you feel. Whatever the situation, your duty and privilege is to pray.

I. Identification with Christ in Prayer

One of the most beautiful things about prayer is the Biblical concept of identifying yourself with Christ.

A. Christ in You

In the second chapter of Colossians, verses 9 and 10, it says:

> For in Christ there is all of God in a human body; *so you have everything when you have Christ,* and you are filled with God through your union with Christ.
> Colossians 2:9-10b, TLB

Can you imagine the excitement of knowing that every time you pray Christ is present with you?

---

[27] *Ibid.*, p. 236.

The Scripture that expresses this is Ephesians 3:12.

> In him and through faith in him we may approach God with freedom and confidence.
>
> Ephesians 3:12, NIV

You must remember that this union with Christ is neither an option nor a temporary discipline, but rather a continual experience of identification with Jesus. This relationship of identification becomes more and more meaningful through the attitude and activities of prayer.

B. A Life Hid with Christ in God

In the third chapter of Colossians it says:

> For you died, and your life is now hidden with Christ in God.
>
> Colossians 3:3, NIV

Just as you have seen the potential of Christ living in you, you also have the wonderful privilege of living that life hid with Christ in God.

This is the activity of living out your life within the scope of His Will.

You must learn to identify yourself with Christ in such a friendship with God that you will live out His Will.

> I don't mean to say I am perfect. I haven't learned all I should even yet, but I keep working toward that day when I will finally be all that Christ saved me for and wants me to be.
>
> Philippians 3:12, TLB

> For because of our faith, he has brought us into this place of highest privilege where we now stand, and we confidently and joyfully look forward to actually becoming all that God has had in mind for us to be.
>
> Romans 5:2, TLB

You are made aware of this Plan day by day as you identify with Him in the communion of prayer.

> But the spiritual man has insight into everything, and that bothers and baffles the man of the world, who can't understand him at all.
>
> How could he? For certainly he has never been one to know the Lord's thoughts, or to discuss them with him, or to move the hands of God by prayer. But, strange as it seems, we Christians actually do have within us a portion of the very thoughts and mind of Christ.
> I Corinthians 2:15-16, TLB
>
> I am crucified with Christ: nevertheless I live; yet not I, but Christ liveth in me: and the life which I now live in the flesh I live by the faith of the Son of God, who loved me, and gave himself for me.
> Galatians 2:20, KJV

II. Intimacy with Christ in Prayer

> ... Prayer continually ...
> I Thessalonians 5:17, NIV

A. God Wants You to Pray

God is eager for you to establish this close relationship with Him. He was so confident that this relationship would work and that man would respond, that He sent His only Son, Jesus.

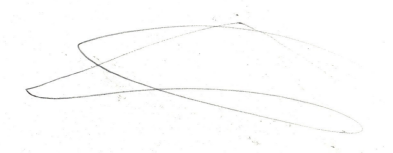

Oswald Chambers states:

> It is not part of the life of a natural man to pray. We hear it said that a man will suffer in his life if he does not pray; I question it. What will suffer is the life of the Son of God in him, which is nourished not by food, but by prayer. When a man is born from above, the life of the Son of God is born in him, and he can either starve that life or nourish it. Prayer is the way the life of God is nourished. Our ordinary views of prayer are not found in the New Testament. We look upon prayer as a means of getting things for ourselves; the Bible idea of prayer is that we may get to know God Himself.[28]

Chambers goes on to say:

> "Your Father knoweth what things ye have need of, before ye ask Him." Then why ask? The idea of prayer is not in order to get answers from God; prayer is *perfect and complete oneness with God*. If we pray because we want answers, we will get huffed with God. The answers come every time, but not always in the way we expect, and our spiritual huff shows a refusal to identify ourselves with Our Lord in prayer. We are not here to prove God answers prayer; we are here to be living monuments of God's grace.
>
> "I say not that I will pray the Father for you: for the Father Himself loveth you." Have you reached such an intimacy with God that the Lord Jesus Christ's life of prayer is the only explanation of your life of prayer? Has our Lord's vicarious life become your vital life? "At that day" you will be so identified with Jesus that there will be no distinction.[29]

---

[28] *Ibid.*, p. 241.
[29] *Ibid.*, p. 219.

In this relationship of prayer, it is beautiful to visualize real prayer as the opening up to Jesus who knocks at your heart and eagerly waits to establish communication.

> "Look! I have been standing at the door and I am constantly knocking. If anyone hears me calling him and opens the door, I will come in and fellowship with him and he with me."
>
> Revelation 3:20, TLB

Through real prayer you can experience the quiet, yet dynamic, opening of the doors representing areas of your life.

This is the exciting relationship with the One Who stands at your heart's door having come for the purpose of establishing a vital union with you as He is permitted to come in and live His life through you. Because He is already acting in this relationship, your first move in prayer is to *respond* to Him, not demand *requests* from Him. You should respond by loving Him back because He first loved you.

E. Stanley Jones painted an effective word-picture of the prayerful heart in one of his prayers:

> O, Father, give me the prayerful heart. Let prayers pervade my soul as blood pervades my body. And just as blood carries sustenance and brings away impurities, so let prayer sustain and cleanse me. Amen.[30]

---

[30] From *The Way To Power And Poise* by E. Stanley Jones. Copyright 1949 by Pierce and Smith. Copyright renewal 1977 by Eunice Treffry Matthews. Used by permission of Abingdon Press.

B. Friendship with Jesus

You can have a continuous friendship with Jesus as compared with occasional feelings of His Presence as you pray. He is most pleased, as your Friend, when you allow His life to be lived through you to the glory of your Father. You have the privilege of taking Jesus where He needs to go each day, and you determine His directions through your prayer relationship with Him. In this way, you are rightly related to Him, and it is a life of freedom and liberty and happiness—you can *be* God's Will.

When you stop in the middle of your prayer and say, "I am not sure—maybe this is not God's Will," you have a problem. You are not well-enough acquainted with God. You are not as well acquainted with Him as Jesus wants you to be. In the Book of John, Jesus said, concerning His relationship to the Father, "I pray . . . that they may be one as we are one" (John 17:20-22, NIV).

> What was the last thing you prayed for?
> Were you devoted to *your selfish desires* or to *God*?

You must ask, through prayer, so that you can get to know God better. The Psalmist David said, *"Delight thyself also in the Lord;* and He shall give thee the desires of thine heart" (Psalm 37:4, KJV). You are encouraged to keep praying in order to get a perfect understanding of God Himself.

When you receive a phone call from someone with whom you have not often talked, it is difficult to recognize the voice. You will probably have to ask him to identify himself, or wait for awhile, as he talks, for a clue as to who he is. But, when your best friend calls, when the first word is spoken, you recognize immediately who he is! The familiarity of the voice instantly lets you know who he is. As you continue to strengthen your daily relationship through communion or communication with your Heavenly Father, you will become more and more confident of His Voice. You can know His Will. Prayer is not only a mechanical *form,* but it also serves as a *dynamic, unifying force*—His power at work within you.

The words of a song written in the nineteenth century by Joe C. Ludgate, and arranged by Stephen Foster, say:

> A Friend when other friendships cease,
> A Friend when others fail,
> A Friend who gives me joy and peace,
> A Friend when foes assail!
>
> Friendship with Jesus!
> Fellowship divine!
> Oh, what blessed, sweet communion!
> Jesus is a Friend of mine.

III. Illustrations of Prayer Forms

In this relationship with God you may communicate using several prayer forms. It may be pointed out again that there will often be an overlap from one prayer form to another. You can generally divide them, however, into at least four forms.

> Praise
> Thanksgiving
> Petition
> Intercession

I urge, then, first of all, that requests, prayers, intercession and thanksgiving be made for everyone—
I Timothy 2:1, NIV

A. Praise

The *prayer of praise* or adoration is a prayer giving honor and glory to God for Who He is.

> ... Think about all you can praise God for and be glad about.
> Philippians 4:8, TLB

> ... that we should praise God and give glory to him for doing these mighty things for us ...
> Ephesians 1:12, TLB

> But true praise is a worthy sacrifice ...
> Psalm 50:23, TLB

Praise should be one of the first forms of prayer offered. If you begin by praising God, you will soon find yourself in such a frame of mind that you will not want to be torn away from this activity of prayer. There are several suggested ways that you can praise God.

1. *You can praise God in your own words.* To praise God is to simply pay tribute or render honor to Him. Mary said, "My soul doth magnify the Lord" (Luke 1:46, KJV). The Psalmist said, "My soul shall make her boast in the Lord: the humble shall hear thereof, and be glad" (Psalm 34:2, KJV). You can tell Him in your own words what you think of

Him in all His greatness. You would not have difficulty admiring or paying tribute to a loved one or a friend. Recall the greatness and the goodness of a majestic and virtuous God. Praise Him for every aspect of His Personality and mighty works as they come to your mind.

2. You can praise God through the Psalms. The Psalmist David made a practice of often praising God in his writings.

> *As an illustration,* the next time you pray, try this: As you are kneeling before God, open your Bible to the Psalms.
>
> *Pick out several good verses* (suggestions: Psalm 8, Psalm 63:1-8).
>
> *Now read them aloud.*
>
> *Read them over again.*
>
> *Memorize them—Visualize them—Personalize them!*
>
> *Now, look up and say them to God.* Make them your own.
>
> *Say His own Words back to Him. Say them in your own words.*
>
> Because the Psalms are great stimulators of praise to God, it is suggested that you repeat them several times. As you repeat them over and over, they will suggest other thoughts to you.

3. You can praise God through songs and music. Have you ever tried to sing your prayer? If you can't carry a tune, just say the words. There are many great songs that will filter through the heart and soul as you strive to praise God. Pray these songs over and over in your heart. Pray the words of "Revive Us Again," written by William P. McKay:

NOTES

> We praise Thee, O God,
> For the Son of Thy love;
> For Jesus who died
> And is now gone above.
>
> We praise Thee, O God,
> For Thy Spirit of Light,
> Who has shown us our Saviour
> And scattered our night.
>
> All glory and praise
> To the Lamb that was slain,
> Who has borne all our sins
> And has cleansed ev'ry stain.
>
> Revive us again;
> Fill each heart with Thy love;
> May each soul be rekindled
> With fire from above.

This will suggest many other things for which to praise Him, such as His *Grace,* His *Mercy,* His *Miracles,* His *Love,* the place He is preparing for you in His *Heaven,* His *Book,* His *Sacrifice* of life itself on your behalf.

Here is another example of a song, the words written by Fanny J. Crosby:

> Praise Him! Praise Him!
> Jesus, our blessed Redeemer!
> Sing, O Earth,
> His wonderful love proclaim!
>
> Hail Him! Hail Him!
> Highest archangels in glory;
> Strength and honor
> Give to His holy name!
>
> Like a sheperd, Jesus will guard His children:
> In His arms He carries them all day long.
>
> Praise Him! Praise Him!
> Tell of His excellent greatness.
> Praise Him! Praise Him!
> Ever in joyful song!

There are many other great songs which will come to mind as you are "on purpose" praying the *prayer of praise* to God. Praise gives rise to faith. When you recognize who He is, you increase the possibility of a stronger faith in Him.

> CHALLENGE:
> (1) Spend 5 minutes yet today, in a prayer of praise only; try to ask for nothing during this prayer.
> (2) While on your knees, quote the 23rd Psalm, and center your thoughts on the character and activities of God.

B. Thanksgiving

The second form of prayer you will study is the *prayer of thanksgiving.* Giving thanks to God, both before and after the answer, expresses not only your belief in His character, but also your appreciation for His love.

> Let your lives overflow with joy and thanksgiving for all he has done.
> Colossians 2:7b, TLB

God appreciates the heartfelt prayers of His grateful children. Is it possible that one of your greatest sins of omission is the sin of not being thankful? Look at Psalm 100:4.

> Go through his open gates with great thanksgiving . . .
> Psalm 100:4, TLB

Thanking God is a great privilege for the Children of God. Thanking God is not only a privilege and responsibility, but it is also the desire of the heart of every grateful Child of God. God responds to our verbal expression of thanks to Him. There is also the personal blessing that you receive as you know He is pleased because you have thanked Him.

> . . . always giving thanks to God the Father for everything, in the name of our Lord Jesus Christ.
>
> Ephesians 5:20, NIV

Just as the lepers asked to be healed and then rushed on without thanking Jesus, so there are many who fail to return to God to thank Him for answers to prayers. Many times you ask God for something, and He sends the answer. But you are so busy that you not only do not acknowledge the answer, but you also do not remember the prayer request.

> Don't worry about anything; instead, pray about everything; tell God your needs and don't forget to thank him for his answers.
>
> Philippians 4:6, TLB

Thanks may be offered, not only for your personal blessings, but also for all the "common" things shared together with God. For example, give thanksgiving for the sunshine, the beauties of creation, and His provisions for your daily needs. Did it ever occur to you that giving thanks to God is a great antidote for doubting, depression, and unpleasantness?

1. *Physical Blessings*

    The old adage is on point: "I complained because I had no shoes, until I met a man who had no feet." If you feel that you have nothing for which to be thankful, then begin naming every physical blessing you enjoy. You will be surprised at your list of blessings for which you can and should be thankful.

2. Spiritual Blessings

How long has it been since you thanked God for your spiritual blessings? You ought to give thanks:

> for God Himself;
>
> for His Son—for His life, death, and resurrection;
>
> for your own personal experience with Him—for the privilege of experiencing the born-again life and the Spirit-filled life;
>
> for His Spirit which led you to Him;
>
> for your church—the building, the staff individually, each program of your church through which He works.

Read aloud one of the best-loved Psalms so you can pray this *prayer of thanksgiving* to God:

Bless the Lord, O my soul: and all that is within me, bless his holy name. Bless the Lord, O my soul, and forget not all his benefits: Who forgiveth all thine iniquities; who healeth all thy diseases; Who redeemeth thy life from destruction; who crowneth thee with lovingkindness and tender mercies . . .

Psalm 103:1-4, TLB

List at least three things for which you can thank God:

_____
_____
_____

C. Petition

A *prayer of petition* is a simple request asking God to meet your needs.

> He does not ignore the prayers of men in trouble when they call to him for help.
>
> Psalm 9:12b, TLB

Even in the Lord's Prayer, you note that petitions are included. God cares about His Children and is pleased to meet their needs.

Paul also claims:

> And my God will meet all your needs according to his glorious riches in Christ Jesus.
>
> Philippians 4:19, NIV

1. Confessional Petitions

> If we confess our sins, he is faithful and just to forgive us our sins, and to cleanse us from all unrighteousness.
>
> I John 1:9, KJV

You must petition or ask for forgiveness for your sins. Forgiveness is not automatic; it is conditional upon your *prayer of petition,* which will include repentance and confession. You have the assurance that your salvation is in His Will.

---

1. What is your motive when you pray the *prayer of petition?*
2. Are you committed enough to God's overall Plan for your life to give Him "elbow room" to work that Plan out through you to His glory?

2. Self-centered Petitions

A problem seems to develop when a Child of God is tempted to develop his own plan and then call on God for extra help to carry it out. This was true of James and John, Jesus' disciples.

> Then James and John, the sons of Zebedee, came to him. "Teacher," they said, "we want you to do for us whatever we ask."
>
> Mark 10:35, NIV

So often you work, plan, and scheme in an effort to accomplish your own plan, and then suddenly you become aware of the fact that you are not getting what your mind was set on. So you quickly turn to the "spare tire" of prayer. You can always use that when all other "tires" fail. So you pray, "God, you get that new car for me"—or, "God, get me out of this bind"—or, "God, do my homework for me." At this point, you are only making prayer a continuation of your "do-for-me" or "give-me" spirit. The *prayer of peition* is not just an additional way to realize your ambitions. As long as you rely on your own self-sufficiency, you do not see the need to ask God for anything.

Perhaps the reason many people never really learn to pray is because they never allow a change of spirit which would *replace a demanding attitude* with a *receptive attitude*.

> And even when you do ask you don't get it because your whole aim is wrong—you want only what will give *you* pleasure.
>
> James 4:3, TLB

3. Acceptable Petitions

You must remember: Prayer is not simply asking for things from God. That is the most immature of the initial forms of prayer. *Prayer is the entering into a right relationship with God,* where you can say, "God, I long to know Your Will and participate in Your Will only." The Bible makes it very clear that you are to ask, but to ask only of God things that are in keeping with His Will.

> And we are sure of this, that he will listen to us whenever we ask him for anything in line with his will.
> I John 5:14, TLB

It is important to note that prayer changes more than just things; it changes people. Based upon the realization of Who God is, through the Word and through the two-way communication of prayer, you learn what His Will is. Thus your way of looking at things is altered.

In conclusion, the following are benefits of the *prayer of petition:*

- As you begin to express your nebulous needs (at least what you thought were your needs), you begin to crystallize them into words.
- With the crystallization of these thoughts you then discover, through the Holy Spirit, whether or not this is, in fact, His Will.
- Then the action. Once the need is defined, and you feel it is in His Will, He provides you with the handles to follow through.

> Don't worry about anything; instead, pray about everything; tell God your needs and don't forget to thank him for his answers. If you do this you will experience God's peace, which is far more wonderful than the human mind can understand. His peace will keep your thoughts and your hearts quiet and at rest as you trust in Christ Jesus.
> Philippians 4:6-7, TLB

D. Intercession

Intercessory prayer is the pleading on behalf of someone else's need.

> "Now take seven young bulls and seven rams and go to my servant Job and offer a burnt offering for yourselves; and my servant Job will pray for you, and I will accept his prayer on your behalf, and won't destroy you as I should because of your sin, your failure to speak rightly concerning my servant Job."
>
> Job 42:8, TLB

1. *The Ministry of Intercessory Prayer*

Intercessory praying is possibly the greatest ministry in the life of the Christian.

> O Jerusalem, I have set intercessors on your walls who shall cry to God all day and all night for the fulfillment of his promises. Take no rest, all you who pray, and give God no rest until he establishes Jerusalem and makes her respected and admired throughout the earth.
>
> Isaiah 62:6-7, TLB

Time will reveal the results of the prayers of the saints of God. Those people are usually the ones whose names have never been broadcast before the public.

In *intercession* you bring the person or his circumstance before God until you are in harmony with God's Will as it relates to that person or his circumstance.

Remember as a Spirit-filled Christian, prayer is not forcing your will on God, but rather discovering His Will. Intercessory prayer is only effective when there is a complete and vital union with Christ. A carnal Christian will often have a problem praying "Thy will be done," *much less carrying a burden for others.*

2. *The Power of Intercessory Prayer*

There is great power in *intercessory prayer*. When you are not sure how you ought to pray, you can rely on Romans 8:26-27.

> In the same way, the Spirit helps us in our weakness. We do not know how we ought to pray, but the Spirit himself intercedes for us with groans that words cannot express. And he who searches our hearts knows the mind of the Spirit, because the Spirit intercedes for the saints in accordance with God's will.
> Romans 8:26-27, NIV

At this point, you can have the assurance of God's harmonious Will being done. What an exciting thought! The Spirit of God has prayed through you according to His Will! The cycle is completed: from God to your spirit by His Spirit; from your spirit back to God by His Spirit. What a miracle! This tremendous, hidden power can now be released!

3. *The Security of Intercessory Prayer*

The very nature of *intercessory prayer* keeps your intimate relationship with God completely undivided. Therefore, Jesus Christ becomes more and more dominant in every interest of life. A heart that is willing to be involved in *intercessory prayer* finds more and more spiritual growth.

There is no pride in *intercessory prayer*. It is a hidden ministry that brings about results which please God.

4. *The Gratitude in Intercessory Prayer*

You are instructed to thank God in advance for His promises and for the fact that He is going to answer your *prayer of intercession.* A classic illustration of this is given in Romans 4:20.

> Yet he did not waver through unbelief regarding the promise of God, but was strengthened in his faith and gave glory to God...
>
> Romans 4:20, NIV

IV. Interpretation of Prayer

A. God Answers Prayer

> "... then if my people will humble themselves and pray, and search for me, and turn from their wicked ways, I will hear them from heaven and forgive their sins and heal their land. I will listen, wide awake, to every prayer made in this place."
>
> II Chronicles 7:14-15, TLB

Prayer is a way of life, not just an occasional exercise. You must see prayer as being as normal as breath is to your lungs and as normal as blood is to your heart. Even though you may not be totally conscious of it, the blood continues to flow and the breathing continues to take place. *If you are obeying God, you are in continual harmony with His Will.* God always answers prayer consistent with His Will, and you must be careful not to question His answer. If you are tempted to be anxious about what seems to be unanswered prayer, you must realize that God may be trying to point out a major truth or rich insight you need to learn.

B. Are You Confident and Obedient Even If . . . ?

What happens to your faith when you pray, and it seems to you that nothing happens? Does it affect your love level? Are you less confident? Do you become less obedient? If it appeared that God says "no," is this an unsatisfactory answer? Do you feel He has sidestepped you? How about the example of Paul when he asked three times for deliverance from the "thorn" in his flesh, and God's answer was a refusal? How does "all the promises of God are yea" fit in this situation? Can you accept the fact that the "refusal" consisted of a revelation to Paul, that it is in man's weakness that God's real strength is made perfect? If God said "no" to you, could you always be sure it will be the kind of "no" which turns out to be a much greater "yes"?

> I will say this; because these experiences I had were so tremendous, God was afraid I might be puffed up by them; so I was given a physical condition which has been a thorn in my flesh, a messenger from Satan to hurt and bother me, and prick my pride. Three different times I begged God to make me well again.
>
> Each time he said, "No. But I am with you; that is all you need. My power shows up best in weak people." Now I am glad to boast about how weak I am; I am glad to be a living demonstration of Christ's power, instead of showing off my own power and abilities. Since I know it is all for Christ's good, I am quite happy about "the thorn," and about insults and hardships, persecutions and difficulties; for when I am weak, then I am strong—the less I have, the more I depend on him.
>
> II Corinthians 12:7-10, TLB

Can you say with Paul, "Let God be true, though every man be false"? Can you say with Job, "Though He slay me yet will I trust Him"? Can you agree with Habakkuk, "Even if the flocks die in the fields and the cattle barns are empty, yet I will rejoice in the Lord"?

Are you so convinced of God's Plan for your life that you will waive all of your own personal rights in favor of pursuing God's Will?

The question is not so much "How does God answer prayer?" The question really is, "Do I really know how to pray, and will I accept God's answers?" God always answers prayer when there is a clean heart, simple faith, and a "God-pleasing" life.

> Dear friends, if our hearts do not condemn us, we have confidence before God and receive from him anything we ask, because we obey his commands and do what pleases him.
> I John 3:21-22, NIV

This chapter has dealt with four very basic areas concerning the subject of prayer. List these areas in the box below.

1. _____
2. _____
3. _____
4. _____

Now that you have listed the four basic areas concerning the subject of prayer, please list the four prayer forms.

1. _____
2. _____
3. _____
4. _____

If you realize the significance of your close relationship with God —that He sent His only Son, Jesus—you can visualize real prayer as the opening up to Jesus Who knocks at your heart's door and eagerly waits to establish communication. You can respond to your Friend through prayer, as you have permitted Him to come in and live His life through you.

Whether you communicate with God through prayers of *praise, thanksgiving, petition,* or *intercession,* the basic and most important desire of your heart must be to seek His Will.

Knowing God's Will
(outline)

I. God Has a "Plan"

A. Nature Would Attest to that Plan

B. The Word of God would Attest to that Plan

1. There is amazing Scriptural evidence that there is a Divine Plan for each redeemed life.
2. There are great examples in the Bible of men who chose to do God's Will.
    a. Old Testament Examples
        (1) David
        (2) Isaiah
        (3) Jeremiah
    b. New Testament Examples
        (1) Jesus
        (2) Paul

II. Man Has a "Problem"

A. Rejection

B. Procrastination

III. You Have a "Procedure"

*My stubborn will at last hath yielded;
I would be thine, and thine alone;
And this the prayer my lips are bringing,
Lord, let in me thy will be done.
Sweet will of God, still fold me closer,
Till I am wholly lost in thee.
Sweet will of God, still fold me closer,
Till I am wholly lost in thee.*
—Mrs. C. H. Morris

Knowing God's Will

The subject of God's Will is at the very heart of the entire concept of Discipling. You must come to grips with the fact that God has a very wonderful and special Plan for your life. You must be able to face each set of circumstances throughout life with the confidence that God not only has a Plan, but can be depended upon to reveal that Plan on a day-to-day basis to those who are His children.

From your earliest spiritual experience through the most advanced lesson in Christian maturity, you find God's Will to be the crux of every situation. It is upon God's Will that all else pivots. It has been explained that faith includes "being so convinced of God's Plan that you waive all of your personal rights in favor of pursuing His Will." Faith's anchor is secure only in God's Will. In the session on "prayer," you were instructed to pray within God's Will. Without being *aware* and *confident* of God's Will, your praying is absolutely powerless. In a future session, you will learn that obedience is the carrying out of God's Will. If you are not aware and confident of God's Will, how can you obey?

Every aspect of your Christian life must then center around this subject of God's Will.

For the Christian, the attitude and activity of forever being in intense pursuit of not only *knowing* but also *doing* God's Will is not an option, but a mandate. In this chapter the subject of God's Will shall be presented in the following manner:

- The Plan
- The Problem
- The Procedure

I. God Has a "Plan"

Once you come to know Christ in the meaningful experiences of the *new birth* and the *Spirit-filled life,* you should realize that God has a very definite Plan and Purpose for your life.

How many good Christian people do you know who theoretically agree that God has a wonderful Plan for their lives, but when being totally honest, many admit they are not totally convinced the theory is true? As a result of their uncertainty, they are of little value to themselves or God's Cause.

There is a course and a goal for everyone. Once this vital fact grips the heart, the whole matter of life takes on a new meaning.

You see, there can be little enthusiasm in people who are seeking something of which they are not convinced.

The fact that God has a definite Plan for your life is abundantly clear.

A. Nature Would Attest to that Plan

Think for a moment of the wonderful Plan for nature: the flowers, the trees, the animals, the cosmos. If His intelligence planned that, consider *how much more* He would plan for His highest handiwork—*man.*

B. The Word of God Would Attest to that Plan

1. There is amazing Scriptural evidence that there is a Divine Plan for each redeemed life. In the following exercise, Scripture from both the Old and New Testament will support this fact.

TAKE TIME TO LOOK UP AND WRITE DOWN THE KEY THOUGHT OF EACH:	KEY THOUGHT
Jeremiah 29:11 (TLB)	
Psalm 143:10 (TLB)	
Isaiah 50:4, 7 (TLB)	
Romans 12:1-2 (NIV)	
Ephesians 5:17 (NIV)	
Colossians 4:12 (NIV)	

2. In addition to the above Scriptural evidence, there are also great examples in the Bible of men who chose to do God's Will. Use the examples in the boxes on the following page as additional resource material.

> a. Old Testament Examples
>   (1) David
>   Psalm 37:23 (TLB)
>   Psalm 139:16 (TLB)
>   (2) Isaiah
>   Isaiah 49:1-9 (TLB)
>   (3) Jeremiah
>   Jeremiah 1:4-10 (TLB)
>   Jeremiah 15:19-21 (TLB)

> b. New Testament Examples
>   (1) Jesus
>   John 4:34 (NIV)
>   John 6:38 (NIV)
>   (2) Paul
>   Acts 20:24 (NIV)
>   II Timothy 4:7 (NIV)

Do not suppose that God's Will includes only ministers or missionaries. The specific Will of God includes everyone. As an example:

- It is the Will of God that all men be saved.

> He is patient with you, not wanting anyone to perish, but everyone to come to repentance.
> II Peter 3:9b, NIV

- It is the Will of God that all men be sanctified.

> It is God's will that you should be holy...
> I Thessalonians 4:3a, NIV

- It is the Will of God that all men carry out the Great Commission.

> "Therefore go and make disciples of all nations, baptizing them in the name of the Father and of the Son and of the Holy Spirit, and teaching them to obey everything I have commanded you. And surely I will be with you always, to the very end of the age."
> Matthew 28:19-20, NIV

II. Man Has a "Problem"

Scripture has assured you that God has a Plan for your life. However, realize that, because of your ability to choose, you have the potential problem of missing God's Plan.

It is possible to miss God's Plan through rejection or procrastination. Both results are the same, i.e., disobedience to God.

A. Rejection

You can completely turn your back on God's Will and be ultimately lost. Here is a classical Biblical illustration of rejection:

> Thus Solomon did what was clearly wrong and refused to follow the Lord as his father David did. So now the Lord said to him, "Since you have not kept our agreement and have not obeyed my laws, I will tear the kingdom away from you and your family and give it to someone else."
> I Kings 11:6, 11, TLB

B. Procrastination

To procrastinate may result in getting into a position that circumstance, age, or condition will not permit you to live out God's best. You, therefore, have to settle for God's second-best.

What about the person who missed God's Will early in his life? He turned his back on God and chose his own sinful and selfish way. Later in his life, he comes to God and, out of a genuine, sincere, committed heart and life, he gives all of his life to Christ. Does that mean he must live a second-rate Christian life? The answer is "no"—not *second-rate,* but *second-best.*

If God called you, at the age of sixteen, into special service, either layman or minister, and you refused to follow that Plan, then at the age of fifty-six you come back to God, there are several facts to consider:

1. Forty years of service have been lost.
2. Forty years of spiritual growth have been forfeited.
3. Scars from sin shall linger long in your functional life, i.e., body, soul, and spirit.

The law of retribution is operative regardless of your spiritual relationship with God.

> Do not be deceived: God cannot be mocked. A man reaps what he sows.
> Galatians 6:7, NIV

Facing this fact is not meant as a *deterrent to achieving spiritual excellence* in your relationship with God.

It is rather to cause you to objectively face the results of wrong decisions and *prod you to WASTE NO TIME in finding and fulfilling God's perfect Will for you today.*

III. You Have a "Procedure"

You may have read accounts and ways of how God has revealed Himself and His Will to man. Can you believe that He will do that for you?

- He appeared to Abraham in physical form.
- He appeared to Moses in the burning bush.
- He sent an angel to instruct Gideon.
- He called Samuel by name—in an audible voice.
- He struck Paul down on the road to Damascus.

Is it necessary or particularly sacred that God must reveal Himself to you in these ways? Romans 12:1 seems to indicate that, now that Christ has come and that this is the dispensation of the Holy Spirit, these methods are no longer necessary.

It is not usually necessary for God to perform supernatural physical acts to guide His people since He has given to them His written, declared, and Living Word. For the most part, your path is clearly spelled out in the written Word. One outstanding Scripture, that deals specifically with the matter of how to know the Will of God, is Romans 12:1-2.

> Therefore, I urge you, brothers, in view of God's mercy, to offer yourselves as living sacrifices, holy and pleasing to God—which is your spiritual worship. Do not conform any longer to the pattern of this world, but be transformed by the renewing of your mind. Then you will be able to test and approve what God's will is—his good, pleasing and perfect will.
>
> Romans 12:1-2, NIV

Note that Paul closes this well-known passage with these words: "That ye may prove what is that good and acceptable and perfect will of God" (KJV). *To prove* means "to establish the certainty of a thing." It means: "to determine for sure—to know beyond doubt."

A. Principles

Examine specifically the question, "Can I know God's Will for my life?" There are four considerations that you must weigh before you answer that question.

1. It is vital for you to consider and vividly remember that God's Plan (or Will) has always been and is right now very clear to Him.

    A classic illustration of this is Jesus in Gethsemane. Even though Jesus struggled with God's Will, it was always there.

    > He withdrew about a stone's throw beyond them, knelt down and prayed, "Father, if you are willing, take this cup from me; yet not my will, but yours be done."
    >
    > Luke 22:41-42, NIV

    It was the voice of human agony that cried out. Christ would not have been human if He had not been affected by this struggle. The Son of God, oppressed by His greatest test, had to fight His way through this temptation to see and accept God's Will.

2. To find God's Will does not mean that you must set aside your own God-given abilities. The thrilling thing is that, many times, God uses our natural functions, i.e., heart and soul, to reveal His Plan. These functions must always be yielded and responsive to His Will.

> In the same way, count yourselves dead to sin but alive to God in Christ Jesus. Therefore, do not let sin reign in your mortal body so that you obey its evil desires. Do not offer the parts of your body to sin, as instruments of wickedness, but rather offer yourselves to God, as those who have returned from death to life; and offer the parts of your body to him as instruments of righteousness.
>
> Romans 6:11-13, NIV

3. The use of Scriptures in knowing God's Will may be twofold.

   a. God may give you the light you seek by a verse. But even this has dangers that must be avoided, because you may find a Scripture that fits "your will" or "your desires" which may not be God's Will.

   b. Secondly, the Scripture that seems to prove your desire should be weighed along with circumstances. This is delicate, but essential.

4. Some people have the idea that God's Will cannot be something that they, too, desire. If you are "crucified with Christ" and have "His mind in you," you are so close to His thinking and so under the control of His Spirit that you will seldom even *want* anything that is *not* His Will.

   > But the spiritual man has insight into everything, and that bothers and baffles the man of the world, who can't understand him at all. How could he? For certainly he has never been one to know the Lord's thoughts, or to discuss them with him, or to move the hands of God by prayer. But, strange as it seems, we Christians actually do have within us a portion of the very thoughts and mind of Christ.
   >
   > I Corinthians 2:15-16, TLB

List three experiences where God has revealed His Will to you.

1. _____
2. _____
3. _____

B. Practical Method

When there is difficulty in determining God's Will in your life, and you are not able to find any clearly written answer from the Word, nor are there any unusual impressions given to you by God, you may want to try the following method that has worked successfully in the lives of many.

> A METHOD TO DETERMINE GOD'S WILL
> 1. *Absolute honesty in wanting God's Will*
> 2. *Choose what seems right and most fulfilling*
> 3. *Depend upon the check of the Holy Spirit.*

1. *Absolute honesty in wanting God's Will*

   Look into your own heart and mind and ask yourself: "Do I want God's Will at any cost?" Absolute honesty is essential at this point. Unless your pursuing of God's Will is motivated by a pure, unmixed motive, you do not have an adequate foundation upon which to build a decision.

   Just as the foundation of a building is an absolute *must* to insure the function, security, and beauty of that building, so is the unquestioned honesty of wanting God's Will a *must* if you are to know and experience His Will in your life.

2. *Choose what seems right and most fulfilling*

If through your spirit or God's Word, you do not clearly know God's Will, then you must use your own heart and soul to choose what seems to be right and the most fulfilling thing for you to do.

Many times God's Will is exactly what you want for yourself because you have the mind of Christ in you. When you are absolutely honest and unmixed in your motive, God's unrevealed Will and your will are often the same (John 14:22-23, TLB), and are never far apart.

> "... Sir, why are you going to reveal yourself only to us disciples and not to the world at large?" Jesus replied, "Because I will only reveal myself to those who love me and obey me. The Father will love them too, and we will come to them and live with them."
>
> John 14:22-23, TLB

A very good rule to remember is that, when evaluating one thing or another, never does God's Will conflict with the Scriptures. As you are praying and pursuing God's direction, be very careful that it does not conflict with the Word of God. When you are about to make a decision about the right and most fulfilling thing to do, know that God's Will never conflicts with His Word.

3. *Depend upon the check of the Holy Spirit*

> Now that you have examined your own heart . . .
>
> Now that you are sure your motive is absolutely pure . . .
>
> Now that you want God's Will at any cost . . .

Now that you have decided to do what seems to be right and the most fulfilling . . . you can have the full confidence that God will check you if it is not His Will. He will bring an uneasiness or heaviness of heart to show you the mistake of your decision.

> If any man will do his will, he shall know of the doctrine, whether it be of God, or whether I speak of myself.
>
> John 7:17, KJV

The principle of this verse is that if your motive is pure and you want only God's Will, He will guide you, and you will know if it is of God or of man.

Therefore, when the Will of God is not one of those clearly written or discerned utterances in your life, there is a very sure method of receiving God's guidance.

Without looking back, list the three steps in this method of knowing God's Will.

1. _____
2. _____
3. _____

Practical Concepts of Commitment
(outline)

I. Commitment of God to Man—Bestowment

  A. Definitions

     1. Commit
     2. Bestowment
     3. Steward

  B. What Did God Commit to Man?

     1. Physical Life
     2. Psychical Life
     3. Spiritual Life

  C. Why Did God Commit to Man?

II. Commitment of Man to God—Consecration

  A. Definitions

     1. Consecrate
     2. Person
     3. Possessions

  B. Consecration of the Person

     1. Physical Life
     2. Psychical Life
     3. Spiritual Life

C. Consecration of the Possessions
   1. Time
   2. Talents
   3. Treasure
      a. The Curse of Selfishness
      b. Tithe and Offering
      c. New Testament Giving

D. Motivations for Consecration
   1. Duty
   2. Reward
   3. Love

*Give of your best to the Master
Give Him first place in your heart;
Give Him first place in your service
Consecrate every part.*
—Mrs. Charles Barnard

Practical Concepts of Commitment

In chapter 1, "Mandate of the Master," it was stated that a disciple is a person who is committed to Christ in obedience and service. In chapter 5, "The Spirit-Filled Life," it was discovered that one of the prerequisites for experiencing the fullness of the Holy Spirit is a total commitment to Christ as Lord. This chapter will explore the different aspects of practical commitment in your everyday Christian life. The study will center around two main thoughts:

    I. Commitment of God to Man—*Bestowment*
   II. Commitment of Man to God—*Consecration*

I. Commitment of God to Man—*Bestowment*

A. Definitions:

1. *Commit:* to give in trust; to put into custody or charge, to entrust, to consign, or surrender for safekeeping.

2. *Bestowment:* that which is given, conferred, or imparted.

3. *Steward:* (1) a man entrusted with the management of the household or estate of another; (2) one who acts as a supervisor or administrator, as of finances and property, etc., for another.

Study the following Scriptures, and see how these definitions can be applied. Underline the key phrases.

> Jesus told his disciples: "There was a rich man whose manager was accused of wasting his possessions. So he called him in and asked him, 'What is this I hear about you? Give an account of your management, because you cannot be manager any longer.' The manager said to himself, 'What shall I do now? My master is taking away my job...'"
> Luke 16:1-3a, NIV

> So then, men ought to regard us as servants of Christ and as those entrusted with the secret things of God. Now it is required that those who have been given a trust must prove faithful.
> I Corinthians 4:1-2, NIV

> He said therefore, A certain nobleman went into a far country to receive for himself a kingdom, and to return. And he called his ten servants, and delivered unto them ten pounds, and said unto them, Occupy till I come.
> Luke 19:12-13, KJV

> For the kingdom of heaven is as a man travelling into a far country, who called his own servants, and delivered unto them his goods . . . His Lord said unto him, Well done, thou good and faithful servant: Thou hast been faithful over a few things, I will make thee ruler over many things: Enter thou into the joy of thy Lord.
> Matthew 25:14, 21, KJV

God has bestowed on you many things that you enjoy today.

> LIST THE THREE THINGS THAT GOD HAS BESTOWED ON YOU THAT, AT THIS MOMENT, SEEM TO BE THE *MOST IMPORTANT* TO YOU.
>
> 1. _____
> 2. _____
> 3. _____

Commensurate with that bestowment comes the responsibility of stewardship. Have you ever considered the fact that God has committed certain entrustments to man?

B. What Did God Commit to Man?

1. *Physical Life*

   a. God entrusted man with the functional, *physical body*. He intended the body to house the psychical functions and spiritual functions of the person.

   b. God has entrusted man with the benefit of His entire physical creation. He intended that man would enjoy and use it as a faithful steward.

2. *Psychical Life*

   God has consigned to man certain attributes that reflect His own Image. These are attributes of emotion, reason, and the ability to choose. Included in this consignment are man's talents, gifts, and abilities to manage.

3. *Spiritual Life*

   God created man in His own Image. This included the bestowment upon man of God's own spiritual character. Man's disobedient mismanagement of God's entrustment resulted in his being charged with breaking that trusted responsibility. However, *God* paid the price to give man an opportunity to be rejoined spiritually to Him through reconciliation by the sacrificial blood of Christ.

C. Why Did God Commit to Man?

1. God created man and conferred upon him countless benefits in order that He might have *fellowship and communion* with man. Man was designed to worship his Creator and to return the love that was given to him by God.

2. Man was also created to *share in God's Image*. Man was entrusted with the management of all of the rest of God's creation.

> And God said, Let us make man in our image, after our likeness: and let them have dominion over the fish of the sea, and over the fowl of the air, and over the cattle, and over all the earth, and over every creeping thing that creepeth upon the earth.
>
> Genesis 1:26, KJV

This supervision was to take place as God Himself worked out His Plan *through* man. God has designed man and bestowed this management position upon him not only for this life, but, contingent upon man's faithfully carrying out his responsibilities here on earth, man will also be assigned responsibilities in eternity.

> "His master replied, 'Well done, good and faithful servant! You have been faithful with a few things; I will put you in charge of many things. Come and share your master's happiness!'"
>
> Matthew 25:23, NIV

II. Commitment of Man to God—*Consecration*

A. Definitions

1. *Consecrate:* to devote to a divinity; to make or declare to be sacred, by certain ceremonies or rites; to appropriate to sacred uses; to set apart or dedicate as holy.

2. *Person:* an individual human being, especially as distinguished from a thing or lower animal.

3. *Possessions:* anything possessed, owned, or occupied.

B. Consecration of the Person

1. *Physical Life*

> I urge you therefore, brethren, by the mercies of God, to present your *bodies* a living and holy sacrifice, acceptable to God, which is your spiritual service of worship.
> Romans 12:1, NASB

Physical life is a bestowment and must be consecrated back to God in the attitude of true commitment. God created you with this indefinable, vital force called "life" that distinguishes you from the inanimate and inorganic.

Life is a sacred commodity, and your physical being was created to house the Spirit of God in Whose Image you were created.

> What? Know ye not that your *body* is the *temple* of the Holy Ghost which is in you, which ye have of God, and ye are not your own? For ye are bought with a price: therefore glorify God in your body and in your spirit, which are God's.
> I Corinthians 6:19, 20, KJV

This verse may be specifically addressed to Christians, but the unconverted must also give an account to God for the responsible management of the physical body. You must take good care of your body and make sure that God's temple is cleansed and Spirit-filled.

> And what agreement hath the temple of God with idols? for ye are the temple of the living God; as God hath said, I will dwell in them, and walk in them; and I will be their God, and they shall be my people. Wherefore come out from among them (the evil doers); and be ye separate, saith the Lord, and touch not the unclean thing; and I will receive you, And will be a Father unto you and ye shall be my sons and daughters, saith the Lord Almighty.
> II Corinthians 6:16-18, KJV

2. *Psychical Life*

> Neither yield ye your members as instruments of unrighteousness unto sin: but yield yourselves unto God, as those that are alive from the dead, and your *members* as instruments of righteousness unto God.
> Romans 6:13, KJV

God has given you *temporary custody* of your psychical attributes. Your mind, with all of its powers, must be consecrated to God and involved in a program of learning how to more perfectly fulfill God's Plan.

Your *emotional* actions and reactions must be dedicated to God. The *desires and ambitions,* the *plans and dreams* that you have held in your "*volitional hope chest,*" must become subservient to the "Master Planner."

3. *Spiritual Life*

As you learned in chapter 5, "The Spirit-Filled Life," there must be a total consecration of your heart . . . your spiritual control center. He must be Lord over all . . . or . . . He is not Lord at all!

4. *The Influence of Your Life*

Influence is a strange phenomenon. It includes all three of your functions, i.e., *physical, psychical,* and *spiritual.* The power of your *influence* is your ability to affect others, without the use of force or authority.

An influential person is one who has weight, credibility, support, strength, and effect. You can be an effective instrument in advancing God's Will if you commit to Him in full consecration all the power of your Spirit-filled influence to be used where, when, and how He directs.

You have your circle of influence. You carry weight somewhere with someone. You must be sure that that weight is thrown always on the side of that which is morally right and helpful to others. Saint Peter's life is an example of a powerful but possibly unconscious influence. Back in New Testament times the people brought the sick out onto the sidewalks in order that the shadow of Peter passing by might overshadow and thereby heal them (Acts 5:15). This indicated the confidence people had in Peter.

There are people who have confidence in you. The shadow of your influence follows you day and night. This kind of influence is an invisible force that results from *what you are,* even more than anything you *say or do.* It is the ability to affect others by the strength of your character, the example of your life, the force of your thought, and the attractiveness of your personality.

Have you committed your influence to the Cause of God? It is God's bestowment, and it is your responsibility to invest it in His work. Your influence will live long after you are gone. This is seen in the example of Elisha, even after he was dead.

> And Elisha died, and they buried him. And the bands of the Moabites invaded the land at the coming in of the year. And it came to pass, as they were burying a man, that, behold, they spied a band of men; and they cast the man into the sepulchre of Elisha; and when the man was let down, and touched the bones of Elisha, he revived, and stood up on his feet.
>
> II Kings 13:20-21, KJV

C. Consecration of the Possessions

1. *Time*

    Commitment includes the consecration back to God of the bestowment of your time while on earth. Time is valuable. Perhaps you have complained about not having enough time but continued to waste it as if you had endless days at your command.

    Time is *duration* measured in years, months, weeks, days, hours, minutes, and seconds—but it is more. It is a stream that carries us silently and relentlessly along toward the final point of accountability in the Presence of God.

Time is opportunity. Are you using or abusing your time? Are you too busy doing *nothing* to accomplish *anything* of real value? The man who is busy senses the value of time far more than the man who is idle. The couplet on the wall motto expresses well the benefits of time:

> Only one life 'twill soon be past;
> Only what's done for Christ will last.

Have you consecrated and dedicated the best use of your time to God? You can waste your time and exist, but only those who use their time wisely can be said to truly live.

Have you set, under the guidance of God, some high goals of accomplishment? What are your plans for today? Have you thought about tomorrow? What does God want you to do? What does He want you to be? Give some serious thought to the wise utilization of your time, and the day will soon come when you can look back and say, "God hath helped me hitherto."

LIST FOUR WAYS THAT YOU COULD MAKE BETTER USE OF YOUR TIME.
1. _____
2. _____
3. _____
4. _____

---

2. *Talents*

You have latent abilities, talents, and capacities which God has entrusted to you and for which you are *responsible*.

Not only must your latent abilities and capacities be committed in consecration to God and His service, but also their potential possibilities become your problem.

> ". . . Your care for others is the measure of your greatness."
> Luke 9:48, TLB

The successful use of your talents is measured by the extent to which you have acquired skills which interest and serve other people. Your personality is your own particular individuality. It is the sum of your distinctive and collective qualities, abilities, and capacities that impress or influence others.

How does *your* personality now serve and interest others? How does it serve God in Kingdom-related concerns? Are you an unselfish, thoughtful person? Are you a keenly aware, tactful, helpful person? Are you interested in self-improvement in character and personality development? What undesirable habits could you break? What new and helpful, more acceptable habits could you diligently develop? Self-improvement comes by doing. Are you willing to become involved in a practical dedication and commitment of all your present and potential abilities, talents, qualities, and capacities in the loving service of God?

LIST THREE ABILITIES THAT GOD HAS GIVEN YOU THAT YOU WOULD LIKE TO FURTHER DEVELOP.

1. _____
2. _____
3. _____

LIST THREE ABILITIES THAT GOD HAS GIVEN TO YOUR HUSBAND, WIFE, OR FRIEND THAT YOU WISH THEY WOULD DEVELOP.

Name of Person _____

1. _____
2. _____
3. _____

3. *Treasure*

The God-directed *management of material possessions* is certainly a part of your total commitment to God.

a. *The Curse of Selfishness*

The curse of selfishness was the burden of the prophet in Haggai 1:2-12 as he stressed the necessity of putting God and the Kingdom first.

Your attitude toward money is usually a good indication of your attitude toward the stewardship management of material things in general. This is true because money is a medium of exchange that represents the value of your possessions.

The necessity of a right attitude toward money is expressed in the following lines:

> Dug from the mountain-side, washed in the glen,
> Servant am I, or the Master of men.
> Steal me, I curse you; earn me, I bless you;
> Grasp me and hoard me, a fiend shall possess you.
> Lie for me, die for me, covet me, take me.
> Angel or devil, I am what you make me!
> I am money.
>
> —Anonymous

The man of wisdom, who wrote the Book of Proverbs, declared:

> It is possible to give away and become richer! It is also possible to hold on too tightly and lose everything. Yes, the liberal man shall be rich! By watering others, he waters himself.
>
> Proverbs 11:24-25, TLB

b. *Tithe and Offering*

The *tithe and a reasonable offering are token requirements* that indicate in a measure the climate of liberality, love, commitment, and consecration you have with your material possessions. Abraham and Jacob are two inspiring examples in the Old Testament. Tithing, of course, is only the starting point or "ABC" of the responsible commitment and management of materiality.

(1) *Abraham*

After the battle of the four kings against five, it was necessary for Abraham to rescue Lot from King Chedorlaomer, who had taken Lot and his family captive. On returning, victorious Abraham was met by Melchizedek, King of Salem, to whom Abraham "gave tithes of all."

This account is further amplified in Hebrews 7:1-13.

(2) *Jacob*

Jacob made his vow at Bethel. God said to Jacob at Bethel . . .

> And behold, I am with thee . . . in all places whither thou goest, and will bring thee again into this land; for I will not leave thee, until I have done that which I have spoken to thee of. And Jacob vowed a vow, saying . . . and of all that thou shalt give me I will surely give the tenth unto thee.
> Genesis 28:15, 20, 22, KJV

c. *New Testament Giving*

One in every six verses of the entire New Testament relates to the subject of giving. Of Christ's thirty-eight parables, sixteen relate to man's attitude toward money. In the four Gospels one verse in every seven deals with this subject. Christ summed it all up in this great commitment statement:

> . . . Render therefore unto Caesar the things which are Caesar's; and unto God the things that are God's.
> Matthew 22:21, KJV

Jesus adds the seal of New Testament authority to the principle of tithing in the words: "These ought ye to have done." The full text reads:

> Woe unto you, scribes and Pharisees, hypocrites! for ye pay tithes of mint and anise and cummin, and have omitted the mercy, and faith! *these ought ye to have done,* and not to leave the other undone.
> Matthew 23:23, KJV

D. Motivations for Consecration

There are at least three possible motivations for consecration.

- Duty
- Reward
- Love

1. Duty

Duty is the first reason for consecration. The Scriptures at the beginning of this chapter clearly teach that the time of accounting will come. You are also warned that it is "appointed unto men once to die, but after this the judgment" (Hebrews 9:27, KJV). Further warnings are given about the need for watchfulness and faithfulness in the following Scripture on responsible management.

> The Lord answered, "Who then is the faithful and wise manager, whom the master puts in charge of his servants to give them their food allowance at the proper time? It will be good for that servant whom the master finds doing so when he returns. I tell you the truth, he will put him in charge of all his possessions. But suppose the servant says to himself, 'My master is taking a long time in coming,' and then begins to beat the men and women servants and to eat and drink and get drunk. The master of that servant will come on a day when he does not expect him and at an hour he is not aware of. He will cut him to pieces and assign him a place with the unbelievers. That servant who knows his master's will and does not get ready or does not do what his master wants will be beaten with many blows."
>
> Luke 12:42-47, NIV

2. Reward

Reward is also a motive for consecration of God's bestowments. Moses was faithful in all responsibilities because he had respect for the rewards of well-doing.

> By faith Moses, when he was come to years, refused to be called the son of Pharaoh's daughter; Choosing rather to suffer affliction with the people of God, than to enjoy the pleasures of sin for a season; Esteeming the reproach of Christ greater riches than the treasures in Egypt: for he had respect unto the *recompence* of the *reward*.
> Hebrews 11:24-26, KJV

Many other Scriptures indicate that the careful custodians of Divine bestowments will be richly rewarded both in this life and in the life to come. It will be worth everything to hear the Master say at the time of your accounting...

> ... Come, ye blessed of my Father, inherit the kingdom prepared for you...
> Matthew 25:34, KJV

What joy to hear God say, "Well done, thou good and faithful servant . . . enter thou into the joy of thy Lord" (Matthew 25:21, KJV)! In times of sacrifice or self-denial you can be encouraged by God's promise to all his followers who put "Kingdom business" first.

> Jesus said to them, "I tell you the truth, at the renewal of all things, when the Son of Man sits on his throne in heavenly glory, you who have followed me will also sit on twelve thrones, judging the twelve tribes of Israel. And *everyone* who has left houses or brothers or sisters or father or mother or children or fields for my sake will receive a hundred times as much and will inherit eternal life."
> Matthew 19:28-29, NIV

3. Love

Love is the ultimate in man's motive for consecration. Christ saved us when we were sinners. He loved us when we were unlovely, and, as Saint Paul declared:

> You see, at just the right time, when we were still powerless, Christ died for the ungodly. Very rarely will anyone die for a righteous man, though for a good man someone might possibly dare to die. But God demonstrates his own love for us in this: While we were still sinners, Christ died for us.
>
> Romans 5:6-8, NIV

When you consider the beneficence of God that provided for your physical, psychical, and spiritual capacities, and when you consider the spheres of influence with which you have been entrusted, then you certainly have reason to consecrate yourself, love Him, and serve Him faithfully.

When you think of the manifestation of His love in supplying protection, provision, and preservation, you have reason to be meticulous in your management of His bestowments.

When you think of the love of God that is shed abroad in your heart by the Holy Spirit which is given you, and remember that He has uprooted all your sinful, selfish desire, covetousness, envy, and greed—then Pure Love becomes the dominating motive for management.

Conclusion

These practical concepts of commitment are for Christ's Disciples of all times.

A Disciple is one who commits all to follow Jesus.

This was especially true of the first Disciples, the twelve which He called to follow Him in the brief period of His earthly ministry.

If you are a true Disciple today, you must turn your back on the old life, the old affections, and the former serving of self, just as the early Disciples did. It necessitates a consecration and a holy abandonment to the Will and Ways of God. "I will follow Thee whithersoever Thou goest."

Obedience
(outline)

I. Past Portraits of Obedience

   A. The Plan of Obedience

   B. Some Pictures of Obedience

      1. Noah
      2. Abraham
      3. Joseph
      4. Moses, Joshua, Gideon
      5. Hannah
      6. Saul
      7. David
      8. Solomon
      9. Isaiah
      10. Jonah
      11. Daniel
      12. Jesus Christ

II. Pertinent Problems with Obedience

III. Practical Principles of Obedience

   A. The Principle of Christ's Formula
   B. The Principle of Confidence as It Relates to Obedience
   C. The Principle of "Insight, Opportunity, and Obedience"
   D. The Principle of "Lag-Time"
   E. The Principle of "Eager-Pursuit"

Conclusion

Obedience must be the struggle and desire of our life. Obedience, not hard enforced, but ready, loving and spontaneous.
—Phillips Brooks

Obedience

OBEY: To be obedient to—execute the commands of; to be ruled or controlled by; to follow the guidance of; to be submissive to restraint, control or command.
—Webster

The importance of the subject of obedience can be seen in the fact that it is the opening and closing theme of the Bible itself.

- In Genesis God is expecting obedience to His command to Adam and Eve to stay away from the fruit of the tree of life in the center of the Garden (Genesis 2 and 3). In fact, when Adam and Eve were driven from the Garden, an angel with a flaming sword was left to insure this obedience.

- In Revelation 14:12 John records these words:

    "Let this encourage God's people to endure patiently every trial and persecution, for they are his saints who remain firm to the end in obedience to his commands and trust in Jesus."
    Revelation 14:12, TLB

- Then John goes on to say, in the final verses of Revelation:

    > Blessed are they that do his commandments, that they may have right to the tree of life, and may enter in through the gates into the city.
    >
    > Revelation 22:14, KJV

From beginning to end and all in between, the Bible emphasizes the necessity of obedience. In this section you will be dealing with three areas of the subject of obedience:

> I. Past Portraits of Obedience
> II. Pertinent Problems with Obedience
> III. Practical Principles of Obedience

If you are to become an effective disciple of Christ, you must cultivate a vital life of complete and immediate obedience.

I. Past Portraits of Obedience

A. The Plan of Obedience

From the beginning of history, God has had one single condition which must be met in order for man to experience spiritual success. *The one single condition has always been quick and complete obedience.* The story of mankind is a pageant, revealing man's response and reaction to God's command to specific obedience. The simplicity of God's singular requirement has been made complex, not by God, but by man.

History is the simple recording of the results of the lives of men and women who individually decided how they were going to handle this conditional requirement of obedience. (Examples: Apostle Paul, Hitler, can you name others?) Just think what would happen in the history of the near future if those who are here desiring to become better Disciples of Christ would decide that, *regardless of the cost, they would obey!*

God *always* honors those who are quickly and completely obedient. The way that God is going to awaken our world today is through *men and women of obedience.* This is the way He has worked through history, and He is looking for men and women through whom He can work even today.

B. Some Pictures of Obedience

Look now at the portraits of some past patriarchs who purposefully planned to please God through pure obedience. These will be character sketches with an opportunity for you to fill in the highlights and shades of color.

1. *NOAH*

God required Noah to perform an unreasonable task—absolutely beyond logic. But Noah responded with an obedience beyond reproach. You will find the following phrase recorded four times regarding this new father of the human race:

> *Noah did everything as God commanded him.*
> Genesis 6:22; 7:5, 9, 16, TLB

2. *ABRAHAM*

Abraham was a friend of God. In this portrait you see Abraham talking with the Angel of the Lord. It was to Abraham that God declared:

> "... I am the Almighty; obey me and live as you should. I will prepare a contract between us, guaranteeing to make you into a mighty nation ... It is a contract that I shall be your God and the God of your posterity ... Your part of the contract ... *is to obey*..."
> Genesis 17:1-9, TLB

God began fulfilling His part of the contract by giving Abraham a son, even in his old age. One son to fulfill the posterity promise! Then God tested Abraham's obedience by saying:

> "Take with you your only son . . . yes, Isaac whom you love so much . . . and go to the land of Moriah and sacrifice him there as a burnt offering . . ."
>
> Genesis 22:2, TLB

Oswald Chambers wrote:

> God's command is—Take now, not presently. It is extraordinary how we debate! We know a thing is right, but we try to find excuses for not doing it at once. To climb to the height God shows can never be done presently, it must be done now. The sacrifice is gone through in will before it is performed actually.
>
> "And Abraham *rose up early* in the morning . . . and went into the place of which God had told him" (verse 3). The wonderful simplicity of Abraham! When God spoke, he did not confer with flesh and blood. Beware when you want to confer with flesh and blood, i.e., your own sympathies, your own insight, anything that is not based on your personal relationship to God. These are the things that compete with and hinder obedience to God.[31]

Abraham obeyed perfectly because his *faith was perfect* and *faith always precedes obedience*. And the Angel of God shouted . . .

> "Lay down the knife; don't hurt the lad in any way . . . for I know that God is first in your life . . . you have not withheld even your beloved son from me . . . I will bless you with incredible blessings and multiply your descendants into countless thousands and millions, like the stars above you in the sky, and like the sands along the seashore . . . *all because you have obeyed me.*"
>
> Genesis 22:12-18, TLB

---

[31]*Op. cit.*, Chambers, p. 316.

> **FAITH ALWAYS PRECEDES OBEDIENCE**

Would you like God to work some great things *through you* like He did through Abraham? Then how does your *obedience level* measure up? Is God really first place in your life? He wants to be!

3. *JOSEPH*

Without the precise obedience of Joseph, the promised posterity of Abraham's seed would no doubt have ended with the starving to death of Jacob and his family. On the obedient shoulders of this seventeen-year-old Joseph, rested the fate of the Israeli nation.

Joseph, whose mother died when he was still a small child, grew up with sibling (family) rivalry that would have made a psychotic out of the most seasoned saint. He was sold into slavery by his own brothers for 20 pieces of silver. Accused of rape by a "has-been" hussy in the palace of Potiphar, Joseph was thrown into jail to rot.

No one has ever lived who has had *more reason to renounce the apparent results of righteousness than Joseph.*

It was almost as if God had to take Joseph to these depths so that later, when He took him to the planned heights, Joseph wouldn't get dizzy and fall. Joseph "kept his head on straight" and obeyed God *quickly and completely every time.* He was aware of God's Plan (Genesis 37:5-10) and responded with perfect obedience.

When Joseph was thirty God placed within those obedient hands the reins of power over the whole known world. By the end of the seven years of worldwide famine, Joseph had gained control over the known world for Egypt. He had traded grain for control of all the known monetary systems. When the money ran out, he traded grain for all the livestock. When the livestock ran out, the starving people traded Joseph "warranty deeds" to their real estate in exchange for grain.

By the seventh year of famine, the starving people from all over the known world came and pledged themselves as servants to Joseph in exchange for grain (Genesis 47:13-26). Joseph had been allowed to gain this control, not with a sword, but by God's bountiful breadbasket.

God planned this entire phenomenon so that a small band of 70 Israelis—yes, Joseph's father, brothers, sisters, and their families—could come to Egypt and live under this kind of control and protection. There in the Land of Goshen, that small tribe of Israel was able to fruitfully multiply for 430 years and grow into a nation numbering over 600,000. Then God told Moses to lead them back home.

What was the common thread of success through Joseph's life?

obedience, Obedience, OBEDIENCE
(Genesis 37—47)

4. MOSES, JOSHUA, GIDEON

Moses, Joshua, and Gideon stand together here for their portraits. They were great men of obedience, *executing God's commands and submitting themselves to His control.*

5. HANNAH

This is the little lady who was willing to obediently give her only begotten son so that God could work His wonderful Plan through the little fellow who grew up to be the great, *fearless prophet of obedience,* Samuel (I Samuel 1-15). It was *SAMUEL* who fearlessly told King Saul:

> ". . . Has the Lord as much pleasure in your burnt offerings and sacrifices as in your obedience? Obedience is far better than sacrifice. He is much more interested in your listening to him than in your offering the fat of rams to him. For rebellion is as bad as the sin of witchcraft, and stubbornness is as bad as worshipping idols. And now because you have rejected the word of Jehovah, he has rejected you from being king."
>
> I Samuel 15:22-23, TLB

6. SAUL

Here in King Saul's portrait, you see him dying—having fallen on his own sword to commit suicide.

> Saul died for his disobedience to the Lord . . .
> I Chronicles 10:13, TLB

7. DAVID

Please notice the flaw there in the beautiful portrait of David. That flaw exists only because of disobedience. (See II Samuel 11 and 12.)

8. SOLOMON

Look closely at Solomon's portrait. *He has absolutely everything—except obedience.*

> . . . even though the Lord had clearly instructed his people not to marry into those nations, because the women they married would get them started worshipping their gods. *Yet Solomon did it anyway . . .* sure enough, they turned his heart away from the Lord . . . *thus Solomon did what was clearly wrong and refused to follow the Lord . . .*
>
> I Kings 11:2-6, TLB

9. ISAIAH

He was the most prolific of the prophets. Look over his shoulder, and see what he is writing.

> Morning by morning he awakens me and opens my understanding to his will. The Lord God has spoken to me and I have listened; I do not rebel nor turn away . . . because the Lord God helps me, I will not be dismayed; therefore, *I have set my face like flint to do his will,* and I know that I will triumph.
>
> Isaiah 50:4b-7, TLB

10. JONAH

Now here's a picture of a man who had a "whale of a time" learning to obey. How are you responding to your "Nineveh"? (See Jonah 1—4.)

11. DANIEL

This is a portrait of "Governor Daniel." Isn't it amazing what God has in store for those who perfectly obey Him? (See Daniel 1—12.)

12. *JESUS CHRIST*

Are you surprised that Christ's portrait is included here? The writer of Hebrews states:

> And even though Jesus was God's Son, he had to learn from experience what it was like to obey, when obeying meant suffering.
>
> Hebrews 5:8, TLB

> READ MATTHEW 26:39-56

Christ Himself testified to His obedience when praying to His Father, as recorded in John 17:4.

> "I brought glory to you here on earth *by doing everything you told me to do.*"
>
> John 17:4, TLB

It was important for Christ, God's Son, to be perfectly obedient to the Will of God. *How can you even think that you can get by with less than complete and instant obedience?*

II. Pertinent Problems with Obedience

Take time to discuss the following problems and relate them to where you are spiritually. (Suggestion: the following section lends itself well to a role-playing situation. See if you can find Scripture references that relate to each.)

NOTES   252

A. I don't know God's Will for my life. Therefore, it is not *possible* for me to obey, because I'm not *responsible* for what I don't know.

B. I would rather *dictate* to God and then ask Him to bless my obedience to *my own* will. "Bless my mess!"

C. I have a problem obeying because of what I think it will *cost others* around me. As an example, my obedience to God may appear to work a hardship on my family.

D. Instead of immediate obedience to what I already know, I would rather build a case, weigh the arguments, seek supportive advice from some of my friends and then, at the best, work out a compromise.

E. I believe in "progressive obedience" and that obedience is optional. I choose to wait and obey *fully*—next time.

F. You may call it a poor attitude, but I don't believe that you can obey with "glad, reckless joy."

G. Instead of instant obedience, I would rather enjoy the luxury of worrying. I'm not convinced that worry is infidelity, as based on Philippians 4:6-7.

H. To me obedience implies submission, and I find it difficult to submit.

I. I simply *don't believe* that it is as necessary for me to obey today as it was for the children of Israel.

J. I find it impossible to believe that I must release the results of my obedience and realize that the outcome is God's problem.

K. My biggest difficulty with obedience in the past was _____ _____.

L. My biggest difficulty with obedience now is _____ _____.

III. Practical Principles of Obedience

You have looked at some past portraits of obedience and have discussed some *problems* with obedience. Now see if you can discover some simple handles which will help you in your everyday life of obedience.

A. The Principle of Christ's Formula

In the Gospel of John, chapter 14, Jesus discloses the formula for success in regard to obedience. He states that "if you love me, you will obey me." The only logical conclusion is that,

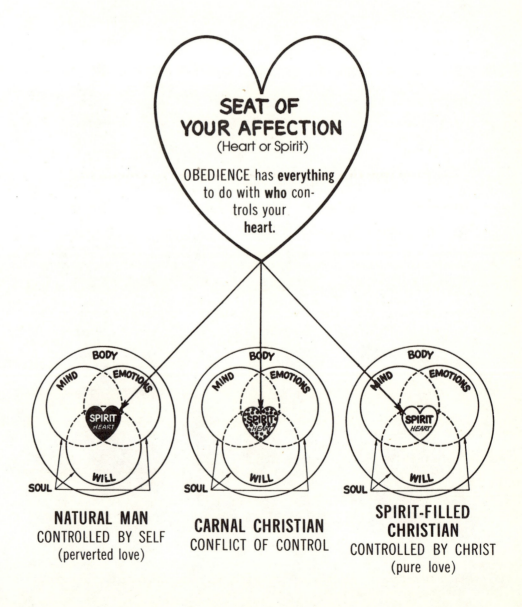

if you don't obey Him, it is because you don't love Him. *If you don't love Him, it is because you love something else instead—self.* Do you see how this so beautifully relates to our diagram?

There will always be a major problem with obedience as long as you have a problem with the question of *who controls the seat of your affection*—your heart. Christ goes on to explain that "if you love me and obey me, I will reveal myself to you." This revelation is all that you need for further obedience. He also adds that He wants to give to those who love Him and obey not only revelation but also a gift of peace of mind and of heart. This peace is not fragile like the peace the world gives, but is the *assurance* that comes when you *love Him completely and obey Him quickly.* Therefore, the principle of Christ's formula is that if you love me, *you will obey* me; if you *love me* and *obey me,* I will reveal myself to you one step at a time and give you the *gift of peace.*

B. The Principle of Confidence as It Relates to Obedience

Hannah Whitall Smith claims she does not know the origin of the following statement but includes it in her book, *The Christian's Secret of a Happy Life.* "Perfect obedience would be perfect happiness if only we had perfect confidence in the power we were obeying."[32] To put it a little more simply, perfect obedience would be perfect happiness if you had perfect confidence in the one you obey. For you see, perfect confidence is when you are so convinced of God's Will that you waive all of your own personal rights in favor of pursuing His Plan. Does that sound familiar? That's *perfect faith!* As you recall, faith implies *action,* and it is the action of faith that becomes the initiation of obedience. *Without perfect faith or confidence, there can never be perfect obedience.* But when

---

[32]Hannah Whitall Smith, *The Christian's Secret of a Happy Life* (Old Tappan, N.J.: Fleming H. Revell Company, 1952), p. 208.

there *is perfect faith* in God's Plan for your life, followed by perfect obedience in carrying out that Plan, the *net result* will be perfect happiness. *This is because you are fulfilling the Plan for which you were created.* There is no greater happiness than this.

> Happy are all who perfectly follow the laws of God. Happy are all who search for God, and always do his will, rejecting compromise with evil, and walk only in his paths.
>
> Psalm 119:1-2, TLB

C. The Principle of "Insight, Opportunity, and Obedience"

Many times something visual can help you understand and retain a concept. Observe visually now this phenomenon of obedience.

GROWTH THROUGH OBEDIENCE

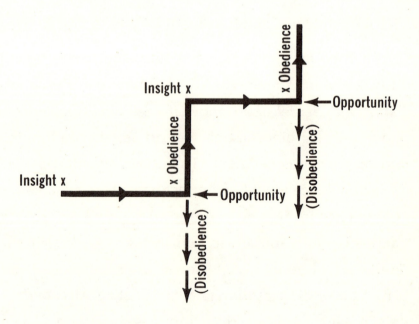

God will give you an insight as to something He wants you to do. This is followed by an opportunity to either obey or disobey.

As you will recall, in the early part of this chapter, it was stated that, *"the story of mankind is a pageant, revealing man's response and reaction to God's command to specific obedience."* Also it was stated that, *"history is the simple recording of the results of the lives of men and women who individually decided how they were going to handle this conditional requirement of obedience."*

So it is at this point of *opportunity* that history is determined. You can either obey or disobey at this point. If you *choose* to take this opportunity to obey, you are then allowed another *insight,* consequently, another *opportunity,* etc., etc.

This is the way spiritual growth and maturity take place. This is the way you allow the growth or influence of the Holy Spirit to, more and more, control the activities of your life. The diagram below is designed to illustrate how the influence of the Holy Spirit can radiate into the physical and psychical areas of your life. *Obedience* is one of the factors which governs this influence in your life.

> No wonder the Psalmist was so insistent that *"growth in wisdom comes from obeying his laws"* (Psalm 111:10, TLB).

D. The Principle of "Lag-Time"

Now that you have briefly looked at Christ's principle of *"love and obey,"* the *principle of "confidence"* as it relates to obedience, and *the principle of "Insight, Opportunity, and Obedience,"* you are ready to investigate another phenomenon that is called *"lag-time."*

Graphically, "lag-time" would look like this:

The period of time that elapses between the time God reveals to you what you should do and when you finally get around to doing it is what is referred to here as "lag-time." *Perhaps this is the most subtle weapon that Satan can use against you concerning obedience.*

You may be confused and don't see it as "lag-time." You may hesitate and claim that you have "placed it in the pigeonhole of suspended judgment." The tragedy lies in the fact that no matter how you rationalize, the end result is still the same, a missed opportunity. You may have been led to believe that being extremely "cautious" is a sign of *wisdom, stability,* and *maturity,* when in reality it could be either lag-time or disobedience.

Satan's approach is to prolong the "lag-time" to the extent that you never get around to obeying what you know you *ought* to do. Even if there is obedience following a period of "lag-time," it is sad to think that God's perfect timing may have been thrown off by your delayed obedience.

Please turn now to the 14th chapter of Numbers and read the awesome account of the Israeli nation. How sad! That day's act of *delayed* obedience resulted in 40 years of despair.

In dealing with this principle of "lag-time" there are two points to be remembered:

1. Your awareness level must increase and your sensitivity must become more acute so that you can more quickly respond to God's will.

2. You must develop the skill of cutting down the "lag-time" to the point where *"knowing"* and *"obeying"* become *synonymous*. The concept of *zero "lag-time"* must be developed.

Zero "lag-time"

E. The Principle of "Eager-Pursuit"

The Psalmist David crystallizes this principle in the first Psalm. He explains that it is not enough to sit back and wait for God to hand down a command for you to obey. He claims that you should always be meditating on God's ways and be creatively thinking about the possibility of your being in *"eager-pursuit"* of new and challenging opportunities for obedience.

> Oh the joys of those who do not follow evil men's advice, who do not hang around with sinners, scoffing at the things of God: But they delight in doing everything God wants them to, and *day and night are always meditating on his laws and thinking about ways to follow him more closely.* They are like trees along a river bank bearing luscious fruit each season without fail. Their leaves shall never wither, and all they do shall prosper.
>
> Psalm 1:1-3, TLB

CONCLUSION

Willful disobedience separates you from God (examples: Eve, Solomon, Judas, etc.).

> But your iniquities have made a separation between you and your God, And your sins have hid His face from you, so that He does not hear.
>
> Isaiah 59:2, NASB

A life of postponed or delayed obedience produces "spiritual fog." In this condition little or nothing is clear; everything is morally gray and out of focus. What you once counted on as a well-defined landmark now becomes a "mobile-situational-ethic," hardly recognizable in the haze of life.

Christ has no responsibility to reveal Himself clearly except in response to instant obedience. If you want to know His Will more clearly—you must obey Him more quickly. His promise is that He will reveal Himself and His Plan only to those who love Him completely and obey Him without hesitation.

> Christ has no responsibility to reveal Himself clearly except in response to instant obedience. If you want to know His Will more clearly—you must obey Him more quickly.

A poorly maintained "love-life" will always result in postponed response. If you think you can afford the luxury of delayed or postponed obedience, then you may as well count on spending the rest of your life stumbling around in "spiritual fog."

The person who chronically complains of the malady of "non-revelation" ("I don't know God's Will") has not only disclosed his symptom but has also, in the same breath, put his finger on the cause. *If you don't know God's Will, it's more than likely due to a delinquent response of obedience to the last installment of revelation.*

For Christ, Who is not the author of confusion, but of light and revelation, promised that He would reveal Himself one step at a time to those who love Him and obey Him. *How imperative it is for you to obey!*

Look back for a moment at Moses' portrait. He's trying to tell you something in closing:

> "Look, today I have set before you life and death, depending on whether you obey or disobey.—Oh, that you would choose life; *that you and your children might live!* Choose to love the Lord your God and obey him and cling to him, for he is *your life and the length of your days.*"
> Deuteronomy 30:15-20, TLB

> "This contract is not with you alone as you stand before him today, but with all future generations of Israel as well."
> Deuteronomy 29:14, TLB

And now Paul adds:

> But some of these branches from Abraham's tree, some of the Jews, have been broken off. And you Gentiles who were branches from, we might say, a wild olive tree, *were grated in.* So now you, too, receive the blessing God has promised Abraham and his children, sharing in God's rich nourishment of his own special olive tree.
>
> Romans 11:17, TLB

Now Christ, with arms outstretched, motions to speak the final word:

> "I have loved you even as the Father has loved me. *Live within my love. When you obey me you are living in my love...*"
>
> John 15:9-10, TLB

The Priorities of the Christian Life
(outline)

I. Your Relationship to His Person

    A. Your Physical Life (Body)

    B. Your Psychical Life (Soul)

    C. Your Spiritual Life (Spirit)

II. Your Relationship to His Purpose

Conclusion

"But seek first His kingdom and His righteousness; and all these things shall be added to you."
—Matthew 6:33, NASB

The Priorities of the Christian Life

PRIORITIES: Precedence in time, order, or importance.

There is no way a non-Christian can fully understand the significance of Christian priorities. His value system is different from that of the Christian; therefore, what is important to the Christian could be, and often is, unimportant to the non-Christian.

However, even with Christians, the problem of priorities must be seriously considered.

- *Establishing priorities is a pervasive problem.* It involves you individually with your assessments . . . and it involves you as a part of the Church, the Body of Believers. It continually affects your life's perspective.

- *Establishing priorities is a personal problem.* It has been stated that four out of five churches today are on the decline. God is not prejudiced: since He wants His church to grow, the responsibility for the decline cannot be placed to His account. But something has to account for the fruitlessness of a church. The responsibility must rest with the priority system of individual church members.

You have heard many good, intelligent people declare an arrangement of how you are supposed to "prioritize" things in your life. They have made lists for you to live by such as the following.

1. God	1. God	1. God
2. Home	2. Church	2. Home
3. Work	3. Home	3. Church
4. Church		4. Recreation

Even the clergy has been guilty of making a static list of priorities in order to support its philosophical position of ministry. Some would say, "If you have good homes, you will have good churches." This isn't necessarily true.

There is a very clear and intelligent priority program in God's Will. The question is, "Are you willing to take God's Plan "regarding your priorities?"

For the Christian, the matter of priorities is an arrangement of the legitimate. As you learned in the chapter on "The Born-Again Life," the Christian no longer engages in sinning. So now it is a matter of how to deal with the life that is already given to God.

There is a Biblical prescription for priorities which not only fits personally, but it is one that furnishes you with a pattern upon which to build a great family and a great church.

Are you willing to listen to God's Voice through His Word and then be quick to respond to His directions? In Colossians 3:1-25 and chapter 4, verse 1, there is a presentation of God's priority system.

The present chapter deals with the following concept of priorities:

      I. Your Relationship to His Person
     II. Your Relationship to His Purpose

I. Your Relationship to His Person

There is little, if any, conflict among those who know Christ as their personal Savior, in regard to their first priority. All Christians agree that nothing is as important as a personal and perpetual relationship with God.

The Apostle Paul, in Colossians 3:1-10, says:

> Since, then, you have been raised with Christ, set your hearts on things above, where Christ is seated at the right hand of God. Set your minds on things above, not on earthly things. For you died, and your life is now hidden with Christ in God. When Christ, who is your life, appears, then you also will appear with him in glory. Put to death, therefore, whatever belongs to your earthly nature: sexual immorality, impurity, lust, evil desires and greed, which is idolatry. Because of these, the wrath of God is coming. You used to walk in these ways, in the life you once lived. But now you must rid yourselves of all such things as these: anger, rage, malice, slander, filthy language. Do not lie to each other, since you have taken off your old self with its practices and have put on the new self, which is being renewed in knowledge in the image of its Creator.
>
>   Colossians 3:1-10, NIV

This relationship involves the total person. From a functional point of view, this is what Paul spoke of in I Thessalonians 5:23.

> . . . May your whole spirit, soul and body be kept blameless at the coming of our Lord Jesus Christ.
>   I Thessalonians 5:23, NIV

The subject of your relationship to His Person will be dealt with as it relates to the three functions of your life, i.e., body, soul, and spirit.

A. Your Physical Life (Body)

> Put to death, therefore, whatever belongs to your earthly nature...
>
> Colossians 3:5, NIV

This verse is saying that if your relationship to God is to be what it ought to be, you must cease from any physical gratification which is out of harmony with God's Will for you. The word *mortify* or *put to death* means a turning of the will from self to God.

B. Your Psychical Life (Soul)

> In your anger do not sin: Do not let the sun go down while you are still angry, and do not give the devil a foothold.
>
> Ephesians 4:26-27, NIV

This is a graphic portrayal of the fact that there is an anger which has its source in the psychical function of the individual and is not a heart condition. The psychical area includes frustration brought on by frayed nerves, emotional stress, and fatigue. It is highly important that this distinction be understood. The important thing to see is that you cannot maintain your priority in relationship to the *Person of God* without this problem being dealt with continually.

C. Your Spiritual Life (Spirit)

> Do not lie to each other, since you have taken off your old self with its practices and have put on the new self, which is being renewed in knowledge in the image of its Creator.
>
> Colossians 3:9-10, NIV

This Scripture is a very graphic picture portraying how priorities encompass the physical, psychical, and spiritual functions in your relationship to His Person.

> . . . Rid yourself of anger, rage, malice, slander . . . Do not lie to each other.
>
> Colossians 3:5-9, NIV

This is a step-by-step explanation of this relationship that you are to establish with God. Unless, and until such a relationship with the Person of God is created and maintained, it will be impossible to live out this system of Biblical priorities. There will be no virtue in following an arbitrary list of priorities unless a vital relationship to His Person is maintained.

II. Your Relationship to His Purpose

What an exciting concept to think of being involved in the Purpose of God! Jesus spoke to this when He said,

> As thou has sent me into the world, even so have I also sent them into the world.
>
> John 17:18, KJV

There are five basic areas in your life: family, church, world, job, and recreation or leisure time. One of the greatest problems is how to "prioritize" these basic areas. Is it possible to have a checklist of preferences by which to live? If it were that easy, everyone would be grateful!

It is impossible to graphically portray all of the implications and interplay of your relationship to God's Purpose in these five areas. However, it is mandatory for you to clearly understand the relationship of these areas to God's Purpose in your individual life. The following diagrams will illustrate this principle.

In this particular illustration, your *job* is taking precedence in time, order, or importance.

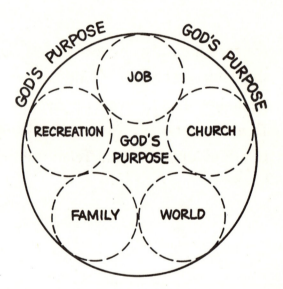

This is a dynamic function. It is not a static listing of these areas. Please note the following characteristics of this principle:

(1) All five of these areas are included in God's Purpose.

(2) They move in a very sensitive manner according to the need of the moment or hour.

(3) All of these are functioning within God's Purpose.

These are all tied into your time frame and are constantly changing based on four very important facts.

PREREQUISITES FOR DETERMINING PRIORITIES

(1) Absolute honesty with God.

(2) A keen sensitivity to circumstances.

(3) A willingness to pay whatever price necessary to fulfill God's Purpose.

(4) Dependence upon the Holy Spirit to reveal the precedence of the priority.

The following incidents will illustrate the different states of precdence and how this principle works in your everyday life.

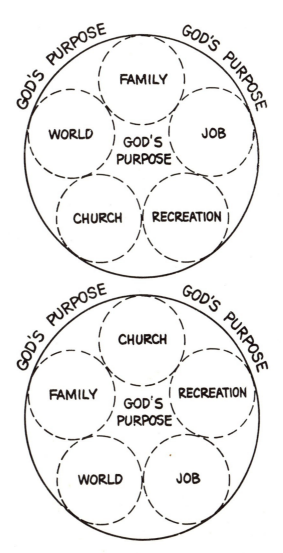

"I won't soon forget the morning when the telephone rang and my son said, 'Dad, I need to see you as soon as you can arrange it.' I turned to my secretary and asked her to rearrange my two appointments at noon and 1:00 p.m., and said, 'Son, I'll see you at noon.' As he talked, I was sensitive to the fact that he had moved into the top spot for the moment, and it was pleasing to God that I deal with his need. It was a part of 'God's Purpose' for me at that moment.

"Several days later he called, and said, 'Dad, I have two good tickets to the pro basketball game, and I want you to go with me.' I struggled for a moment because there is no one I would enjoy going with more than him, and no one I'd rather see play my favorite game than the home team. As I thought about my responsibility to the church, the Discipling program, and the people I was to teach, there was an awareness that this was a part of 'God's Purpose' for my life at that moment. I then expressed my sorrow to my son, and said, 'I'd better teach my class.'"

One of the enigmas of life is that there are many people who have won their families to themselves and their home, but have lost them to God and the church. Can you ever recall any incident when a family has won their children to God and the church, but lost them to their homes?

It is very possible to use this dynamic principle as a rationalization to fulfill your own selfish purpose. All of these areas are included in God's Purpose, and a violation of at least one of these areas would have to occur to fulfill your selfish purpose as opposed to God's Purpose. However, the four previously mentioned necessities (absolute honesty with God; keen sensitivity to circumstances; willingness to pay whatever price necessary; dependence upon the Holy Spirit) make it impossible for anyone to rationalize and still stay consistent with God's Purpose.

In the previous incident, had the father chosen to go to the ballgame with his son rather than teach his Discipling class, this would have been an example of arbitrarily placing his will over God's priority for that moment.

The diagram to the right shows how man, by his own choice, can selfishly choose to rearrange this precedence of God's Purpose, thereby destroying the harmony of God's Will.

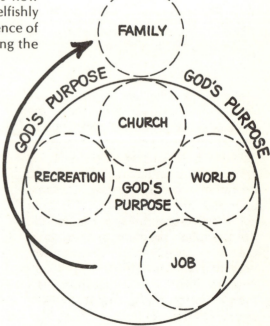

How many times has God's harmony become discord by *your* arbitrarily choosing *your* own selfish precedence over God's Purpose? You may have done this by a failure to be absolutely honest in your relationship with Him. It may be that you were not as keenly sensitive to the circumstances as you ought to have been.

Perhaps you were not willing to pay the price necessary. Or your life may be out of balance today because you don't have complete confidence in the fact that the Holy Spirit can and wants to reveal His desired priority in your life.

CONCLUSION

As you have found in this chapter, God's priorities are not a static list which can be used in all instances. You have discovered that God's priorities are dynamic, ever-changing positions to fulfill the imperative of "Seek first the kingdom of God."

In reality, you have learned in this chapter that your relationship to His Person is absolutely primary. Based upon this right relationship with His Person, your relationship to His Purpose naturally follows. God's priorities are not a static list, but, rather, are a dynamic precedence in harmony with His Purpose.

It takes more emphasis on the relationship to His Person when dealing with a dynamic concept of priorities than it does when you are dealing with a static list. It is possible to live according to a static list of priorities and miss God's perfect Purpose because of a lack of rightness in a relationship to His Person.

True harmony in the life of a Disciple comes when the five areas of his life (family, church, world, job, recreation) are "prioritized" through the revelation of the Holy Spirit, based upon an up-to-date, meaningful relationship to His Person.

REVIEW EXERCISE

A. List the Pedagogy of Discipling.

1. _____
2. _____
3. _____

B. List the Five Principles of Obedience.

1. _____
2. _____
3. _____
4. _____
5. _____

C. List the Four Prerequisites for Determining Priorities.

1. _____
2. _____
3. _____
4. _____

Worship
(outline)

I. Worship Defined

    A. The Attitude of Worship

    B. The Activities of Worship

II. Worship Designed

    A. The Purpose of Worship

    B. The Practices of Worship

        1. Worship God in Spirit
        2. Worship God in Truth

III. Worship's Decline

    A. Time—The Friend of Worship

    B. Time—The Foe of Worship

IV. Worship Denotes Growth

    A. The Mandate of Growth

    B. The Meaning of Growth

V. Worship Demonstrates Commitment

    A. Worship Includes Service

    B. Worship Includes Sacrifice

VI. Worship Demands Communication

    A. The Human Need for Communication

    B. The Divine Need for Communication

VII. Conclusion

Worship is giving God the best that He has given you. Be careful what you do with the best you have. Whenever you get a blessing from God, give it back to Him as a love gift.

—Oswald Chambers

Worship

You were created to worship God. Worship is a result of your seeing Who God is in comparison to yourself and who you are. In the chapter on God's Will, you discovered that God has a special Plan for your life. By fulfilling that Plan, you bring praise, honor, glory, and fellowship to God. You, who are God's Children, worship Him when you actively and increasingly participate in His Will on a moment-by-moment basis each day of your life. You present yourself as a living sacrifice in order to mirror and magnify His Image so that you can glorify Him.

In this chapter, the subject of Worship will be viewed from the following divisions:

     I. Worship Defined
    II. Worship Designed
   III. Worship's Decline
   IV. Worship Denotes Growth
    V. Worship Demonstrates Commitment
   VI. Worship Demands Communication.

I. Worship Defined

WORSHIP: (1) To adore, to pay divine honor to as a deity, to reverence with supreme respect;

(2) To have intense love or admiration for.
—Webster

A. The Attitude of Worship

Worship may include many activities, duties, and privileges that you choose to do as a response of love to your Heavenly Father. However, you may come into a beautiful sanctuary and sing songs of praise and enter into corporate prayer and find that these activities may only be conveniences which are designed to help you enter into an attitude of worship. All the ritual of the Old Testament was introduced as a means of helping the children of Israel to focus, not only the attention of their physical eye on God, but more importantly, to focus the attention of their inner eye of motive and attitude (spirit or heart) on God, so that they could worship Him in truth.

"You may worship no other God than me."
Exodus 20:3, TLB

"Now if you will fear and worship the Lord and listen to his commandments and not rebel against the Lord . . . then all will be well."
I Samuel 12:14, TLB

"Make sure now that you worship the Lord with true enthusiasm, and that you don't turn your back on him in any way."
I Samuel 12:20b, TLB

"Trust the Lord and sincerely worship him; think of all the tremendous things he has done for you."
I Samuel 12:24, TLB

My soul doth magnify the Lord.
Luke 1:46, KJV

> What I want from you is your true thanks; I want your promises fulfilled. I want you to trust me in your times of trouble, so I can rescue you, and you can give me glory.
> Psalm 50:14-15, TLB

B. The Activities of Worship

Not only does worship include inner attitudes or inner dispositions which will be directed toward God and His Son, Jesus, but it also includes external acts of divine service. You can outwardly express your service in the following ways: faith, prayer, fasting, material help to the needy, singing Psalms and hymns, the involvment in religious instruction and preaching, and the offering of yourself as a living sacrifice.

> "For it's not where we worship that counts, but how we worship—is our worship spiritual and real? Do we have the Holy Spirit's help? For God is Spirit, and we must have his help to worship as we should. The Father wants this kind of worship from us."
> John 4:23, TLB

II. Worship Designed

A. The Purpose of Worship

You were created to worship God and to have fellowship with Him. Recall the Genesis account where God said, "Let us make man in our image, after our likeness." God came down in the cool of the evening to walk through the Garden and would talk to Adam and Eve.

He intended to fellowship with them and expected them to respond to Him in worship. Later, Paul, in Ephesians 1:9-12, speaks to God's Purpose for man, to respond to Him with glory and praise.

> God has told us his secret reason for sending Christ, a plan he decided on in mercy long ago; and this was his purpose: that when the time is ripe he will gather us all together from wherever we are—in heaven or on earth—to be with him in Christ, forever. Moreover, because of what Christ has done we have become gifts to God that he delights in, for as part of God's sovereign plan we were chosen from the beginning to be his, and all things happen just as he decided long ago. God's purpose in this was that we should *praise God* and *give glory to him* for doing these mighty things for us, who were the first to trust in Christ.
> Ephesians 1:9-12, TLB

If you are going to worship God, you must live in a holy relationship with Him. This worship relationship finds you presenting yourself as a living sacrifice, purposefully, actively, hour-by-hour, for the rest of your life.

> And so, dear brothers, I plead with you to give your bodies to God. Let them be a living sacrifice, holy—the kind he can accept. When you think of what he has done for you, is this too much to ask? Don't copy the behavior and customs of this world, but be a new and different person with a fresh newness in all you do and think. Then you will learn from your own experience how his ways will really satisfy you.
> Romans 12:1-2, TLB

In chapter 6, *faith* was defined as your "being so convinced of God's Plan for your life that you waive all of your own personal rights in favor of pursuing His Will."

Worship, then, is an active participation in response to God's Will on a moment-by-moment basis for the rest of your life. Through worship, you grow closer and become more and more mature in your love response to God: "I will serve Thee because I love Thee—You have given life to me."[33]

---

[33]Words by William J. and Gloria Gaither. © Copyright 1969 by William J. Gaither. All Rights Reserved. International Copyright Secured. Used by Special Permission of the Publisher.

B. The Practices of Worship

1. *Worship God in Spirit*

Look at the diagram and remember that the seat of your affection is your heart or spirit. Your motivation, pure or perverted, comes from your spirit.

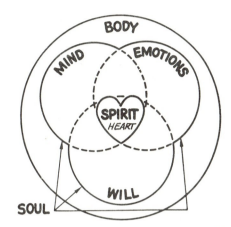

SPIRIT-FILLED CHRISTIAN

Therefore, the only true worship must come from your spirit, the very citadel of your life. Worship is rooted in the inner attitude and disposition of your heart. True worship stems from pure love, and the reflection of God's own Image and Love, motivating you to respond back to Him. True worship will have a purity of intention and will be accompanied by an internal attitude and motivation to give yourself totally to Him.

There are many helps or *aids to worship*. For example, the church (both the physical structure and the corporate group), songs, nature, sermons, prayer, all help spark your appreciation and direct your attention to worship which is from the spirit.

> Mary responded, "Oh, how I praise the Lord."
> Luke 1:46, TLB

> But we Christians have no veil over our faces; we can be mirrors that brightly reflect the glory of the Lord. And as the Spirit of the Lord works within us, we become more and more like him.
> II Corinthians 3:18, TLB

> *Oh, magnify the Lord with me,*
> *Ye people of His choice.*
> *Let all to whom He lendeth breath*
> *Now in His Name rejoice.*
> *For love's blest revelation,*
> *For rest from condemnation,*
> *For uttermost salvation.*
> —Mrs. C. H. Morris

2. *Worship God in Truth*

You discussed in chapter 2 the need to become acquainted with Truth.

By way of review:

a. You must saturate yourself with the Scripture, i.e., God's *written Word.*

b. You must avail yourself of the *declared Word,* i.e., teaching, preaching, singing.

c. You must become better acquainted with the Person of Jesus Christ, i.e., the *Living Word,* as you identify with Him, and as you establish a closer and more intimate relationship with Him.

III. Worship's Decline

The Christian experience usually commences with a sense of joy and excitement which produces a willingness to do all you can for Christ. However, later there may be a tendency to become less and less excited and, as a result, less and less involved. Service, at this point, becomes a duty rather than a delight. The important question is, "Why does this happen?"

> LIST AND DISCUSS AS MANY REASONS AS YOU CAN THINK OF THAT MAY CONTRIBUTE TO THE DECLINE OF WORSHIP.
>
> 1. _____ 4. _____
> 2. _____ 5. _____
> 3. _____ 6. _____

One of the most prevalent problems in the decline of worship is *time*. There are two very important aspects that relate to the effect time has on worship. One is the positive aspect; the other is the negative aspect.

A. Time—The Friend of Worship

Time is your friend as it affects heartache and tragedy. For example, in the event when you experience a serious disappointment or a death in the family, the load seems so heavy and the sorrow so great that you wonder if you will ever recover. God created you with the ability to forget. A few days after a tragedy, the hurt is not quite so keen. God knew that there was no way your human mind and emotions could ever adjust to adding one heartache after another. He knew it would be more than you could humanly stand. You can be thankful that, through the help of the Holy Spirit, the scars of the past begin to fade away.

Under these conditions, then, this benefit is twofold:

1. Your mind was created so that time tends to take the edge off the hurt.

2. You have the advantage of the fact that time allows you to adjust to your circumstances. This adjustment affords you the opportunity of worshiping God because of the growth that has taken place.

B. Time—The Foe of Worship

Time can also affect good relationships in a negative manner. Satan may use the process of time to deteriorate your worship. Here, you must consider the fact that time also takes the edge off your memory as it relates to the vivid recollection of past blessings, or many other good things.

> RECALL AND LIST THREE BLESSINGS OF THE PAST, THE AWARENESS OF WHICH MAY HAVE BEEN DULLED BY TIME.
> 1. _____
> 2. _____
> 3. _____

Time poses the problem of broken promises. An example: "Oh God, if you will heal my son, I'll serve you better and do everything I can at the church for the rest of my life to show you my love." Several days later, the promise to obey is not so keen. A year later, the specific details of the promise are very foggy. In fact, you are not sure that you ever said that—seems like maybe that was someone else!

> RECALL PERSONAL PROMISES THAT WERE FORGOTTEN.
> 1. _____
> 2. _____
> 3. _____

You must be very careful in your devotion to God, in your worship response, to not allow time to destroy the keen edge of your relationship. You must not allow "time adjusting" to phase out your close communication and worship relationship with Him. Determine that your worship will be an on-purpose, active participation in God's Will on a moment-by-moment basis for the rest of your life. In light of the fact that time can work against you in your worship relationship, purposefully guard against the following:

1. Do not allow time to take the original, fine edge off your desire to respond to God. Respond obediently. Express your acts of worship to Him through an "on-purpose" commitment and communication.

2. Do not permit time to cause your relationship to be dimmed by rationalizing, and thereby miss God's Will. You will recall the discussion about "lag-time" in the chapter on "Obedience." Lag-time can become disobedience—thus the loss of an opportunity.

> So when you talk to God and vow to him that you will do something, don't delay in doing it . . .
> Ecclesiastes 5:4a, TLB

> "When you make a vow to the Lord, be prompt in doing whatever it is you promised him, for the Lord demands that you promptly fulfill your vows . . ."
> Deuteronomy 23:21, TLB

There can be continuous joy and excitement in your attitude and activities of worship. Because time can be a negative factor, you must actively, and on purpose, look for ways to worship God out of a "heart" response of reflective love.

Worship is a disciplined response out of a heart of love. However, you must depend upon the Person of the Holy Spirit to help you worship more perfectly.

IV. Worship Denotes Growth

A. The Mandate of Growth

Growth brings about ripe fruit. The growth of your worship must be real. This growth must be progressive, and the days, weeks, and months should ripen your worshipfulness so that the fruit of your worship can develop and become increasingly mature. If your relationship is alive, it must grow.

For example, if a farmer goes out to plant a crop just for an experience, that is one thing. But usually he goes out to plant a crop for the purpose of harvest. He works hard. He plants the seed in the ground. He counts on the fact that he will soon see growth. Ultimately, he'll have the fulfillment of harvest. Just planting with no expectation of growth makes no sense to the average person.

Another example of growth expectation is that of a small baby. There is nothing so beautiful and so miraculous as a tiny baby. He is so cute! He is so much the pride of his father and mother.

They couldn't want anything any more perfect if they could have ordered him from Heaven's own catalog. However, they will naturally be looking for signs of growth in the months and years ahead. What a tragedy should their baby remain twenty-one inches long and ten pounds at age ten years! Even though the baby is perfect for today, he *must* grow.

B. The Meaning of Growth

God is the Object of love if you are being motivated from a pure spirit. Growth in worship becomes more dynamic and *meaningful* as you learn to abandon comfort and pleasure in order to become more self-sacrificing and devoted to God.

> But grow in the grace and knowledge of our Lord and Savior Jesus Christ. To him be glory both now and forever! Amen.
>
> II Peter 3:18, NIV

> ". . . a time is coming and has now come when the true worshippers will worship the Father in spirit and truth, for they are the kind of worshippers the Father seeks."
>
> John 4:23, NIV

In the Book of John, chapter 15, it speaks of abiding in the Vine. You can experience a growing life where God's Spirit can flow through you and nourish your spirit. The natural fruit (or response) will be to honor and serve Him. Worship includes saying "yes" to God's Will. You must resolve the *problems* and *reservations* if you are going to allow growth to take place as the Heavenly Father lives His life through you.

V. Worship Demonstrates Commitment

A. Worship Includes Service

Worship includes giving back to God everything that He has given to you. Oswald Chambers states:

> Worship is giving God the best that He has given you. Be careful what you do with the best you have. Whenever you get a blessing from God, give it back to Him as a love gift. Take time to meditate before God and offer the blessing back to Him in a deliberate act of worship. If you hoard a thing for yourself, it will turn into spiritual dry rot, as the manna did when it was hoarded. God will never let you hold a spiritual thing for yourself, it has to be given back to Him that He may make it a blessing to others.[34]

Do you recall the game children often play called "hot potato"? Someone throws an item, and the object of the game is to receive it, and then see how fast it can be passed on to someone else. Are you willing to receive a blessing from your Heavenly Father, and then, as an act of worship, see how fast you can pass it on to someone else, for His glory?

> "'For I was hungry and you fed me; I was thirsty and you gave me water; I was a stranger and you invited me into your homes, naked and you clothed me; sick and in prison, and you visited me.' Then these righteous ones will reply, 'Sir, when did we ever see you hungry and feed you? Or thirsty and give you anything to drink? Or a stranger, and help you? Or naked, and clothe you? When did we ever see you sick or in prison, and visit you?' And I the King, will tell them, 'When you did it to these my brothers, you were doing it to me.'"
>
> Matthew 25:35-40, TLB

---

[34]*Op. cit.*, Chambers, p. 6.

Oswald Chambers commented regarding service, as follows:

> Service is the overflow of super-abounding devotion ... To serve God is the deliberate love-gift of a nature that has heard the call of God ... The Son of God reveals Himself in me, and I serve Him in the ordinary ways of life out of devotion to Him.[35]

B. Worship Includes Sacrifice

> "No one has greater love than the one who lays down his life for his friends. You are my friends if you do what I command. I no longer call you servants because a servant does not know his master's business. Instead, I have called you friends, for everything that I learned from my Father I have made known to you."
>
> John 15:13-15, NIV

Most of the time it would be much easier to reach a point of commitment where you would be willing to, once and for all, *die physically* for the cause of Christ *rather than live out His Will in a daily life of obedience.*

Jesus has not necessarily asked you to *die* for Him, but rather, to *live* for Him. You can glorify your Father in Heaven by "laying down your life for Him" as a living act of worship.

> If I am a friend of Jesus, I have deliberately and carefully to lay down my life for Him. Salvation is easy because it cost God so much, but the manifestation of it in my life is difficult. God saves a man and endues him with the Holy Spirit, and then says in effect—"Now work it out, be loyal to Me, whilst the nature of things round about you would make you disloyal. I have called you friends." Stand loyal to your friend, and remember that His honour is at stake in your bodily life.[36]

---

[35] *Ibid.*, p. 17.
[36] *Ibid.*, p. 168.

I eagerly expect and hope that I will in no way be ashamed, but will have sufficient courage so that now as always Christ will be exalted in my body, whether by life or by death. For to me, to live is Christ and to die is gain.

Philippians 1:20-21, NIV

Therefore, I urge you, brothers, in view of God's mercy, *to offer yourselves as* living sacrifices, holy and pleasing to God—which is your spiritual worship. Do not conform any longer to the pattern of this world, but be transformed by the renewing of your mind. Then you will be able to test and approve what God's will is—his good, pleasing and perfect will.

Romans 12:1-2, NIV

You also, like living stones, are being built into a spiritual house to be a holy priesthood, offering spiritual sacrifices acceptable to God through Jesus Christ.

I Peter 2:5, NIV

Through Jesus, therefore, let us continually offer to God a sacrifice of praise—the fruit of lips that confess his name.

Hebrews 13:15, NIV

VI. Worship Demands Communication

A. The Human Need for Communication

There is not a wife, husband, or child who does not long for genuine love to be expressed. Every normal person seeks reassurance: "How did I do?" "What did you think?" "Give me some positive input."

As an example, a father loved his little girl very much. He would do everything from day to day that he knew to do for her to show her his love and care.

Yet, in the back of his mind, there was always the question, "I wonder if she still loves me today?"

You see, the little girl had the right to choose to love, and the father was aware of this. He wondered if her friends might have become more important to her than he was. Perhaps her toys or her little horse had captured her attention.

What a great moment for the father, however, when his lap was available, and his little girl would come running and climb up onto his lap and throw her arms around his neck and whisper in his ear, "I love you, Daddy!" In that moment, and for that moment, all of the questions regarding her love were settled.

She had given him the reassurance that she still loved him. No one else nor any other thing had taken his place in her heart. Everyone has a need for the expression of love and reassurance.

B. The Divine Need for Communication

God longs for you to communicate your position of love to Him on a regular basis. Part of your responsibility in worship is to tell Him, "I love you, Heavenly Father."

> What I want from you is your true thanks; I want your promises fulfilled. I want you to trust me in your times of trouble, so I can rescue you, and you can give me glory.
> Psalm 50:14-15, TLB

The paraphrase of Psalm 63:1-8 is so beautiful in the musical, *Celebration of Hope,* by Paul Johnson.

NOTES 294

> Oh God, You are my Father;
> Each morning I'll seek Your face.
> My soul cries out for Your mercy;
> I long for a touch of Your grace.
>
> Though it seems I'm often surrounded
> By a dry and desolate land.
> I behold Your power and glory,
> And I know that I'm safe in Your hand.
>
> Your love is better than life—
> And my heart longs to offer You praise,
> So I'll lift up my hands and I'll worship You,
> And be satisfied all of my days.
>
> When I make my bed in the darkness,
> I will sing with joy a new song,
> And recall all the times that You've rescued me;
> And I'll worship You all my life long.[37]

VII. Conclusion

There are six basic thoughts about worship to be reviewed:

A. You were created to worship God and to have fellowship with Him. You must worship Him in spirit and in truth.

B. As you present yourself a living sacrifice to God, you mirror and magnify His Image.

C. Time can work for or against you in worship.

D. True worship includes spiritual growth. The Heavenly Father wants to live His life through you to His glory.

E. The committed life of worship includes giving back to God everything that He has given to you.

---

[37] © Copyright 1972 by Lillenas Publishing Co. All rights reserved. Used by special permission of the publisher.

F. Just as you have the human need for communication, so God has need for your communication with Him: "I love you, Heavenly Father." You can live out the Purpose for which you were created: to worship and have fellowship with Him.

REVIEW EXERCISE

1. Give your definition of worship.

2. Write one Scripture from memory dealing with worship.

3. List four aids to worship.

4. What effect does time have on worship?

5. Explain the "hot-potato" concept in worship.

6. What does Romans 12:1 have to do with worship?

Temptation
(outline)

I. Temptation Is Natural

II. Temptation Is Neutral

III. Temptation Is Necessary

    A. Dealing with Temptation

    B. Different Levels of Temptation

        1. The Physical
        2. The Psychical
        3. The Spiritual

Conclusion

In Him we have peace. In Him we have power!
Preserved by His grace throughout the dark hour.
In all our temptations He keeps us, to prove
His utmost salvation, His fulness of love.
—John Wesley

Temptation

TEMPT: (1) To put to trial, to test;
(2) To endeavor to persuade, to induce, incite.
—Webster

In a previous chapter, it was pointed out that God is glorified when man *worships* Him by choosing righteousness. It is the "on-purpose" act of the will in selecting alternatives that determines your moral relationship with God. In the chapters on "The Born-Again Life" and "The Spirit-Filled Life," it was learned that man is continuously confronted with the choice of alternatives. True Christian character is built as a result of successfully handling those encounters. The outcome of *temptation* will always reveal the true source of your *faith* and the *object* of your *dependence*. It will, likewise, reveal your spiritual "readiness level" . . . i.e., can you be trusted with the next installment of "insight-opportunity-obedience"? (See chapter on "Obedience.")

Confrontation, then, assists in the preparation of man to become all that God had in mind for him to become. It gives man an opportunity to crystallize his desires and, by choice, determine his ultimate destiny.

NOTES 300

Temptation is not to be taken lightly, for within each occasion of temptation, there lies the possibility of moral conflict, defeat, and eventual damnation.

How, then is TEMPTATION related to the concepts of CONFRONTATION and CONFLICT that you learned about in the chapters on "The Born-Again Life" and "The Spirit-Filled Life"? For discovering that relationship, look closer now at the following definitions:

TEMPT:	(1)	to put to trial, to test;
	(2)	to endeavor to persuade, to induce, incite
PERSUADE:		to argue into an opinion or procedure
INDUCE:		to move by persuasion or influence
INCITE:		arouse to action
TEST:		examination or trial, subjection to conditions that show the real character

In the space below fill in the definitions for "Confrontation" and "Conflict." (If you need help in recalling these definitions, please turn back to page 102.)

```
CONFRONTATION _____
              _____
CONFLICT _____
         _____
```

For purposes of this study, you may define *temptation* as follows:

> TEMPTATION: an endeavor to *persuade* a person to actively *select* a *certain alternative* by means of argument and influence. (This usually carries the connotation of being tempted to do evil.)

Confrontation is simply where you are faced with moral alternatives. Then comes an endeavor (a "sales pitch") to persuade, induce, and incite you to *choose one* of the *alternatives* . . . this is *temptation*. *Conflict* comes when you begin to recognize that there is something inside you that wants *both alternatives*.

You begin to identify first with one alternative, then the other. This moral conflict is a clash, a struggle, a battle for mastery of your spiritual control center . . . your heart. But this conflict can also affect your psychical and physical functions. The price of *truce* to such a conflict is always the activity of the will. You must choose an alternative.

In this chapter you will be directed to consider three important aspects of temptation.

I. Temptation is Natural
II. Temptation is Neutral
III. Temptation is Necessary

I. Temptation Is Natural

> No temptation has overtaken you but such as is *common* to man; and God is faithful, who will not allow you to be tempted beyond what you are able, but with the temptation will provide the way of escape also, that you may be able to endure it.
> I Corinthians 10:13, NASB

Many good Spirit-filled Christians are confused at the point of temptation. Their reasoning is this: "If I am filled with the Holy Spirit, how can I be tempted to think and react as I sometimes do?"

Temptation always comes through the natural desires and functions of man and is a consequence of free moral agency being worked out in a world torn between evil and righteousness. If God is to be glorified by man's freely choosing righteousness, then man must be subjected to a *probationary position* to see if, *in fact, he will choose correctly.* He must be placed in a position of confrontation where he becomes aware of both alternatives, i.e., *righteousness* and *evil.* He must be exposed to the persuasion and solicitation of the evil representative as well as the wooing and convincing appeal of righteousness. God allowed man to be subjected to this position with the inevitable cost of the possibility that man might choose evil and reject righteousness. Temptation was permitted because there was no other way human obedience could be tested and perfected. W. T. Purkiser states: "Man is tempted to use his natural desires in the wrong way or for a wrong goal. Unless there is desire, there is no temptation."[38]

Even if you are a Spirit-filled Christian, you still retain certain natural susceptibilities to sin. Every natural, legitimate, lawful function of your person is vulnerable to cause an occasion for temptation.

However, your most likely point of vulnerability *will probably not be* the same as that of the person next to you. You are most susceptible at the point of your own affinity, i.e., your personal likes and dislikes, which will largely determine your potential areas of confrontation and temptation. You will usually be tempted in an area where you are most sensitive to a particular type of appeal. For example: You would not be tempted to cheat on your income tax if you had not made enough money that year to be required to fill out a tax form.

---

[38] *Op. cit.*, Purkiser, p. 430.

Stop now, and consider the statement in the box below. Then, proceed to fill in the blanks.

> THE AREAS IN MY LIFE IN WHICH I AM MOST SUSCEPTIBLE TO TEMPTATION
> 1. _____
> 2. _____
> 3. _____
> 4. _____
> 5. _____
> 6. _____

You can be sure that every temptation that confronts you comes because it exactly suits your condition. Satan knows you very well. He knows your likes and dislikes. He, therefore, is extremely successful in knowing exactly where and when to tempt you. He will naturally use any avenue of moral or amoral desire as an occasion to persuade you to actively select an evil alternative that would pervert the good and separate you from God.

> God created man male and female, with righteousness and true holiness, having the Law of God written in their hearts, and power to fulfill it; and yet under a possibility of transgressing, being left to the liberty of their own will which was subject to change.
> From the WESTMINSTER CONFESSION

> As the most dangerous winds may enter at little openings, so the devil never enters more dangerously than by little unobserved incidents, which seem to be nothing, yet insensibly open the heart to great temptations.[39]

---

[39] *Op. cit.*, Wesley, *Plain Account of Christian Perfection*, p. 100.

II. Temptation Is Neutral

> For we do not have a high priest who cannot sympathize with our weaknesses, but one who has been tempted in all things as we are, *yet without sin.*
> Hebrews 4:15, NASB

Down through the years, many good, sincere Christians have been robbed of living the victorious life. This robbery was due to their having been taught that even the slightest evil thought passing through the conscious mind was absolute and sure proof that they were still evil. That brought about insurmountable discouragement, and they fell, often from the very fear of having fallen.

Temptation, in and of itself, *is not sin.*

Sin is in the *response.*

> But each one is tempted when he is carried away and enticed by his own lust. Then when lust has conceived, it gives birth to sin; and when sin is accomplished, it brings forth death.
> James 1:14-15, NASB

James is saying, here, that when wrong desire has conceived . . . (that is, when man's free will, his power of choice, has been married to the perverted use of that legitimate instinct) . . . *when he has consented to it,* and joined himself to it, then the child of that marriage is "SIN."

Seeing that temptation is not sin has brought liberation to many Christians who have had unwarranted condemnation imposed upon them due to the misunderstanding of their instincts and desires. Usually, as a consequence, their *Christian profession* was nothing more than hypocrisy because, inside themselves, they had a secret contradiction to what they were claiming.

> Recall and write the definition of SIN as an *Act:* _____
> _____
> _____,
> which brings: _____
> _____
> _____.
>
> (see page 83)

L. T. Corlett summarizes the nature of temptation:

> Temptation is always accompanied by a desire to follow the suggestion. First in the process the attention is drawn either to a mental contemplation or to an object outside of man. If that attention is centered on either one, a legitimate desire is aroused for that object. The suggestion is made from the tempter that it would be advantageous to enjoy the situation. The next step is the suggestion of how to obtain this end. Then the will is attached and the individual must make a decision as to whether or not the suggestion for satisfaction in an illegitimate manner will be carried out.
>
> The desire will at times be very strong and it may last for a period of time, but the guilt and condemnation do not come to an individual because of the desire. Temptation has not become sin simply because desire has been awakened. Temptation becomes sin only when the will decides in favor of the suggestion of the tempter. At times the battle is intense . . . but, as long as the will is held steady in alignment with the will of God and against the suggestion to evil, the individual has not sinned.[40]

---

[40]Lewis T. Corlett, *Holiness in Practical Living* (Kansas City, Mo.: Beacon Hill Press, 1948), p. 56.

III. Temptation Is Necessary

A. Dealing with Temptation

> Dear brothers, is your life full of difficulties and temptations? Then be happy, for when the way is rough, your patience has a chance to grow. So let it grow, and don't try to squirm out of your problems. For when your patience is finally in full bloom, then you will be ready for anything, strong in character, full and complete.
> James 1:2-4, TLB

Temptations, met and mastered, are the only high road to stabilization of character. For, *character is the sum total of all the alternatives which you have chosen*. There is no way that *spiritual progress* can take place without your choosing that *alternative which is consistent* with the desires and nature of the Holy Spirit.

> We can rejoice, too, when we run into problems and trials for we know that they are good for us—they help us learn to be patient. And patience develops strength of character in us and helps us trust God more each time we use it until finally our hope and faith are strong and steady. Then, when that happens, we are able to hold our heads high no matter what happens and know that all is well, for we know how dearly God loves us, and we feel this warm love everywhere within us because God has given us the Holy Spirit to fill our hearts with his love.
> Romans 5:3-5, TLB

You can depend upon God's love and assistance to help you choose the correct alternative in every situation of temptation. Times of testing *are essential* to your progress and maturity. *Christian maturity will not take place without choice*. In order to have choice, there must be at least two alternatives. These alternatives will be based on desires. Desires will ultimately be governed by your basic motivation. Basic moral motivation stems from your heart.

The heart is controlled by either carnal selfishness, or righteousness, i.e., . . . the Holy Spirit. That is why it is so important for you to have a Spirit-filled and controlled life when it comes to dealing with temptation.

> The best means of resisting the Devil is, to destroy whatever of the world remains in us, in order to raise to God, upon its ruins a building all of love, then shall we begin in this fleeting life, to love God as we shall love Him in eternity.[41]

God does not exempt His Children from times of examination and testing.

> "I know, my God, that you test men to see if they are good men."
> I Chronicles 29:17, TLB

He counts on His Children *coming through the trials* stronger than ever and more dependent upon *His* love and power.

> And we know that all things work together for good to them that love God, to them who are the called according to his purpose.
> Romans 8:28, KJV

The existence of temptation and testing in your life must never be allowed to become a point of discouragement. Difficulties are not *intruders,* but rather, *opportunities* for spiritual growth and maturation. They give opportunity for worship and praise to God.

> What I want from you is your true thanks; I want your promises fulfilled. I want you to trust me in your times of trouble, so I can rescue you, and you can give me glory.
> Psalm 50:14-15, TLB

If you have Christ living in you through the Holy Spirit, you already, potentially, have victory over any given situation, for, "Greater is He that is in you than he that is in the world." Christ has already overcome the world and makes that "overcoming power" available to you . . . NOW!

---

[41]*Op. cit.*, Wesley, p. 99.

NOTES

> I would like to accept Christ's offer for spiritual victory over the following *areas of difficulty* in my life.
> _____
> _____
> _____
> _____
> _____

Even though God uses times of difficulty and temptation for your spiritual maturation and growth, yet, you can be assured that *God never solicits you to do evil.*

> When tempted, no one should say, "God is tempting me." For God cannot be tempted by evil, nor does he tempt anyone . . .
>
> James 1:13, NIV

B. Different Levels of Temptation

It is difficult for the human mind to grasp the fact that it was necessary for Jesus to undergo examination and be subjected to temptation by Satan. It is of great interest to observe that Christ's period of temptation immediately followed the descending of the Holy Spirit upon Him in the form of a dove and the announcement by the Voice out of Heaven saying, "This is my beloved Son, in whom I am well pleased" (Matthew 3:17, KJV).

> Some of your most crucial temptations will follow immediately on the heels of a "spiritual high point."

Look now at Christ's experience with temptation, and observe the way temptation affected His different functional levels.

1. *The Physical*

> Then Jesus was led up by the Spirit into the wilderness to be tempted by the devil. And after He had fasted forty days and forty nights, He then became hungry. And the tempter came and said to Him, "If You are the Son of God, command that these stones become bread." But He answered and said, "It is written, 'MAN SHALL NOT LIVE ON BREAD ALONE, BUT ON EVERY WORD THAT PROCEEDS OUT OF THE MOUTH OF GOD.'"
>
> Matthew 4:1-4, NASB

It seems that Satan always appeals on the level of the physical desires first. Such was the case with Eve. If Satan can trip you up on this level, he need go no further.

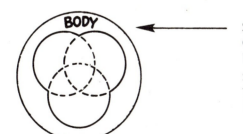

Satan appealed *first* to Christ on the physical level. Christ was hungry: "Command that these stones become bread."

This is a common temptation, and often results in *conflict* in the born-again Christian's life. It would be characterized by the *perverted* or *out-of-balance accumulation* of things that would satisfy the *legitimate physical needs;* examples: clothes, cars, food, sex, recreation, etc.

2. *The Psychical*

> Then the devil took Him into the Holy City; and he stood Him on the pinnacle of the temple, and said to Him, "If You are the Son of God throw Yourself down; for it is written, 'HE WILL GIVE HIS ANGELS CHARGE CONCERNING YOU; AND ON THEIR HANDS THEY WILL BEAR YOU UP, LEST YOU STRIKE YOUR FOOT AGAINST A STONE.'" Jesus said to him, "On the other hand, it is written, 'YOU SHALL NOT TEMPT THE LORD YOUR GOD.'"
> Matthew 4:5-7, NASB

With suave subtlety, Satan, then, appealed to Christ's psychical function. He *"reasoned"* with Him by actually quoting Scripture to Christ. Satan also was trying to persuade Jesus, through His *emotions* to *do* the "spectacular" . . . be the miracle worker . . . "jump off the roof."

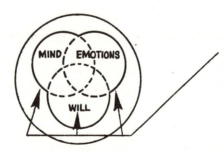

Satan secondly appealed to the psychical function of Christ, i.e., His reason, emotions, and will.

3. *The Spiritual*

> Again, the devil took Him to a very high mountain, and showed Him all the kingdoms of the world, and their glory; and he said to Him, "All these things will I give You, if You fall down and *worship me.*" Then Jesus said to him, "Begone, Satan! For it is written, 'YOU SHALL WORSHIP THE LORD YOUR GOD, AND SERVE HIM ONLY.'" Then the devil left Him; and behold, angels came and began to minister to Him.
>
> Matthew 4:8-11, NASB

Here Satan was the most subtle. He dealt, in this temptation, with *worship.* As you have previously learned, you must worship in spirit. Satan was headed directly toward the "control room" . . . the heart.

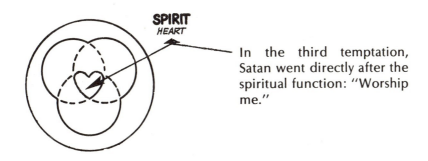

In the third temptation, Satan went directly after the spiritual function: "Worship me."

This is the most subtle, because even the most seasoned saint is vulnerable at this point. . . *misdirected worship.* These are temptations dealing with spiritual attitudes and may manifest themselves in varied forms . . . from *self-pity* to *spiritual pride.* Is there anything in your life that you are worshiping other than God?

Yes ☐   No ☐

It is important to note here that Christ never answered Satan in any of His temptations with a simple "no" that might have left the nagging temptation unrelieved. But rather, by the *use of God's Word,* He gave a triumphant positive that swallowed up the negative. That technique and power is available to you today! "Well," you might say, "if temptation is so necessary for growth and, in fact, if temptation is so good, then let's go find some!" But Christ gives a very clear warning at this point when He makes the admonition to pray, "Lead us not into temptation, but deliver us from evil," and when He advises that you "Watch and pray lest ye enter into temptation." Temptation is not to be taken lightly—much less with an unwise spirit of "bravado." In dealing with temptation on any level, you must recognize the Source of your strength and victory.

CONCLUSION

You have now learned that confrontation is the facing of moral alternatives and that temptation is an endeavor to persuade you to actively select a certain alternative by means of argument and influence. You have also learned that temptation is: (1) Natural, (2) Neutral, and (3) Necessary. Between you and each level of spiritual maturation that God has designed for you, stands a situation that, of necessity, includes temptation.

When you have faced that real life and death struggle, one where the facts on the one hand look so sweet, so sensible and so secure . . . yet . . . on the other hand there is an awareness of the simple, consistent "oughtness" of God's persuasion . . . and when you have come through that situation, having chosen what you know to be "right" . . . then you move from a position of theory and "simple lip service to God" to a position of whole-hearted willingness to obey Him regardless of the personal cost.

Let John Wesley's prayer be yours . . .

> Oh may thy love possess me whole
> My joy, my treasure; and my crown
> *Strange fires far from my heart remove*
> My every act, word, thought, be love.[42]

---

[42] *Ibid.*, p. 7.

Personal Evangelism
(outline)

I. The Principles of Personal Evangelism

   A. Every Christian Must Be a Witness

   B. Every Christian Must Be a Trainee

   C. Every Christian Must Be a Trainer

II. The Problems of Personal Evangelism

   A. Fear of Failure
      1. Your Sense of Inadequacy
         a. Inadequate Understanding
         b. Inadequate Spiritual Experience
         c. Inadequate Communication Training
      2. Your Overactive Imagination
      3. Your Uncertainty of the Other Person's Intention

   B. Facing Objections

   C. Finding New Prospects
      1. People Visiting Your Own Local Church
      2. Parents of the Sunday School Children
      3. People in Your Own Surroundings

III. The Pedagogy of Personal Evangelism

   A. Understand

   B. Experience

   C. Communicate

IV. The Presentation of Personal Evangelism

A. Basic Outline

1. Qualification
2. Presentation for the Born-Again Life
3. Follow-through and Discipleship After Presentation and Acceptance of the Born-Again Life
4. Presentation for the Spirit-Filled Life
5. Follow-through and Discipleship After Presentation and Acceptance of the Spirit-Filled Life

B. Outline Plus Reasons and Scriptures

1. Qualification
2. Presentation for the Born-Again Life
3. Follow-through and Discipleship After Presentation and Acceptance of the Born-Again Life
4. Presentation for the Spirit-Filled Life
5. Follow-through and Discipleship After Presentation and Acceptance of the Spirit-Filled Life

C. Sample Presentation in Conversation Form

1. Qualification
2. Presentation for the Born-Again Life
3. Follow-through and Discipleship After Presentation and Acceptance of the Born-Again Life
4. Presentation for the Spirit-Filled Life
5. Follow-through and Discipleship After Presentation and Acceptance of the Spirit-Filled Life

Give me one hundred preachers who fear nothing but sin and desire nothing but God, and I care not a straw whether they be clergymen or laymen; such alone will shake the gates of hell and set up the "Kingdom of heaven on earth."

—John Wesley

Personal Evangelism

EVANGELISM: A preaching of, or a zealous effort to spread, the Gospel

—Webster

In the previous thirteen chapters of this material, you have been presented with the basic concepts that will help you not only enter into a vital relationship with Christ, but also help you become an established, victorious Christian. However, there is now an additional step that you must take. The Master wants you not only to be a *Disciple* . . . but also a *Discipler*. There is no way you can fulfill the *Great Commission* without *sharing* your faith. The sharing of this great new life with those around you will be accomplished through *Personal Evangelism*.

Perhaps the most encouraging single revelation in the evangelical world today is the vast army of unused laymen! This is the *most strategic key* to evangelizing the world. You are a part of that great potential army. Only when you become *trained, motivated,* and *involved* will you be able to *change your world*. What if this sleeping army would awaken and confront the known world with the claims of the Gospel? What a privilege it is to be a part of that awakening army through Personal Evangelism!

The subject of Personal Evangelism will be presented in this chapter and will include the following areas for your consideration:

    I. The Principles of Personal Evangelism
   II. The Problems of Personal Evangelism
  III. The Pedagogy of Personal Evangelism
  IV. The Presentation of Personal Evangelism

I. The Principles of Personal Evangelism

A. Every Christian Must Be a Witness

Christ's directive to "go and make disciples" does not make allowance for any exceptions. There is no logic flexible enough to release any Christian from this order. Exactly how and when you are to witness is not clearly revealed. But the *necessity of your witnessing is essential.*

Christ began His ministry with the words, "Come, follow me . . . and I will make you fishers of men" (Matthew 4:19, NIV). *He closed His ministry* with the words, "go and make disciples" (Matthew 28:19, NIV). The Discipling activities of the early church are recorded in the Book of Acts. The first-century church was characterized *by its love and enthusiasm for Personal Evangelism.*

B. Every Christian Must Be a Trainee

There is no way you can become proficient in any area without training.

> Study to shew thyself approved unto God, a workman that needeth not to be ashamed, rightly dividing the word of truth.
> II Timothy 2:15, KJV

The imperative declared here by Paul is not for the clergy alone ... it is for everyone! More than 99% of the Christian world is composed of laymen. If this great, potential army of laymen is to be *effective* ... *it must be trained*. The duty of the Christian minister is to see to the training of his people.

> It was he who gave some to be apostles, some to be prophets, some to be evangelists, and some to be pastors and teachers, to prepare God's people for works of service, so that the body of Christ may be built up ...
> Ephesians 4:11-12, NIV

As a Disciple, you must be involved in a program of becoming better equipped to share your faith.

C. Every Christian Must Be a Trainer

Professional ministers are not the only ones who need to be trained. Neither are these ministers the only ones who need to be *actively involved in training others.* There is a limit to the number of people any professional minister or church leader can train.

Some years ago in industry, there was a study undertaken to determine the number of people any one person could supervise effectively. The results of that study show that, in most cases, one person could effectively supervise only seven to twelve people.

Dr. James Kennedy has claimed that 95% of those who are Christians never lead anyone else to Christ. Part of the problem lies in the lack of sufficient numbers of trainers. You, and all of the born-again believers that you know, must become actively involved in training others if the masses of the world are to be confronted with the claims of the Gospel.

II. The Problems of Personal Evangelism

It won't take you long, if you honestly want to share your faith with those in your world, to learn that there are problems inherent in this great task of evangelism. The mistaken idea is, that because you are dealing with spiritual issues, God will automatically remove all obstacles. This is unrealistic. You cannot ignore problems and simply expect them to go away. This is not only foolish, but also fatal. Perhaps the three most pressing problems are:

- Fear of Failure
- Facing Objections
- Finding New Prospects

A. Fear of Failure

Essentially, the problem of fear arises from three sources:

- Your sense of inadequacy
- Your overactive imagination
- Your uncertainty of the other person's intention.

1. *Your sense of inadequacy*

    A sense of inadequacy may stem from an:

    - Inadequate understanding
    - Inadequate spiritual experience
    - Inadequate communication training.

a. If you sense a fear of inadequacy stemming from what appears to be a lack of understanding, go back and review chapters 3 ("Man"), 4 ("The Born-Again Life"), and 5 ("The Spirit-Filled Life"). It is further suggested that you pray, asking God for wisdom.

James, in his Epistle, states,

> If any of you lacks wisdom, he should ask God, who gives generously to all without finding fault, and it will be given to him.
> James 1:5, NIV

b. If your fear comes from an inadequate relationship with Christ, it must be immediately remedied. A present, vital relationship with Christ is an imperative. The point of greatest encouragement is that God wants continuous fellowship with you. His drawing, and your responding, will re-establish that fellowship.

c. If your fear is based on a feeling of inadequate communication training, you are now reading the appropriate chapter. This chapter will explore the techniques of approach, presentation, and follow-up. When you complete this chapter, you will have some practical handles for presenting the claims of the Gospel.

2. *Your overactive imagination*

Many times your overactive imagination creates situations and conjures up pictures which do not exist . . . and probably never will. A subtle fear is to presume that, because of a person's position or abilities, he does not need God. This is a trick of Satan to defeat you and the person to whom God has led you. The personal evangelist must remember that *everyone needs what Christ has to offer.*

3. *Your uncertainty of the other person's intention*

Another cause of fear is the uncertainty of the prospect's intentions, possible reactions, and ultimate response. The command of Jesus was simple: "go and tell." The responsibility for the results of that sharing does not lie with the personal evangelist . . . *but with the Holy Spirit.* Your success is not judged on whether the person to whom you witness accepts Christ, but rather, on the fact *that you have shared.* This should eliminate the fear of failure for those who share.

> "But if you warn him to repent and he doesn't, he will die in his sin, and you will not be responsible."
>
> Ezekiel 33:9, TLB

B. Facing Objections

When you present the Gospel, you can expect to face some objections. This is because you are dealing with pride, prejudice, preconceived ideas, and the influence of a personal devil. *The way you face these objections* may tend to be influenced by your own personality.

Some will meet the objections "head-on." *Some will* push the "panic button." *Others will* "shrink," "fall back," and even "freeze."

However, you must accept these objections with grace. You are to be more interested in winning *a person* than winning *a point*. When someone questions your statement, or specifically disagrees with you, the best way to keep the issue *objective,* and not *subjective,* is to say, "Thank you for that point . . . I really appreciate it." As a result, the person is kept from being on the defensive.

Are you really looking for objections? The answer is "no!" But it is always good when the person with whom you are dealing, feels free to object, and feels as though you are willing to face any question he might have.

Here are three ways you can face objections.

1. The objection may be simple and may not hinder your presentation. If so, deal with it *simply* and *quickly.*

2. If it is something you will be dealing with later in your presentation, simply state, "That is a good point . . . and we will talk about it in a few minutes, if this is all right."

3. There is a possibility that some questions or objections will be presented to you that you are unable to answer. First of all, don't be embarrassed or threatened. Just simply take out a pen or pencil, write it down, and tell the person that you are going to find the answer. This kind of interest, and careful writing of his question, shows your genuineness and concern for him.

C. Finding New Prospects

There has never been a day in modern history when prospects seemed more available than today. The *awareness of need,* the popularity and *acceptance of evangelical Christianity,* the *futility of affluence* and artificiality, and the *realization of Christ's soon return* . . . all tend to make people willing to discuss spiritual matters.

In the church, there are several ways that have proved helpful in contacting new prospects.

1. *People visiting your own local church* are some of the best prospects. This is because:

   a. they have visited those of you who will be coming to visit them;

b. they have received help from your service which they attended;

c. they have felt the warmth of the Body of Christ which helps to break down prejudices and preconceived ideas.

2. *Parents of the Sunday School children* in your church are also *prime prospects*. This is because:

a. they normally appreciate your interest in their families;

b. they should feel guilt for not being to their children what they ought to be spiritually;

c. they probably have a deep, though not always acknowledged, desire to have a right relationship with God.

3. *People in your own surroundings can be some of the most likely prospects.* New people in your community, and men's or women's service groups, are only a few of the potentials for prospects.

Whatever system is used, there must be a constant realization that there are more prospects than there are converts. This means that you and your church must be constantly reaching out to a hurting world if you are to carry out the Great Commission.

> "... a man's worst enemies will be right in his own home! If you love your father and mother more than you love me, you are not worthy of being mine; or if you love your son or daughter more than me, you are not worthy of being mine. If you refuse to take up your cross and follow me, you are not worthy of being mine."
> Matthew 10:36-38, TLB

III. The Pedagogy of Personal Evangelism

As you will recall from chapter 1, "Mandate of the Master," the basic teaching method of this entire Discipling Curriculum has been:

- Understand
- Experience
- Communicate.

In chapters 3, 4, and 5—"Man," "The Born-Again Life," and "The Spirit-Filled Life"—the major emphasis was on *Understanding* and *Experiencing*. Chapters 6-13 centered around the *concepts of spiritual growth* through *Understanding* and *Experiencing*. In this chapter on *"Personal Evangelism,"* you will apply the third ingredient of *Communicating* those things which you have understood and experienced. It is important now for you to apply this same pedagogy (Understand, Experience, Communicate) to Personal Evangelism.

A. Understand

There are many Christians within the fellowship of the church who possess a spiritual experience which *far surpasses their understanding*. This need not—and should not—be true. If you are going to be an effective personal evangelist, you will need to *know who and what* man is (chapter 3, "Man") and *his condition* prior to his conversion (chapter 4, "The Born-Again Life").

The degree to which you understand *man's need* and *God's provision* will have a direct bearing on your effectiveness.

B. Experience

There are some within the church, and many outside it, who have an *understanding far beyond their experience*. There are few instances when you, as a personal evangelist, will lead someone else to an experience with Christ beyond what you presently possess.

Perhaps the greatest single factor going for you as a personal evangelist is *your own personal relationship with God.* There are three elements which contribute to experience:

- spiritual condition
- consistency
- credibility.

Your good life will do much to prepare the heart of the possible convert.

When a personal evangelist is sensitive to the Spirit of God in his own life, the timing, the wording, and the atmosphere all work together.

C. Communicate

Once understanding and experience are in harmony, you are in a position to share Jesus Christ. The word *communicate* has its basis in the word *commune,* which simply means, "to share" or "have in common." It could best be expressed in terms of the personal evangelist as, "One person sharing with another the message of salvation."

Perhaps the greatest single reason for a formal study of Personal Evangelism is to prepare you to the very greatest degree possible to help you communicate what you have learned and experienced during these first 13 chapters.

IV. The Presentation of Personal Evangelism

As a review, please list the eight elements included in the *Born-Again Crisis*.

BORN-AGAIN CRISIS

LIST THE FOUR RESPONSES
1. _____
2. _____
3. _____
4. _____

LIST THE FOUR RESULTS
1. _____
2. _____
3. _____
4. _____

Also, list the eight elements included in the *Spirit-Filled Crisis*.

SPIRIT-FILLED CRISIS

LIST THE FOUR RESPONSES
1. _____
2. _____
3. _____
4. _____

LIST THE FOUR RESULTS
1. _____
2. _____
3. _____
4. _____

It is the intention of this chapter to *equip* you with some *simple, practical handles* which will enable you to *share* that which you have learned in the previous chapters. You are now going to be able to *share this "good news"* with those around you.

Recall the diagram describing the Discipling Building Blocks. Notice how the fulfillment of the *"Mandate of the Master"* is achieved through the final step of *"Personal Evangelism."* This process becomes the *life cycle of the true Disciple.*

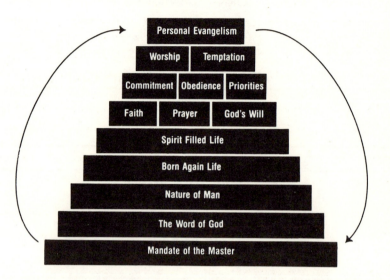

The Discipling Building Blocks are designed to bring you from the point of being a *Disciple* to that of becoming a *Discipler*. This section of the chapter on "Personal Evangelism" will be divided into three sections:

- Basic Outline
- Outline Plus Reasons and Scriptures
- Sample Presentation in Conversation Form.

A. Basic Outline

1. *Qualification:* To identify the position of the prospect

    a. *Approach #1*—To prospects who have attended your church

    (1) Identify their secular background

    (2) Identify their church background

    (3) Identify their relationship with your church

    (4) Identify their relationship with God

> Go to either the Presentation for the Born-Again Life (2)
> or the Presentation for the Spirit-Filled Life (4).

    b. *Approach #2*—To prospects who have not attended your church

       (1) Identify their secular background

       (2) Identify their church background

       (3) Identify their relationship with God

> Go to either the Presentation for the Born-Again Life (2)
> or the Presentation for the Spirit-Filled Life (4).

2. *Presentation for the Born-Again Life*

    a. Divine Initiative

    b. Awareness of Need

    c. Awareness of Moral Choice

    d. Man's Response

3. *Follow-through and Discipleship After Presentation and Acceptance of the Born-Again Life*

    a. Forgiveness

    b. Justification

    c. Regeneration

    d. Adoption

    e. Involvement

4. *Presentation for the Spirit-Filled Life*

    a. Divine Initiative

    b. Awareness of Need

    c. Awareness of Moral Choice

    d. Man's Response

5. *Follow-through and Discipleship After Presentation and Acceptance of the Spirit-Filled Life*

   a. Heart Purity
   b. Heart Perfection
   c. Infilling of the Holy Spirit
   d. Empowering of the Holy Spirit
   e. Involvement

B. Outline Plus Reasons and Scriptures

1. *Qualification*

   It is important to qualify the prospect by identifying his position regarding both his secular and spiritual life. If you are going to help meet that person's need, you must *first identify the need*. The approach will be varied based upon whether the prospect's acquaintance was made through the church or the "workaday world."

   a. *Approach #1—To prospects who have attended your church*

      (1) *Identify their secular background*
      Reason: to establish rapport and find a "common ground" for communication.

      (2) *Identify their church background*
      Reason: establish rapport and discover the prospects' past theological affiliation and to determine the attitude they maintain toward their church and background.

      (3) *Identify their relationship with your church*
      Reason: to establish rapport by allowing them to disclose their feelings and responses to *your church* and its ministry.

(4) *Identify their relationship to God*

Reason: based upon, and utilizing, the rapport that has been established, *determine their present spiritual position* and *discover their need.* The *outcome* of this identification *will determine* whether this visit should become a *situation for the presentation of the Gospel,* or simply *a "public relations" visit,* where you proceed to find out how your church can serve them.

b. *Approach #2—To prospects who have not attended your church*

(same as Approach #1—except "Identify their relationship with your church" has been left out)

(1) Identify their secular background

(2) Identify their church background

(3) Identify their relationship with God

2. *Presentation for the Born-Again Life*

a. *Divine Initiative—God reaching out to man.*

> *"For God so loved* the world that *he gave* his one and only Son, that whoever believes in him shall not perish but have everlasting life."
> John 3:16, NIV

> But God commendeth his love toward us, in that, *while we were yet sinners,* Christ died for us.
> Romans 5:8, KJV

b. *Awareness of Need—Man recognizing his sinful condition.*

> . . . for *all have sinned* and fall short of the glory of God . . .
> Romans 3:23, NIV

> "And He, when *He* comes, *will convict* the world concerning sin, and righteousness, and judgement . . ."
> John 16:8, NASB

c. *Awareness of Moral Choice—Man realizing his moral responsibility.*

> "*Whoever puts his faith in the Son* has eternal life, but *whoever rejects the Son* will not see that life, for God's wrath remains in him."
>
> John 3:36, NIV

d. *Man's Response—Man reacting to his moral responsibility.*

> "Here I am! I stand at the door and knock. *If anyone hears* my voice *and opens* the door, I will go in and eat with him, and he with me."
>
> Revelation 3:20, NIV

> *If we confess* our sins, *he is faithful* and just and will forgive us our sins and purify us from all unrighteousness.
>
> I John 1:9, NIV

3. *Follow-through and Discipleship After Presentation and Acceptance of the Born-Again Life*

This section is to be used to explain to the new Disciple *what has happened in his life.*

a. *Forgiveness—the pardon given to man to free him from the penalty of his sinful acts.*

> "All the prophets testify about him that everyone who believes in him receives *forgiveness* of sins through his name."
>
> Acts 10:43, NIV

> If we confess our sins, he is faithful and just and *will forgive us* our sins and purify us from all unrighteousness.
>
> I John 1:9, NIV

b. *Justification—just as if you had never sinned; a legal act of satisfying the Law.*

> God presented him as a sacrifice of atonement, through faith in his blood. He did this to demonstrate his *justice* . . .
>
> Romans 3:25, NIV

c. *Regeneration—to be "born again"; new life through Christ.*

> Therefore, if anyone is in Christ, he is a *new creation;* the old has gone, the *new has come!*
> II Corinthians 5:17, NIV

d. *Adoption—being received into the Family of God with all privileges of sonship.*

> So you are no longer a slave, *but a son;* and since you are a son, God has made you *also an heir.*
> Galatians 4:7, NIV

> The Spirit himself testifies with our spirit that we are *God's children.* Now if *we are children,* then *we are heirs—heirs of God* and *co-heirs with Christ* . . .
> Romans 8:16-17, NIV

e. *Involvement*

After the prospect has become a born-again Christian, help him to immediately get *involved* in an *active Discipling group.* This will give him the opportunity to become exposed to the "Mandate of the Master," experience the plan of *growth* God has designed for him, and help him see that he, too, can share his faith through *Personal Evangelism.*

4. **Presentation for the Spirit-Filled Life**

> NOTE: Use this presentation only after the qualifying of the prospect has determined the need for his being Spirit-filled.

Diagram the twofold aspect of sin.

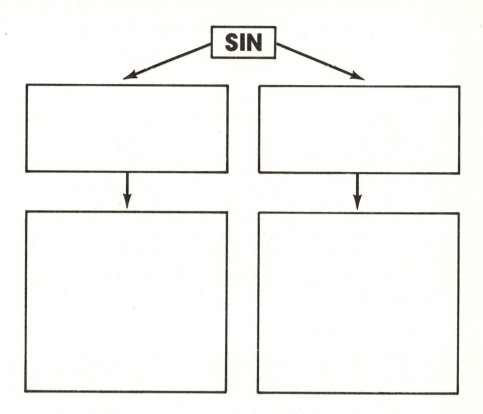

a. *Divine Initiative—God reaching out to deliver man from indwelling sin.*

> And so Jesus also suffered outside the city gate to make *his people holy* through his own blood.
> Hebrews 13:12, NIV

b. *Awareness of Need—Man recognizing his sinful nature.*

> What a wretched man I am! Who will rescue me from this body of death?
> Romans 7:24, NIV

> Blessed are they which do hunger and thirst after righteousness: for they shall be filled.
> Matthew 5:6, KJV

c. *Awareness of Moral Choice—Man realizing his responsibility to seek deliverance from indwelling sin.*

> But just as he who called you is holy, so be holy in all you do; for it is written: "Be holy, because I am holy."
>
> I Peter 1:15-16, NIV

d. *Man's Response—Man reacting to his need for the Spirit-filled life.*

> . . . *present your bodies a living sacrifice,* holy, acceptable unto God, which is your reasonable service.
>
> Romans 12:1, KJV

5. *Follow-through and Discipleship After Presentation and Acceptance of the Spirit-Filled Life*

This section is to be used to explain to the new Spirit-filled Disciple *what has happened in his life.*

a. *Heart Purity—God's act of cleansing your heart from the pollution of original sin.*

> "He made no distinction between us and them, for he *purified their hearts* by faith."
>
> Acts 15:9, NIV

> Cleanse your hands, ye sinners; and *purify your hearts,* ye double minded.
>
> James 4:8b, KJV

b. *Heart Perfection—restoration of God's moral nature through perfected affections and motives.*

> May God himself, the God of peace, *sanctify you through and through.*
>
> 1 Thessalonians 5:23a, NIV

> "*Be perfect,* therefore, *as your heavenly Father* is perfect."
>
> Matthew 5:48, NIV

> Herein is *our love made perfect,* that we may have boldness in the day of judgment: because as he is, *so are we in this world.*
>
> I John 4:17, KJV

c. *Infilling of the Holy Spirit—the Holy Spirit fills and abides within the heart of the believer.*

> . . . *be filled* with the Spirit.
>
> Ephesians 5:18, NIV

> ". . . and he shall give you another Comforter, that he may *abide with you* forever . . . for *he dwelleth with you,* and *shall be in you.*
>
> John 14:16-17, KJV

d. *Empowering of the Holy Spirit—the Power that is received when the Holy Spirit comes to abide.*

> "But you will *receive power* when the Holy Spirit comes on you . . ."
>
> Acts 1:8, NIV

> . . . but tarry ye in the city of Jerusalem until ye be endued with power from on high.
>
> Luke 24:49, KJV

e. *Involvement*

After the prospect has received the Holy Spirit, you should help him to immediately get involved in an active Discipling group, if he is not already. This will give him the opportunity to become exposed to the "*Mandate of the Master,*" experience the plan of *growth* God has designed for him, and help him see that he, too, can share his *born-again* and *Spirit-filled* experience through *Personal Evangelism.*

C. Sample Presentation in Conversation Form

We live in a world where the artificial and insincere seem to dominate interpersonal relationships. If someone says he "really cares" about you, the question may arise in your mind, "What is it he really wants?" or "What strings are attached?"

Everyone seeks genuineness in personal relationships. He is looking for *that one person who is sincerely and genuinely interested in him* . . . a person in whom he can place his trust. To become a person in whom trust is placed, you must *earn the right* by being sincerely interested in the other person. You must establish identification with that person in order for you to share Christ.

> When I am with those whose conscience bothers them easily, *I don't act as though I know it all* and don't say they are foolish; the result is that they are willing to let me help them. Yes, whatever a person is like, *I try to find common ground with him so that he will let me tell him about Christ* and let Christ save him. *I do this to get the Gospel to them* and also for the blessing I myself receive when I see them come to Christ.
> I Corinthians 9:22-23, TLB

1. *Qualification: To identify the position of the prospect*

    (Memorize all Key Statements, Key Questions, and Key Scriptures.)

    a. *Approach #1—To prospects who have attended your church*

    (1) *Identify their secular background*
    Those first few moments of introduction and conversation are very important. To be overly serious would be disastrous. Occasionally, a bit of humor and light conversation will help you open the door to friendship with them.

KEY STATEMENT

> Example: "HELLO, MR. AND MRS. BROWN, MY NAME IS CHARLIE SMITH, AND I'M FROM _____ CHURCH. WE WERE DELIGHTED TO HAVE YOU AND YOUR FAMILY WORSHIP WITH US A FEW DAYS AGO. WE WANTED TO COME BY AND VISIT WITH YOU FOR A LITTLE WHILE."

As you enter the house and are ready to be seated, be aware of something about which to converse, i.e., trophies, musical instruments, family portraits, plants, antiques, etc. Be sure you are talking about *their interests, their lives, their families,* and the *non-controversial* matters of interest to them. *Do not* talk about yourself or your interests *except as they relate to them,* and then only briefly.

(2) *Identify their church background*

If you can become aware, to some degree, of their theological background, their depth of training, and special interests, you will be better prepared to handle the questions that may arise.

KEY STATEMENT

> "WHAT AN EXCITING DAY TO BE A PART OF A GOOD CHURCH!"

KEY QUESTION

> "WHAT CHURCH DO YOU REGULARLY ATTEND?"

(3) *Identify their relationship with your church*

KEY QUESTION

> "HOW DID YOU HAPPEN TO VISIT OUR CHURCH?"

If their answer is . . . friends, special services, or advertising, you may wish to respond, *"That's exciting, Mr. Brown. We are always interested in the way people learn about our church!"* If friends . . . *"They're such nice folk"* (if you know them). If special service . . . *"That was an especially meaningful time for me."* If advertising . . . *"That was an attractive ad or commercial."*

"WHAT DID YOU LIKE BEST ABOUT OUR CHURCH?"	KEY QUESTION

(a) If they speak to a particular ministry, such as the music or the pastor's message, your response may be: *"More than anything else, we want to be a church who sincerely cares about meeting the needs of people in our world. Every ministry in our church is committed to this end."*

(b) If they speak about the warmth and friendliness of the congregation, your response may be: *"The reason that you sensed that warmth and friendliness is because our relationship to Christ is the most meaningful experience in our lives."*
Note: Regardless of their response, continue with this KEY STATEMENT in a *reflective manner.*

"AS I LOOK BACK OVER MY LIFE, OUR CHURCH HAS BEEN SO IMPORTANT IN HELPING ME, NOT ONLY TO ACCEPT CHRIST, BUT TO LEARN TO KNOW HIM SO MUCH BETTER. THE MANY KINDS OF MINISTRIES IN THE CHURCH HELP ME (and my family) GROW IN THE LORD."	KEY STATEMENT

Note: Remember, *you are continuing to earn the right to later ask them the real question,* concerning their relationship with God. Remember too, that *the Holy Spirit is actively involved* in this situation and is extremely interested in the results.

(4) *Identify their personal relationship with God*

You will be dealing with prospects in one of four spiritual conditions:

- Those who profess to be a Christian and *have a vital relationship with God.*
  Requires public relations call

- Those who profess to be a Christian but *do not have a vital relationship with God.*
  Requires Born-Again Presentation (p. 342)

- Those who *do not profess* to be a Christian but are somewhat interested in the benefits of the Christian life.
  Requires Born-Again Presentation (p. 342)

- Those who *are born-again Christians* and are seeking the Spirit-filled life.
  Requires Spirit-Filled Presentation (p. 349)

The following approach can be used in dealing with a person *in any one of the above spiritual conditions.*

"BILL OR JANE, IT HAS BEEN SO GREAT VISITING WITH YOU." (Wait for a response.)	KEY STATEMENT
"YOUR INTEREST IN SPIRITUAL THINGS IS EVIDENT IN OUR CONVERSATION." (Wait for a response.)	KEY STATEMENT
(With great tenderness) "HAVE YOU EVER KNOWN CHRIST AS YOUR PERSONAL SAVIOR?" (Wait for a response.)	KEY QUESTION
"IS YOUR RELATIONSHIP WITH CHRIST MEANINGFUL AND SATISFYING TO YOU?"	KEY QUESTION

Note: There are occasions when people will not be totally honest at this point, but this still gives no reason to argue. It is better to win a person than a point. God knows their heart, and He can deal judgment or conviction—you can only manifest love and acceptance.

If their answer is *"YES,"* then your conversation becomes a *public relations visit,* and *proceed to find out how your church can better serve them.*

If their answer is *"NO,"* your next question is:

"BILL OR JANE, I'M SURE YOU WOULD ALLOW ME TO SHARE SOME SCRIPTURE WITH YOU, WOULDN'T YOU?"	KEY QUESTION

You then proceed with the "Presentation of the Born-Again Life."

  b. *Approach #2—To prospects who have not attended your church*

   (1) *Identify their secular background*

   (2) *Identify their church background*

   (3) *Identify their personal relationship with God*

   Note: You may use the same format as is used in Approach #1, with the exception of references to the church.

   (Number 3 of Approach #1 has been deleted as it deals with your own church which they have not yet attended.)

 2. *Presentation for the Born-Again Life*

  a. *Divine Initiative*

KEY QUESTION	"BILL OR JANE, DO YOU REALIZE THAT GOD IS REACHING OUT TO MAN?"

The Scriptures declare:

KEY SCRIPTURES	**For God so loved** the world, that **he gave** his only begotten Son, that whosoever believeth in him should not perish, but have everlasting life.
	         John 3:16, KJV
	But God commendeth his love toward us, in that, while we were yet sinners, Christ died for us.
	         Romans 5:8, KJV

KEY STATEMENTS	"GOD KNOWS AND **LOVES YOU AND ME** VERY MUCH. HE HAS DESIGNED A SPECIAL PLAN FOR YOUR LIFE. ISN'T THAT EXCITING?" "GOD HAS NOT WAITED FOR YOU TO REACH OUT TO HIM, BUT IS RIGHT NOW REACHING DOWN TO SAVE YOU FROM YOUR SINS AND SHARE WITH YOU HIS PLAN."

b. *Awareness of Need*

"BILL OR JANE, DO YOU REALIZE THAT GOD HELPS MAN RECOGNIZE HIS SINFUL CONDITION?"	KEY QUESTION

Paul clearly establishes the fact that all have sinned.

. . . For all have sinned and fall short of the glory of God . . . Romans 3:23, NIV	KEY SCRIPTURE

(1) When we look around at our world, as great as it is, we are all aware that something is wrong.

(2) It is the work of the Holy Spirit to bring all men to this awareness of their sins.

". . . And He, when He (the Holy Spirit) comes, will convict the world concerning sin . . ." John 16:8, NASB	KEY SCRIPTURE

c. *Awareness of Moral Choice*

"BILL OR JANE, DO YOU REALIZE YOUR GREATEST POWER IS THE POWER TO CHOOSE?"	KEY QUESTION

The Bible is very clear in confronting man with the important fact of a moral choice.

"**Whoever puts his faith in the Son** has eternal life, but **whoever rejects the Son** will not see that life, for God's wrath remains on him." John 3:36, NIV	KEY SCRIPTURE

It is an important moment when you recognize things in your life that are *not pleasing to God*. To simply realize they are wrong is not enough.

Many would like *for God or someone else* to make that moral choice for them. But that would reduce man to a mechanical robot or machine. *The power to choose* that God gave to man is his *greatest power*. However, with this great power comes *grave responsibility*.

d. *Man's Response*

KEY QUESTION
> "BILL OR JANE, DO YOU REALIZE THAT EVERYONE RESPONDS TO GOD ONE WAY OR ANOTHER?"

Everyone gives a response to God. Either he repents of his sins and accepts Christ, or he rejects God's loving call.

Christ is beautifully pictured in Revelation, saying,

KEY SCRIPTURE
> "Here I am! I stand at the door and knock. If anyone **hears my voice** and **opens the door,** I will go in and eat with him, and he with me."
> Revelation 3:20, NIV

KEY QUESTION
> "BILL OR JANE, YOU MAY ASK, 'HOW DO I OPEN THE DOOR?'"

John makes it very clear when he says,

KEY SCRIPTURE
> **If we confess** our sins, he is faithful and just and **will forgive** us our sins and purify us from all unrighteousness.
> I John 1:9, NIV

KEY QUESTION
> "BILL OR JANE, DOES THIS MAKE SENSE TO YOU?"

If their answer is *"NO,"* then you simply and softly say, "WHAT PART OF IT TROUBLES YOU?" Then you begin to deal with their questions systematically.

If their answer is *"YES,"* you then move to the next question.

KEY QUESTION

> "BILL OR JANE, IS THERE ANY GOOD REASON WHY, RIGHT HERE IN THE PRIVACY OF THIS ROOM, YOU WOULDN'T WANT TO ACCEPT (or— RENEW YOUR RELATIONSHIP WITH) JESUS CHRIST AS YOUR PERSONAL SAVIOR?"

If their answer is *"YES,"* remember, regardless of the reason, you are more interested in winning a person than a point. Therefore, if it is a matter of misunderstanding something, clear that up simply and softly; but if they are backing down, let them do so with warmth and continued acceptance.

If their answer is *"NO,"* simply recapitulate the presentation in no more than sixty seconds, and then suggest that you have a simple prayer together.

When they say *"NO,"* suggest that you pray a brief *prayer of thanking God that Bill and Jane have decided* to accept Christ; then *if they know how to pray,* suggest they follow your prayer—but if *they don't know how,* or would like some help in praying, then simply pray a prayer of confession, faith, and thanks for them, and ask them to repeat each phrase.

NOTES

3. Follow-through and Discipleship After Presentation and Acceptance of the Born-Again Life

a. Forgiveness

KEY QUESTION
> "ISN'T IT A GREAT FEELING TO KNOW THAT YOUR SINS ARE FORGIVEN, AND THAT YOU HAVE BEEN PARDONED?"

KEY SCRIPTURE
> If we confess our sins, he is faithful and just and will forgive us our sins and purify us from all unrighteousness.
> I John 1:9, NIV

b. Justification

KEY STATEMENT
> "BILL OR JANE, CHRIST HAS NOT ONLY FORGIVEN YOU, BUT YOU HAVE ALSO BEEN JUSTIFIED, WHICH MEANS YOU NOW STAND BEFORE GOD, JUST AS IF YOU HAD NEVER SINNED."

KEY SCRIPTURE
> God presented him as a sacrifice of atonement, through faith in his blood. He did this to demonstrate his justice, because in his forbearance he had left the sins committed beforehand unpunished—
> Romans 3:25, NIV

c. Regeneration

KEY STATEMENT
> "YOU HAVE BEEN FORGIVEN, JUSTIFIED, AND REGENERATED, WHICH MEANS, BILL OR JANE, YOU HAVE NOW RECEIVED **NEW LIFE** THROUGH CHRIST."

> Therefore, if anyone is in Christ, he is a new creation; the old has gone, the new has come!
> II Corinthians 5:17, NIV

KEY SCRIPTURE

d. *Adoption*

> "BILL OR JANE, YOU HAVE BEEN FORGIVEN, JUSTIFIED, REGENERATED . . . AND ALSO ADOPTED. YOU HAVE NOW BECOME A CHILD OF GOD."

KEY STATEMENT

> The Spirit himself testifies with our spirit that we are God's children. Now if we are children, then we are heirs—heirs of God and co-heirs with Christ...
> Romans 8:16-17, NIV

KEY SCRIPTURE

> "ISN'T IT A **GREAT FEELING** TO KNOW THAT YOU ARE A BORN-AGAIN CHRISTIAN?"

KEY QUESTION

e. *Involvement*

> "NOW THAT YOU HAVE BECOME A BORN-AGAIN CHRISTIAN, BILL OR JANE, THERE ARE TWO THINGS IN WHICH YOU SHOULD BECOME INVOLVED: (1) AN ACTIVE DISCIPLING GROUP, AND (2) A VITAL, DYNAMIC, SPIRITUAL CHURCH."

KEY STATEMENT

BRIEF EXPLANATION: Occasionally, you will be dealing with a person who has *become aware of his need for the Spirit-filled experience.* Under the *direction of the Holy Spirit, prayerfully proceed* with the Presentation of the Spirit-Filled Life. Included at this point, for *your convenience,* is a review of the Qualifying Procedure that was used previously.

> 1. IDENTIFY THEIR SECULAR BACKGROUND
> 2. IDENTIFY THEIR CHURCH BACKGROUND
> 3. IDENTIFY THEIR RELATIONSHIP WITH YOUR CHURCH
> 4. IDENTIFY THEIR RELATIONSHIP TO GOD
>
> *Note:* Final Key Question is: "Bill or Jane, I'm sure you would allow me to share some Scripture with you, wouldn't you?"

Review and be prepared to utilize the following diagrams as "tablet talk" while you present the Spirit-Filled Life.

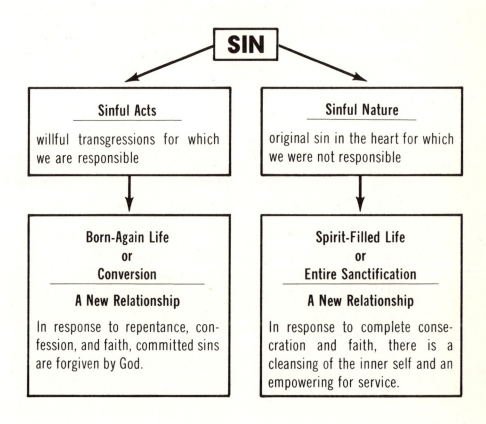

"DARK HEART"   "MIXED HEART"   "CLEAR HEART"

The Christian Experience

CRISIS	CONTINUATION	CRISIS	CONTINUATION
1. Divine Initiative 2. Awareness of Need 3. Awareness of Moral Choice 4. Man's Response	CONFLICT	1. Divine Initiative 2. Awareness of Need 3. Awareness of Moral Choice 4. Man's Response	ABSENCE OF CONFLICT
1. Forgiveness 2. Justification 3. Regeneration 4. Adoption	Confrontation & Temptation—Confrontation & Temptation	1. Heart Purity 2. Heart Perfection 3. Infilling of the Holy Spirit 4. Empowering of the Holy Spirit	Confrontation & Temptation—etc.—etc.
BORN-AGAIN		SPIRIT-FILLED	

4. *Presentation for the Spirit-Filled Life*

   a. *Divine Initiative*

"BILL OR JANE, I HAVE SOME GREAT NEWS FOR YOU. DO YOU REALIZE THAT GOD HAS A PLAN WHEREBY YOU CAN BE FREE FROM THIS INNER CONFLICT THAT YOU SENSE IN YOUR LIFE?"	KEY QUESTION

And so Jesus also suffered outside the city gate to make his people holy through his own blood. Hebrews 13:12, NIV	KEY SCRIPTURE

b. *Awareness of Need*

KEY STATEMENT

"BILL OR JANE, THIS IS PERHAPS THE GREATEST DAY IN YOUR LIFE, BECAUSE YOU HAVE RECOGNIZED YOUR NEED FOR GOD TO DELIVER YOU FROM THIS SELFISH, SINFUL NATURE. CHRIST HAS PROMISED, THROUGH THE HOLY SPIRIT, TO MEET THIS NEED."

KEY SCRIPTURES

What a wretched man I am! Who will rescue me from this body of death?
Romans 7:24, NIV

Blessed are they which do hunger and thirst after righteousness: for they shall be filled.
Matthew 5:6, KJV

c. *Awareness of Choice*

KEY QUESTION & STATEMENT

"BILL OR JANE, DO YOU REALIZE THAT YOUR GREATEST POWER IS YOUR POWER TO CHOOSE? (Wait for a response.) JUST AS YOU HAD TO MAKE A CHOICE TO ENTER INTO THE BORN-AGAIN LIFE, SO YOU ALSO HAVE TO MAKE A MORAL CHOICE TO RECEIVE A CURE FOR THE SELFISH, SINFUL NATURE."

KEY SCRIPTURE

But just as he who called you is holy, so be holy in all you do; for it is written: "Be holy, because I am holy."
I Peter 1:15-16, NIV

d. *Man's Response*

"NOT ONLY IS GOD **REACHING OUT** TO YOU AND HELPING YOU **BECOME AWARE** OF YOUR NEED, BUT, BILL OR JANE, YOU HAVE THE PRIVILEGE OF RESPONDING TO YOUR SPIRITUAL NEED BY:
 	
    presenting yourself as a living sacrifice to God, and also
    accepting the infilling and cleansing power of the Holy Spirit."
	KEY STATEMENT

I beseech you therefore, brethren, by the mercies of God, that ye present your bodies a living sacrifice, holy, acceptable unto God, which is your reasonable service. Romans 12:1, KJV	KEY SCRIPTURE

"BILL OR JANE, THIS WONDERFUL GIFT OF THE HOLY SPIRIT CAN BE YOURS TODAY, SIMPLY BY:
 	
    acknowledging your need
    confessing this need to God
    committing everthing you are and have to God
    believing that God accepts your commitment and cleanses and infills you **NOW** with the Holy Spirit.
 	
BILL OR JANE, DOES THIS MAKE SENSE TO YOU?"
	KEY STATEMENT & QUESTION

If their first answer is *"NO,"* then you simply and softly ask, "WHAT PART OF IT TROUBLES YOU?" Then you begin to deal with their questions systematically.

If their answer is *"YES,"* then you move to the next question.

KEY QUESTION

> "BILL OR JANE, IS THERE ANY GOOD REASON WHY, RIGHT HERE IN THE PRIVACY OF THIS ROOM, YOU WOULDN'T WANT TO ACCEPT THIS SPIRIT-FILLED LIFE?"

If their answer is *"YES,"* remember that, regardless of the reason, you are more interested in winning a person than a point. Therefore, if it is a matter of misunderstanding something, clear that up simply and softly, perhaps with the use of another one of the diagrams. But if they seem to be backing down, let them do so with warmth and continued acceptance.

If their answer is *"NO,"* simply review the presentation in no more than sixty seconds, and then suggest that you have a simple prayer together. Inasmuch as Bill and Jane are already Christians, they will probably have no difficulty praying. However, if there is any hesitation, lead them in a prayer of *acknowledgment, confession, commitment, faith,* and *thanks.*

5. *Follow-through and Discipleship After Presentation and Acceptance of the Spirit-Filled Life*

   a. *Heart Purity*

"ISN'T IT A GREAT **FEELING** TO **KNOW** THAT ALL OF THE POLLUTION AND CORRUPTION FROM YOUR OLD SINFUL NATURE HAS BEEN CLEANSED?"	KEY QUESTION
"He made no distinction between us and them, for he **purified their hearts by faith.**" Acts 15:9, NIV	KEY SCRIPTURE

   b. *Heart Perfection*

"BILL OR JANE, GOD HAS NOT ONLY **PURIFIED YOUR HEART** BUT HAS ALSO **RESTORED HIS** MORAL NATURE IN YOU. HE HAS PERFECTED YOUR AFFECTIONS AND MOTIVES."	KEY STATEMENT
"Be perfect, therefore, as your heavenly Father is perfect." Matthew 5:48, NIV and Herein is our **love made perfect,** that we may have boldness in the day of judgment: because as he is, so are we in this world. I John 4:17, KJV	KEY SCRIPTURES

c. *Infilling of the Holy Spirit*

KEY STATEMENT

> "ONE OF THE EXCITING FACTS ABOUT THE SPIRIT-FILLED LIFE IS THAT HE COMES IN AND COMPLETELY FILLS YOUR HEART. BILL OR JANE, THIS MEANS THAT THE MORAL CONFLICT IS GONE AND THE HOLY SPIRIT **ABIDES, COMFORTS,** AND **ASSISTS** YOU IN YOUR SPIRITUAL GROWTH."

KEY SCRIPTURE

> . . . and he shall give you another Comforter, that he may abide with you for ever . . . for he dwelleth with you, and shall be in you.
>
> John 14:16-17, KJV

d. *Empowering of the Holy Spirit*

KEY QUESTION

> "BILL OR JANE, DURING THE TIME YOU EXPERIENCED THE BORN-AGAIN LIFE, DID YOU EVER WISH THAT YOU HAD MORE **POWER** TO LIVE THAT LIFE CONSISTENTLY?" (Wait for a response.)

KEY STATEMENT

> "THE THRILLING FACT ABOUT THE SPIRIT-FILLED LIFE IS THAT, WHEN THE SPIRIT COMES IN TO ABIDE, HE **FURNISHES THE POWER** NECESSARY TO LIVE A **VICTORIOUS LIFE.** THIS SPIRITUAL POWER IS POSSIBLE BECAUSE OF:
>
> an absence of moral conflict in the cleansed heart
>
> the indwelling presence of the Holy Spirit, Who is your **POWER SOURCE.**"

> "But you will receive power when the Holy Spirit comes on you . . ."
> Acts 1:8, NIV

KEY SCRIPTURE

e. *Involvement*

> "BILL OR JANE, WITHOUT DOUBT, THIS IS THE **GREATEST DAY** IN YOUR SPIRITUAL DEVELOPMENT.
>
> YOU NOW KNOW CHRIST AS YOUR **SAVIOR** AND **LORD**.
>
> NOW THAT YOU HAVE BECOME SPIRIT-FILLED, BILL OR JANE, THERE ARE TWO THINGS IN WHICH YOU SHOULD BECOME INVOLVED:
> (1) AN ACTIVE DISCIPLING GROUP, AND
> (2) A VITAL, DYNAMIC, SPIRITUAL CHURCH.
>
> I WOULD LIKE TO MAKE MYSELF AVAILABLE TO YOU TO HELP YOU IN ANY WAY I CAN AS YOU BECOME AN INVOLVED, SPIRIT-FILLED CHRISTIAN."

KEY STATEMENTS

CONCLUSION

In this study, *DYNAMICS OF DISCIPLING,* the "Mandate of the Master" ("go and make disciples") has been aimed at helping you...

- Understand
- Experience
- Communicate

...the dynamics of the Christian life.

As you will recall, this material has been developed from the standpoint of "Discipling Building Blocks."

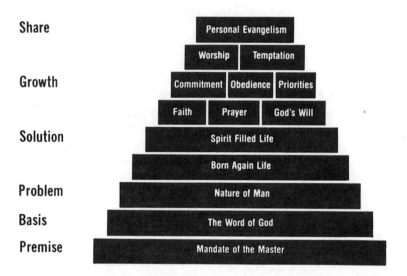

If you have approached these fourteen chapters with a "learner's heart," you will find a rewarding experience in looking back at the *you* who began chapter 1, and the *you* who has completed this final chapter. Pause right now and...

THANK GOD FOR YOUR SPIRITUAL GROWTH.

This is your final exercise of this study. Write in the box below:

> FIVE AREAS OF GROWTH THAT CAN BE ATTRIBUTED TO THE HOLY SPIRIT'S USE OF "DYNAMICS OF DISCIPLING."
>
> 1. _____
> 2. _____
> 3. _____
> 4. _____
> 5. _____

Acknowledgments

We gratefully acknowledge the following authors and publishers for use of their material in DYNAMICS OF DISCIPLING.

Scripture quotations are from the *New American Standard Bible,* © The Lockman Foundation 1960, 1962, 1968, 1971, 1972, 1973, 1975, and are used by permission.

New International Version of the New Testament, Copyright © New York Bible Society International, 1973. Used by permission.

Verses marked (ILB) are from *The Living Bible,* copyright 1971, Tyndale House Publishers, Wheaton, Illinois. Used by permission.

and the

King James Version of the Holy Bible.

Quotations cited at the beginning of each chapter were taken from the writings of . . .

Mrs. Charles Barnard
Phillips Brooks
Oswald Chambers
Martin Luther
Mrs. C. H. Morris
Hannah Whitall Smith
and
John Wesley.